Resource Management in Academic Libraries

Edited by
David Baker
Director of Information Strategy and Services,
University of East Anglia, Norwich

Library Association Publishing
London

© This compilation: David Baker 1997
© Articles: the contributors 1997

Published by
Library Association Publishing
7 Ridgmount Street
London WC1E 7AE

Library Association Publishing is wholly owned by The Library Association.

First published 1997

British Library Cataloguing in Publication Data
A catalogue record for this book is available from the British Library.

ISBN 1-85604-036-4

Typeset from contributors disks in 11/13pt Palermo and Arial by Library Association Publishing.
Printed and made in Great Britain by Bookcraft (Bath) Ltd.

Contents

14 Space planning and management / 189
Andrew McDonald

15 Special bids / 207
David Baker

16 Models for the future: implementing a resource management strategy / 219
David Baker

List of Contributors

David Baker MA MMus MLS PhD FLA FRCO FRSA is Director of Information Strategy and Services and University Librarian at the University of East Anglia (UEA) Norwich. He has over 90 publications, including 12 books/collections of essays and six commissioned reports, to his credit and is editor of a refereed electronic journal and a major training and development series. He has undertaken major consultancies and lecturing engagements in Europe, the Middle East and Africa, including for the World Bank, ODA and EU. The largest projects consisted of advising the Kuwaiti Government in revitalizing the library system after the Gulf War and a $40m acquisitions programme for Nigerian academic libraries. His professional interests include strategic planning, information strategy, staff training and development and library finance.

Professor Peter Brophy is Head of Library and Learning Resource Services at the University of Central Lancashire and also heads the University's Centre for Research in Library and Information Management (CERLIM). He has led a large number of research and development projects funded by bodies such as the European Commission, the British Library and the Higher Education Funding Council's Joint Information Systems Committee. His publications include *Quality management for information and library managers* (with K. Coulling) and *Management information and decision support systems in libraries*. He is a Fellow of both The Library Association and Institute of Information Scientists and serves on a number of national committees and other bodies.

Professor Colin Harris is University Librarian at Manchester Metropolitan University. He studied Sociology, Social Policy and Librarianship at the University of Hull, McMaster University, University of Western Ontario and the Open University. He is a Fellow of The Library Association and Fellow of the Institute of Information Scientists. He has worked at Newcastle Polytechnic and was Director of the Centre for Research on User Studies at the University of Sheffield and University Librarian and Director of Academic Information Services at the University of Salford. He is the Editor of *New review of academic librarianship* and Editorial Coordinator of *New review of information networking;* a Director of BLCMP Library Services. He was a member of the sub-group on Management of Libraries of the Follett Review and the 1996 RAE panel on Library and Information Management; a member of the CEI Development Programme Working Group and a member of the team conducting the evaluation of the HEFCE UK Pilot Site Licence Initiative.

Elizabeth Hart is currently Assistant Director of Library Services at the University of Huddersfield with responsibility for staffing and staff development, financial management and quality and performance measurement. She began her career in special libraries in the water and pharmaceutical industries before moving to the education sector. As well as having a professional interest in financial systems and methods she is currently undertaking research into performance measurement methods.

John Hutchins has worked as an academic librarian after graduating from the University of Nottingham and attending the London School of Librarianship: first at the Universities of Durham and of Sheffield, and since 1971 at the University of East Anglia. In recent years as Sub-Librarian with responsibility for Resources Development, he has undertaken costings of library activities and in particular has successfully introduced and implemented a formula for allocating acquisitions funds. Outside the library, his principal interest has been machine translation, and he has written many articles and two books on the subject. He is currently president of the European Association for Machine Translation and chief editor of *MT news international*, a thrice-yearly news magazine.

Ian Lovecy commenced work as a cataloguer at Manchester University Library after completing a degree in English and a PhD in mediaeval literature at Cambridge. He subsequently became Deputy Librarian at UMIST and then at Reading University, before being appointed Librarian at Bangor; he was appointed Director of Information Services there in 1991. He is a Fellow and Honorary Fellow of The Library Association, a member of LISC (Wales), and a member of the Council of the National Library of Wales.

Andrew McDonald became Director of Information Services at the University of Sunderland in 1995, before which he was Deputy Librarian at the University of Newcastle upon Tyne. He sits on Library Association Council and chairs its Academic and Research Libraries Committee. He is a member of SCONUL Executive and chairs the Advisory Committee on Buildings. He has published and lectured widely, and has consulted for the British Council all over the world, mostly in the areas of library planning and design and strategic planning. He also sits on IFLA's Buildings Committee. In addition to space planning, he is keenly interested in automation for self-service, electronic delivery and service quality.

Bernard Naylor was educated at Balliol College, Oxford, and University College, London. He became University Librarian of the University of Southampton in 1977, and before that was Secretary of the Library Resources Coordinating Committee of the University of London (1974–77), and Librarian of the University of London Institute of Latin American Studies (1966–74). He has been Vice-Chair (1984–86) and Chair (1986–88) of the Standing Conference of National and University Libraries (SCONUL), and has chaired several of its subcommittees with resource management themes, such as Performance Indicators and Scholarly Communication. He has chaired the British Library Lending Division Advisory Committee (1981–85), the British Council Libraries Advisory Committee (1986–95) and the Executive Committee of the Hampshire Technical Research Industrial and Commercial Service (HATRICS) (since 1982). He was appointed a non-executive member of the Board of the British Library in 1995. He is a frequent contributor to professional conferences and meetings, many of his contributions having been published, and he also regularly publishes original articles and book reviews in the professional press.

Julie Parry is Director of Library and Information Services at Bath College of Higher Education, where she is responsible for managing library services and open access computer facilities across two sites. Her particular interest is staff management and her publications cover staff induction, recruitment, appraisal and continuing professional development among other topics. She also lectures on the MSc in Information and Library Management at the University of Bristol, where she is Unit Organizer for 'The management of people in libraries'.

Jean Steward has worked at the University of East Anglia since 1974 and is currently Director of Library Services. She was responsible for introducing a Library Service Level Agreement in 1996. Jean has worked with The Library Association, serving on the Council, as Chair of the East Anglian Librarians Consultative Committee and as President of the Association of Library Assistants. Through this work she has presented conference papers on a wide variety of topics and has also undertaken consultancy work in Nigeria, Bulgaria and Ethiopia.

Keith Webster BSc(Hons) MLib ALA MIInfSc is Sub-Librarian at the University of Newcastle upon Tyne. Previous posts include Reference Librarian at Glasgow Caledonian University, and Manager of the Scottish Library and Information Council. He is currently Honorary Secretary of the Institute of Information Scientists.

Foreword

Dame Elizabeth Esteve-Coll
Vice-Chancellor
The University of East Anglia, Norwich

Universities and colleges the world over are under pressure: pressure to succeed, to maintain income, to pursue research, to be excellent. So too are their libraries. Academic librarians face ever greater demands from their users for services and an increased effectiveness and accountability from those who fund them. Human, financial and technological resources need to be justified and managed more effectively than ever before.

This book looks at many aspects of resource management. It contains a wealth of information from respected senior practitioners in UK academic librarianship. That must surely be one of its strengths: the authors draw on their own work and applications of theory to the 'real world'. In addition, it covers the key areas of resource management, from politics to total quality management (TQM) and special bidding to routine operating costs.

We face an ever more challenging and uncertain future in education. There is much in David Baker's book that is applicable not just outside higher education, but outside the UK too. Library Association Publishing is to be commended for producing the collection. It will be a valuable addition to the literature at a time when academic libraries need helpful advice on both short-term and long-term development of their services.

I recommend *Resource management in academic libraries* to all who have an interest in the subject.

Introduction

DAVID BAKER

Resource management in academic libraries

What I have long realized at the University of East Anglia (UEA) Library, Norwich, is that if we academic librarians did not improve and refine our approach to resource management in the 1990s, it was hard to see us surviving and prospering in the academic world in which we were already living; hence the need to find ways to enable us to manage and develop our library, on a strictly limited resource base, for the good of our parent institution and its members.

I may not deem myself to be an expert in every resource management technique, but I can certainly claim a good deal of experience in being in charge of library resources in an academic institution under a good deal of pressure – pressure which will increase significantly over the next decade. The University of East Anglia has seen its unit of resource drop since the late 1970s as government funding cuts have taken their toll; now expansion – in competition with every other university and former polytechnic in the United Kingdom – will drive down unit costs and increase the need for effective and efficient management even further.

The growth in student numbers at East Anglia has been in new as well as existing subject areas. Services and collections have to be developed in these areas – but at what effective and appropriate cost? The increased emphasis on research quality and productivity requires us to target funds towards those areas of the university which are deemed to be the (actual or potential) 'high ground', whether in terms of income generating ability or quality, or both.

Materials price rises have also taken their toll; book and periodical price inflation in particular has crippled our library's acquisitions budget and this is a situation common to many academic institutions. The need to fund technological developments – whether it be computers for library housekeeping activity or the various forms of online bibliographic access – competes with the continuing demands for traditional library materials.[1] At the University of East Anglia, we have also run out of space, with only limited prospects of funding for an extension.

In addition to the kinds of internal pressure described above, I perceive that the ways in which institutions of higher and further education are funded will become increasingly volatile as competition for scarce resources grows. Because of this, and as the overall unit of resource continues to dwindle and internal effectiveness and efficiency are seen as important factors in external success, questions will inevitably be asked about the nature and level of funding of the academic library.

Academic libraries consume a substantial amount of an institution's resources. Space, heating, lighting, staff, computers, equipment, furniture, books, journals and other materials are resources that could be allocated to other activities and cost centres if the parent institution saw fit. In consequence, the library has to compete internally for funds in a more hostile environment than has been seen for very many years.

Being competitive means having your wits about you, and in the present and likely future climate, that means effective and efficient management of available resources: justifying allocation decisions, spending money and deploying resources to maximum advantage and benefit, using money to attract money, costing out new activity and setting those costs against other alternatives, cutting expenditure where it can be cut, increasing efficiency, targeting resources, measuring effect and, if necessary, modifying approach and above all, being, and being seen to be, credible.

As well as being credible, academic librarians are also having to become entrepreneurial, just as all other unit heads within the institution are having to do so. As central funds have become a smaller proportion of many academic institutions' income, so has the drive to earn money from other sources. Full-cost students, contract research, sale of services, appeals and donations are but examples of the increasingly varied range of 'income streams' which need to be tapped for funds if an institution is to survive.

The library must therefore aim to generate income to supplement its 'central' allocation and to participate in income-generating activity for the good of the University as a whole. All this takes time, effort, strategic decision-taking and a deployment of resources. It also requires librarians to take risks – the higher the risk, the greater the chance of financial success or failure; librarians need to know how best to develop and maintain their income-generating capacity.

What is said here is typical of academic libraries, in Britain and elsewhere. Judging by the literature, North American academic libraries are in a similar position. The situation is even more acute in eastern Europe and the developing countries. Nor is this experience restricted to the higher education sector: further education and other similar types of academic library all face the same problems.

Hence my wish to edit *Resource management in academic libraries*. It is obvious that there is no one clear solution, no single answer and no unique cure-all approach to the question of resource management, whether at the 'nuts and bolts' level of internal library allocation processes or at the macro level of strategy and politics. The world of academic libraries and their parent institutions is far too complex for that. What this book aims to do is to steer the reader through the issues and problems which face academic institutions and those which face their libraries in particular, looking at possible approaches and solutions.

The emphasis is inevitably on financial resource management. Without money, all but minor projects and activities are difficult if not impossible to implement and manage. Financial performance, whether in terms of efficient budgeting or effective allocation, income generating capacity or simple financial solvency, will be one of the key measures – if not the key measure of an academic institution's performance in the 1990s and into the next century. That situation is bound to impact upon the library.

Much has changed in academic librarianship since this book was first conceived. Information technology (IT) developments in particular have altered the nature of library and information provision to a greater extent than could have been envisaged even four years ago.

More fundamental changes are likely to come.

And yet it is my perception that the traditional 'book' is not yet dead. Something that has not been studied in academic librarianship to any great extent so far is the relative cost-effectiveness of different types of library provision. Is the IT-based library really more cost-effective than the traditional hardcopy one? That is one of the fundamental issues of resource management, and one which is covered in this book.

In this context, the text incorporates references to the *Follett Report* and its related working papers and reports. While these documents are primarily of importance for librarians in Britain, they summarize much that will be of concern to academic librarians in many other countries, and especially where the concept of the 'virtual library' is being introduced as one of the ways of tackling the increased demand for library services at a time of reduced resource levels.

It is my view that managing resources can only be done effectively if those who are doing the managing understand the environment and the culture in which they have to operate. Just as important is a comprehension of the pressures and forces which will inevitably shape institutional attitudes towards any new strategies and techniques for the management of library resources. Organizational politics is a key factor in the shaping and the success of any resource management strategy.

My own experience, reinforced by discussions with colleagues and an analysis of the literature, suggests most strongly that it will be difficult to develop an effective resource management style without a basic infrastructure – an infrastructure which, for example, gives the library resource manager the ability to access or collect information ranging from 'ready reckoner' payroll costs to snapshot or longitudinal statistics of given activities or the ability to develop performance indicators which will feed back into the evaluation of the resource management process.

Since income generation is such a vital part of the library resource manager's responsibilities, this is dealt with on its own. Given that bidding for funds, whether within or outside the institution, is an increasingly important aspect of the library resource manager's work and one way of generating income, special attention is also paid to this activity.

Specific chapters are devoted to special types of resource. The headings of Information Technology, Space, Operating Costs, and Research Collections being arguably the areas where academic librarians are likely to be most concerned about the effective and efficient deployment and management of the resources at their disposal in the future.

Reference

1 See, for example, Lee, S. H. (ed.), *Library material costs and access to information*, New York, Haworth, 1990; Lee, S. H. (ed.), *Pricing and costs of monographs and serials: national and international issues*, New York, Haworth, 1987.

Acknowledgments

Many people have contributed, whether wittingly or unwittingly, to the production of this book. Above all, however, I would like to thank all those authors who have contributed to the book. Their expert contributions have significantly increased the publication's worth.

I would also like to express my gratitude to the many librarians who have over a period of time sent details of their own approaches to resource management and the associated techniques adopted and who have been willing to share ideas with me.

A special word of thanks is due to Joan Welsby, who acted as editorial assistant for the book and without whom the project would not have been completed – certainly not so efficiently.

Dr David Baker
The Library
The University of East Anglia
Norwich

1

Academic Libraries

DAVID BAKER

Introduction

Academic libraries come in all shapes and sizes. Two basic comparative measures relating to the academic library are the size of the population being served and the size of the stock housed or controlled by
the library. Other, more specific comparisons can be made regarding
the relative spending on the library, the annual intake of material and
the yearly usage of stock and services. Average sizes vary from country to country. British universities have long been regarded as having
relatively small student populations compared with their counterparts in North America or certain European countries such as
Germany, though the expansion of the early 1990s has meant a 'catch-
ing up' in size of user population.

In collection size, too, British academic libraries tend to be smaller
than their equivalents in countries such as the United States, though
larger, in general, than most developing countries' libraries.
Academic libraries in the former Communist countries may seem
large judging by the numbers of volumes in stock, although the figures often relate to large numbers of multiple copies and hence small
numbers of actual titles held.

A different way of categorizing academic libraries is to look at the
ways in which they are funded. In Britain, the vast majority are publicly funded, though not all through the same funding body. Even
where they are funded through the same mechanism, as for example
the Higher Education Funding Councils of England, Wales and
Scotland, the actual allocation of monies, and the way in which indi-

vidual university librarians are allowed to distribute it internally, is very much a matter for local decision and variation.

Despite the diversity of academic libraries within the United Kingdom, there are several common characteristics which can be identified as being important aspects and determinants of the whole practice of resource management.

Present nature and purpose

What all academic libraries have in common, virtually regardless of country or history, is their basic position, role, aims and objectives. An academic library is a central service or unit of operation set up to provide a location, materials and facilities for the study, teaching and research being carried out in the institution overall. It is not a universal or public library, except insofar as most of the capital or recurrent costs associated with its operation are met from public funds allocated either directly or indirectly for the purpose of creating and maintaining such a service. Otherwise the parent institution is a private one, not reliant on government or other public financial support for its income.[1]

While the academic library may also have a regional or a national role by virtue of its geographical location, its special collections or some other major feature of its stock or its services, it is primarily a unit which exists for the members of the academic institution of which it forms a part. It is funded to support those members, and those members alone. Access and services provided beyond the academic community will be a matter for local decision according to a number of factors, whether political, social or financial. They are subject, at least in Britain, to the provisions relating to public use of library materials in the light of, for example, agreements governing the siting of European Documentation Centres. In addition, access and services *within* the parent institution will be subject to policy, constraints and priorities set outside the library as much as inside it.

The subject basis of the academic library

It could be argued that the traditional university library in Britain, and almost certainly many other countries, is an amalgam of single-subject special libraries catering for a series of special client groups. 'The majority of staff [in these special client groups] owe their immediate allegiance to their own cost centre and may even have more allegiance to an external professional association [than to the institution]'[2]

This amalgam poses a fundamental problem for academic library resource managers. Similarly, the mixture of purposes to be supported by the academic library: study, teaching and research, presents a further problem. Line[3] has identified and described the tensions which emerge as a consequence of serving, or attempting to serve, these different client groups and purposes. Is the library supporting study and teaching or research? Is it providing just-in-time information or long-term research collections? Does it exist for the scientist or the humanist, the scholar or the teacher? Is it an archive or an information centre? Does it have a hard copy or a technology base? The questions are almost endless, but they can be summarized in the fundamental one: what is the role of the academic library within its parent institution?

It is easy enough to compose a 'mission statement' for an academic library which will incorporate, if not answer, all the basic questions listed above. That statement is likely to be applicable and acceptable to most librarians, simply because it will be an all-embracing comment on what the academic library should be doing. However, while it used to be possible to give equal importance to every subject and every group of users, to each new and existing storage format, to all types of need and activity, it is no longer possible to do so now. Academic library managers are having to reconcile the competing claims of the campus users, the institution's directorate, a variety of external forces and a host of other pressures (for example to earn money) as best they can.[4]

Cultures and structures

A university has no comprehensive chain of command. It is not a hierarchy. Instead there is a proliferation of centres of initiative and decision making. There are few in a university who can take a broad view across the institution, as the majority of staff owe their immediate allegiance to their own cost centre and may even have more allegiance to an external professional association. Universities cannot at the same time devolve budgets to multiple cost centres and then be surprised that it proves impossible to establish and enforce strategic priorities.[5]

Having said that, most UK academic institutions will have one or more central coordinating committees which determine or develop policy for implementation within the organization. There is likely to be a Planning or Policy and Resources Committee which is responsible overall for both the institution's strategic planning process and the management and allocation of resources to achieve the objectives laid down in that plan. Such bodies will incorporate 'lay' members (i.e. people external to the institution) and will report to the highest governing committee or council of the university or college. Additionally, certain officers of the institution: Vice-Chancellor/ Principal, Registrar/Secretary, Director of Finance, will be charged with overall responsibility for not only the institution's strategic direction but also the effective allocation and management of its resources, as well as their attraction and enhancement in the first place. The effectiveness and appropriateness of the library resource manager's relationship to these committees and officers will always be of crucial importance.[6]

Research versus teaching

Universities and other institutions of higher education have two basic functions: to teach and to research. The extent to which they do both varies from institution to institution. The way in which British universities are now funded discretely for teaching (T) and research (R) activity may well lead to a situation where some institutions, whether by accident or design, have teaching of students at first and possibly taught course postgraduate level as their primary, if not their only, aim. The incorporation of the former polytechnics in Britain into a single funding body alongside the universities has at the same time created a group of 'new universities' with a tradition of teaching students but, in some cases at least, an aspiration to undertake research work in the way that the older universities have been doing for the last thirty years or more.

In pure 'T' institutions, the librarian may find it easier to support the aims and objectives of the parent body than is likely to be the case in 'R' institutions and especially in 'X' institutions – those universities where research is to be carried out formally in only some subject areas, with the other academic units concentrating on the teaching of students.[7] However, one of the traditional characteristics of many higher education systems is that those who teach also do research; they research in order to broaden and deepen the subject, their knowledge of it and, in consequence, enhance their teaching.

What in reality is happening, both in Britain and other countries, is that R, X and T categorizations denote how universities are funded rather than what they may be doing or how they are spending their money to do it. While only a very foolish institutional management would fly completely in the face of the implicit and explicit messages which form part of central funding allocations, there is likely to remain a fair degree of difference between the official position on what an institution is meant to be doing and what is actually happening in practice.

The technological imperative

Information technology (IT) is now changing the shape and nature of academic libraries, and 'the challenge to library managers is clear'.[8] UK academic libraries have for some time been party to information technology strategies, which are documents required by the national funding bodies as part of a drive towards effective and efficient deployment of equipment funds primarily allocated for the purchase of computing equipment. More recently, the UK higher education community has been preoccupied with the development of *information* strategies which encompass the provision of all kinds of information, whether via technological or other means.[9]

These developments all have an impact upon the ways in which library resources are likely to be allocated, deployed and managed in the future. The rate of technological change and expectation amongst the UK Higher Education community is also gathering pace. The Electronic Libraries (e-Lib) programme alone has spawned over 60 major projects designed to transform the ways in which 'academic' information and knowledge is stored and transmitted. Many of the e-Lib projects will have turned into system-wide products well before the year 2000. University libraries will never be the same again.[10]

Financial uncertainty

The financial position in academic institutions is increasingly uncertain. Central grants are rarely known well in advance and library budgets can often only be guessed at until after the year has actually begun. There is nothing particularly new in this; not since the 1970s has the British higher education system had a forward planning system which gave universities a clear forecast of what government money would be made available to them. Since that time, many have found that the loss of government income can be made good by an increasingly 'commercial' approach to activities carried out within the institution. What is making the situation more difficult are the major changes that are taking place: growth, selectivity, competition, *they* add the volatility to the uncertainty.

If the parent institution is rarely sure from year to year of the amount of money which it will earn or be allocated, it is hardly surprising, then, that libraries will have little advance warning of their annual budget. A major difficulty facing academic librarians in this respect is the way in which money is allocated to the library by the senior management of the institution. Traditionally, many academic libraries have been funded on the basis of a percentage of the institutional expenditure. What constitutes 'institutional expenditure' in this respect is open to debate. As long as the bulk of an institution's income comes from central government, then there is perhaps less of a problem; the library's share, if calculated as a proportion of the government allocation, is still potentially a respectable element of overall spend.

Once the government grant becomes only a part of the total, with non-governmental income accounting for 50% or more of total available funds in some institutions, then any unit whose entire allocation is locked into the government grant only will suffer, not simply from a disproportionate loss of income, but from an inability to support much of the activity which is generating the non-governmental income at institutional level.[11]

Diversification of funding

Wherever there is a diversification of activity there is likely to be an increase in the number of income streams flowing into the institution. Without a coherent mechanism for channelling some of the income from these streams into support services like the library, not only will resourcing of such units be inappropriate and inadequate, but effective resource allocation of available funds will also prove extremely difficult. The allocation process within the library will still be hard to apply even if all the parent organization's income streams are taken into account when the 'library grant' is calculated.

Lack of flexible and rational budgeting

Even if this is not a problem, it is rare, as Webster points out,[12] to find a budget process in academic institutions which can be manipulated readily 'to study the effect of a specific change on the other parts of the budget'. Units such as academic libraries are complex institutions and, in consequence, many of the product-based techniques of financial and resource management techniques developed in industry and commerce may be difficult to apply.[13] Yavarkovsky[14] also points out the problems faced by academic librarians when the library is perceived as a cost centre similar to all the other cost centres within the institution:

> this problem of university management perceptions of the library is serious if [they] interfere with rational dialogue between university library managers and university budget managers... it [will be] virtually impossible for the librarian to justify legitimate incremental needs except as solutions to crises. In this case the library is condemned to marginal growth and internal resource shifts to meet ever more demanding programme requirements.

Moving from a 'historical' to a 'dynamic' funding model of the academic library can be of benefit, especially at times of growth, whether in terms of student numbers or research activity. At least the library will obtain additional funding for additional students under a formulaic approach which recognizes the inevitable price tag on central support services of increased class sizes.[15]

Income generation

Such central funding initiatives as have been launched in Britain in recent years have emphasized the maximizing of investment in existing and likely future resources and enforced an increasing degree of standardization on local developments. Academic and administrative computing are two areas which have been particularly influenced by central funding initiatives and planning directives in Britain.[16] The tone of official government documents stresses efficiency and accountability.[17] It can also be seen in the way in which public services are increasingly being asked to tender. Universities bid for students; libraries bid for funds.[18]

The last ten years have seen a move in British and many other countries' academic libraries towards a 'market economy' which encourages library managers to generate income to supplement existing allocations and even to fund new developments. However, as Winkworth points out:

> academic libraries are not typically set up to generate income. Their function is usually to perform a shared community service, financially supported by some kind of taxation on general institutional income. Typically 90% of library income comes from taxation, and no more than 10% from income generation.[19]

Nicholson[20] has identified the various levels of risk involved in income generation within an academic library, from the 'selling biros' end of the market to the fully-blown commercial information service. Low-risk activity is likely to bring low rewards – so low that the administrative and overhead costs could outweigh the income actually earnt. High-risk activity requires substantial capital investment and an entrepreneurial approach which is not yet part of academic culture. It could also detract from the provision of essential services to the library's primary client base – the members of the campus. It will certainly require a full cost accounting process as part of its management if it is to be truly commercial. In the middle are the relatively safe earners. Photocopying services are probably the most obvious example in academic libraries, where a self-contained activity is also self-financing, at least in terms of the direct and possibly some of the indirect costs.[21] Equally important in UK academic libraries is the ability of the institution to recover costs or 'overheads' on the increasing amount of contract research work carried out in universities and other institutions of higher education and the willingness of the local resource allocating bodies to pass on a share of that overhead to the library, once funded.[22]

Wilkinson comments of the North American experience of fundraising (much more developed than in Britain, for example) that

> success in fundraising appears to be related to raising the most money with the minimum expenditure in a way which increases the likelihood

of future long-term support and continues to attract new donors. Few other rules seem to apply generally, although institutional leadership and sustained financial commitment are vital. Success is largely due to the sustained effort of library staff to raise money.[23]

Charlene Clark, writing of the American situation, comments:

... fund raising will become a financial imperative and a key component of strategic planning. Successful fund raising will require that new and existing tools and support groups be mobilized for maximum effectiveness...The challenge is to pursue selective, stimulating, and profitable activities which make use of effective fund raising strategies[24]

Wilkinson comments, somewhat ruefully, that 'the UK, particularly before 1980, was the envy of many Americans, who long ago came to understand the limitations and the disadvantages of dependence on private philanthropy for essential services'.[25] For Second World countries, the move to 'market economies' is bringing the same kinds of tension to higher education as in Western countries such as Britain, except that the resource levels are significantly worse.[26] The problem for developing countries countries is even greater: the challenge is to 'catch up', but in their own terms rather than those of the West.

Fee or free?

The question of charging for services has been a topic of considerable interest to library resource managers for the last ten years and more.[27] This is a complex and emotive issue. Much depends upon the ways in which the individual academic library is funded in relation to its primary goals and objectives. If a library is clearly funded to provide certain services and to meet given aims to a specific user group or groups, then it is not easily possible to charge those users for the services provided. Charges may be levied for additional services, or the same services to a higher or broader level, or to different user groups (e.g. external users and non-members of the parent institution).

Winkworth sums up the approach towards income generation which most UK academic librarians would currently take:

I have no quarrel with income-generating activities if they meet an agreed objective and are properly costed. But it is important that:

- the financial profit or loss sought is clear before work begins
- that the focus is on the objective and not the activity
- that financial (and other) performance is monitored against clear targets

With these control processes in place, then income generation is a valuable aid to library management. If not, it can be an embarassing albatross, disruptive of the main purpose of the library.[28]

Importance and vulnerability of the academic library

If the library is a servant rather than a master or mistress in the academic environment, it is nevertheless an important servant, which the parent institution ignores at its peril. In Britain, for example, it is clear that, despite the projected major expansion at minimum cost in student numbers, there is an underlying concern with the likely adequacy of library provision in these (considerably) changing circumstances.[29]

Not that there is any room for complacency. Despite considerable efforts to increase income-generating capacity within academic libraries, the main source of funding will always be a central allocation from the parent institution, to which the academic librarian may be allowed to add some or all of any income earned in addition. The policy and practice of determining the level of library resourcing will therefore largely be determined within the university or college, typically by a 'planning and resources committee' charged with the task of distributing funds across the institution as a whole.[30] The librarian's scope for flexibility in attracting and allocating funds is likely to be governed and limited by the attitude and approach of senior management within the institution.

The automatic support which academic librarians could count upon from their faculty colleagues has long gone. When resources are strictly limited, the altruism which says that funds should go to academic support services such as the library rather than academic units is in short supply. As Ehikhamenor suggests: 'In times of economic depression, public services whose contributions to the socio-economic development of a country or whose default cannot be immediately felt or quantified, stand the risk of being forced into walking a budgetary tightrope or even deleted from budget estimates'.[31]

In addition to this, any money that does go to the library is scrutinized closely when it is perceived as a resource hard-earned by groups of academics teaching ever more students or winning increased numbers of contracts. 'Their' (i.e. academics') money is not to be spent lightly and certainly not in the interests of other groups within the institution. In addition, in many Western countries, there has been a considerable drive over the last decade towards 'value for money' and 'greater accountability' in the public services within which higher education is no exception.

If the 'big earners' within an institution – whether teachers or researchers (or both) are not being supported by the library or, as importantly, do not *perceive* themselves as being supported, then the library will have major difficulties. Not only will it lose the political and financial support of the powerful groups within the organization, but it will also risk the scenario in which rival, departmentally-based library services are established. This is a logical enough move for those who wish to control spend on library materials and services and to exclude others (who may be thought of as not paying for the privilege of using the materials or the services) from access to 'their' collections or facilities.[32]

However, too often academic librarians have not played to their strengths. As Brian Enright comments:

At a time when there is increased need for more precise targeting of library resources to match university selectivity and priorities and there is a desperate requirement on the part of academics to publish in the competitive 'bibliometrical' survival battle, the library's unique ability to analyse and assess use, evaluate document delivery and exposure, and provide information regardless of where or how it is stored, could make an invaluable contribution to the effectiveness and competitiveness of a university... The special role of libraries in relating 500 years of printed sources with information in multi-media and electronic formats opens up the possibility of their participating in assisting staff and postgraduates in publishing academic works and research reports using high quality desk-top publishing systems, an interesting revival of classical and medieval library traditions.[33]

Summary

This chapter has looked at the nature of the academic library, the context in which it operates and some of the key trends and issues which surround the management of academic libraries in the 1990s and beyond. Later chapters look in more detail at different types of academic libraries in the UK. Perhaps the most important point to note from this general introduction is that the academic library can only develop its own strategy within the context of the parent institution's strategy. If the latter aims to maintain, say, research activity in all subjects taught within the institution, then there is little the library and the library staff can do but to support that strategy to the best of their ability and within the available resource structure.

It is to be hoped that library staff have an opportunity to point out the implications of such a strategy and any attendant difficulties of library provision. One might even expect that the parent strategy would be altered or determined by the ability of the major support services, for example library, computing and media services, to give effective and appropriate input to the activity. However, in the final analysis, the library's position is only one factor to be taken into account when strategic decisions about present and future academic developments are being taken. This will always be borne in mind by the astute resource manager.

References

1   For a comparative description of the way in which higher education is funded in Western Europe, *see* Commission of the European Communities, *The Education structures in the member states of the European Communities*, Brussels/Luxembourg, The Commission, 1986.

2   Quoted in Breaks, M., 'Information systems strategies', *British journal of academic librarianship* **6** (2), 1991, 69–70.

3   Line, M., '"Library goodness" – perception of quality and value', in Line, M. (ed.), *Academic library management*, London, Library Association Publishing, 1990, 185–95.

4   See, for example, Davinson, D., *Academic libraries in the enterprise culture*, London, Library Association Publishing, 1989. (Viewpoints in LIS: 2) – a short but pithy summary of the British position.

5   Breaks, M., *op. cit.*, 69–70.

6   For a further discussion on the recent governance of UK universities, see Committee of Vice-Chancellors and Principals, *Report of the Steering Committee for Efficiency in Universities* [The Jarratt Report], London, The Committee, 1985 and Universities Funding Council, *Follow up to the Jarratt Report*, Circular letter 16/89, July, 1989.

7   I have used the basic categorization of R, X and T first put forward by the Advisory Board for the Research Councils (ABRC) *A strategy for the science base: a discussion document prepared for the Secretary of State for Education and Science*, London, HMSO, 1987, Chairman Sir David Phillips ('The Phillips Report'). See also Baker, D., 'Fears for tiers: academic rationalisation and university libraries', *UC&RS newsletter* **24**, 1988, 3–7.

8   Getz, M., 'The elctronic library: analysis and decentralization in collection decisions', *Journal of library acquisitions*, **14** (3), 1991, 83.

9   Joint Information Systems Committee [of the Higher Education Funding Councils] *Guidelines for developing an Information Strategy*. Bristol, The Committee, 1995. See also: Joint Information Systems Committee, *Five-year strategy, 1996–2001*. Bristol, JISC, 1996; Joint Information Systems Committee, *Electronic libraries programme*, 3rd ed. Bristol, HEFCE, 1996

10   Baker, D., 'Overdue for change', *Managing HE*, **5**, 46–8, 1996.

11   For an analysis of UK higher education expenditure, see *Universities Statistical Record, University statistics, v3: finance*, Cheltenham, USR, annual.

12   Webster, D., 'Issues in the financial management of research libraries', *Journal of library administration*, **3** (3/4). 1982, 14.

13   See, for example, Innes, J. and Mitchell, F., *Activity based costing*, London, Chartered Institute of Management Accountants, 1991.

14   Yavarkovsky, J., 'Planning and finance: a strategic level model of the university library', *Journal of library administration*, **3** (3/4), 1982, 54.

15   See, for example, Cooper, J.M., 'Financing academic libraries: making the transition from enrollment growth to quality enhancement', *College and research libraries*, **47** (4), 1986, 354–9.

16   See, for example, the discussion of information systems strategies relating to UK universities in Breaks, M., 'Information systems strategies', *British journal of academic librarianship*, **6** (2), 1991, 66.

17   See, for example, HM Treasury, *Public expenditure analyses*, London, HMSO, annual.

18 'Tendering may spread to all library activities'; 'Civil Service libraries facing market testing', *Library Association record*, **94** (7), 433–4, 1992.

19 Winkworth, I., ' "Turnover is vanity. . . " a philosophy for library income generation', *UC&R newsletter*, 38, 1993, 5. See also Winkworth, I., 'Turnover is vanity: how to raise cash in libraries', *Library Association record*, **95** (5), 290–1, 1993.

20 Nicholson, H., 'Uncomfortable bedfellows: enterprise and academic libraries', *British journal of academic librarianship*, **22** (1), 1992, 9–13.

21 Nicholson, *op. cit.*, 11.

22 See, for example, Committee of Vice-Chancellors and Principals, *Sponsored university research: recommendations and guidance on contract issues*, London, The Committee, 1992.

23 Wilkinson, J., *op. cit.*, 191.

24 Clark, C., 'Getting started with annual funds in academic libraries', **12** (4), 1990, 85.

25 Wilkinson, J., *op. cit.*, 191.

26 See, for example, Akifarin, A., 'Acquisitions of library materials in Nigeria's university libraries: problems and prospects', *Taking stock: journal of the National Acquisitions Group*, **1** (1), 1992, 12–16.

27 See, for example, The National Commission on Libraries and Information Science', 'The role of fees in supporting library and information services in public and academic libraries', *Collection building*, **8** (1), 1986, 3–17.

28 Winkworth, *op. cit.*, 5.

29 'New Funding Council to review library provision in higher education . . . ', Higher Education Funding Council for England, circular 1/92, 17 June, 1992.

30 See, for example, Baker, D., 'Resource allocation in university libraries', *Journal of documentation*, **48** (1), 1992, 11; Council of Polytechnic Librarians [COPOL], *Working papers on bookfund allocation*, ed. D. Revill, Oxford, COPOL, 1985, 7.

31 Ehikhamenor, F. A., 'A formula for allocating book funds: the search for simplicity and flexibility', *Libri*, **33** (2), 1983, 148.

32 Enright, B., 'Concepts of stock: comprehensive vs selective', in Line, M., *Academic library management*, London, Library Association Publishing, 1990, 44.

33 Enright, *op. cit.*, 45.

2

Resource Management –
The Context

DAVID BAKER

Introduction

'Resource management' is a phrase often used in library and information work. Judging by the literature, it can be defined in many
ways. Much depends upon the context and the culture in which those
who are responsible for a given set of resources are allowed, are able
and wish to manage. There is no single or obvious definition of
resource management, perhaps because libraries, as public rather
than private institutions, have not traditionally been fully in control
of all the resources which are used to provide the total service. A
study of standard thesauri suggests that 'to manage' involves administering, directing, engineering, overseeing, controlling, handling,
manoeuvring, manipulating, coping, faring, functioning and simply
surviving. Most academic library resource managers will recognize
all those alternatives: they are not so much substitutes for the term
'management' as aspects of it.

The standard synonyms for the term 'resource' are perhaps less
obvious to academic librarians. They relate to assets, capital, fortune,
riches, wealth, means, property, substance and similar words, terms
and concepts. They are words from commerce, business and accounting. Yet, increasingly, they symbolize attitudes and approaches which
higher education will have to adopt. The library becomes an asset to
the university, college or other institution of which it forms a part.
The building, equipment and collections are assets. The whole provides a service which attracts resources ('fortune', 'riches') and which
as a result contributes to the overall wealth of the institution, whose

'property' the library is. What is the 'resource' to be managed? It may be money or people, buildings or furniture, books or journals, networks or standalone workstations, remote databases or in-house CD-ROMS. It may only be some of these, depending upon the extent to which the individual resource manager has control over the allocation and management process relating to the unit being managed.

Who are the resource managers?

It is tempting to assume that resource managers in academic libraries are only the most senior staff – notably the Director or Chief Librarian and the Deputy or Associate Directors. Much will depend upon the organizational structure of the library service. While it is true to say that final responsibility and accountability for resources and finances must always rest with such people, the increased involvement of other library staff in the resource allocation and management process is both desirable and necessary if real efficiency and effectiveness is to be achieved. Good professionals in any walk of life should be concerned with the effective and efficient management and deployment of the resources at their disposal.

Because of the increased pressures and demands described in the first chapter, more effort will inevitably be spent on the process of resource management in academic libraries in future. The Director will not be able to respond to these pressures and demands alone. Much of the basic data (as for example processing and usage statistics, relative time spent on different operations) which resource managers require in order to forecast, budget, assess and manage will be provided by their colleagues in charge of, or working within the various parts of the library. They will have a more detailed knowledge of the work associated with the data being provided and will have a 'feel' for the trends which the information may or may not indicate. In some structures, the degree of budgetary devolution within the library is such that a number of staff may have budgetary responsibility if not control for specific areas of operation and may be budget managers within their own 'cost centre'.

The historic position

According to Webster:[1]

the past financial management practices of academic libraries have been characterized by limited fiscal control, unevaluated development of collections, reliance on single source funding, multiple missions, hopeful but not purposeful funding, segmented functions, multiple people working in isolation, and what might be called reactive management.

Certainly, until recently, resource management for many academic librarians meant:

1   An annual bid, based on estimates of need and previous budgets, for funds to buy materials (books, periodicals, other media) and to cover operating costs.
2   A separate bid for capital equipment and associated maintenance costs.
3   Periodic bids for posts to be added to the staffing establishment, or, if there were vacancies on an existing establishment, for the 'release' of the post for filling by permanent or temporary appointment.
4   Occasional requests for more resources in other areas – most notably space.
5   Allocation/distribution of the available resources between the various spending heads (payroll/non-payroll, materials/operating costs, books/journals/other media).
6   Monitoring of the rate of spend of the resources made available under each major heading in response to the various bids submitted.
7   Production of an annual report and summary financial statement for transmission to the officers of the parent institution.
8   Regular cost-cutting exercises, mainly driven by a central directive concerning a percentage reduction in projected spend.
9   Periodic reviews of actual and potential capacity/opportunity for income generation, either/both within and/or outside the institution.

In many libraries, both in Britain and abroad, this pattern is still the norm. Major resources such as staff, space, heating and lighting[2] have been centrally funded and are not therefore fully under the control of the librarian as resource manager. It is primarily the management of the non-payroll funds in general and the amount made available for the acquisition of materials (the acquisitions budget) which have traditionally taken up much of the time of the academic librarian, along with the periodic major bids for capital resourcing of equipment and space. Because the other expenditure heads have not been allocated to the library as a 'cost centre' but have instead been 'absorbed' as central costs or 'overheads', the true cost of library activities has typically been masked.[3] This position is now changing, however, with an increased move towards full devolution in many library systems and their parent institutions.[4]

Planning cycles

Resource management in academic libraries, then, is typically undertaken on an annual, or at least a regular, cyclical basis. Much of the timetable is driven not by the university or college, but by external agencies. In the UK, the funding bodies will set the resource agenda and the timetable, both on an annual and a longer term strategic basis. Ultimately, it is the annual funding 'settlement' with government that drives the level of resource allocation to universities. In times of poor settlements, capital and long-term strategies tend to suffer at the expense of protecting immediate annual budgets, though to their great recent credit, the UK Higher Education Funding Councils aim to take long-term views wherever possible.[5] While other funding bodies, especially 'private' and commercial organizations, may not work to a single cycle, it is the governmental funding year which still sets much of the resource management timetable within universities. This situation is likely to continue for at least the foreseeable future.

This annual timetable pervades the internal resource allocation and management processes, whether it be the submission of estimates, the bidding for special funds, the approval of variations from the agreed spending plan, or the submission of annual reports on activities carried out and resources expended in the process.

The payroll budget

Academic institutions are labour intensive. Spend on staff overall can account for 60% or even more of total recurrent expenditure.[6] Academic libraries, traditionally, have had a relatively low spend on staff as a proportion of total recurrent expenditure, not least because of the need for budgets for materials acquisitions and operating costs. Academic units have typically invested the bulk of their annual resources in teaching, research and support staff, with relatively small operating cost budgets. Equipment expenditure (often accounting for large sums of money, especially in research-orientated science departments) has in the past been accounted for separately, as part of an annual capital allocation to, and within, the institution.

The extent to which the library resource manager controls the payroll budget varies from institution to institution. Reference is made later in this chapter to budgetary devolution. Librarians have often had only limited control over the amount of spending on staff as opposed to materials, the payroll budget being a 'given', with additional spending or transfers of money to and from the payroll budget only being agreed after agreement with a university-level committee. Such lack of 'local' control may or may not have extended to income-generating activities (most usually photocopying and duplicating services) and use of the monies earned.

The acquisitions budget

Within the non-payroll budget, it is in the area of acquisitions expenditure that the relative spending of library funds is most apparent to the user community in general and the academic staff in particular. It is in this area that the most detailed work has been undertaken and it is with this area that much of the literature relating to resource management is concerned.[7] Later chapters consider the various techniques and approaches which can be, and have been, adopted to 'manage' the acquisitions budget in the sense of distributing the amounts made available between (usually) subjects or academic departments and types of materials (books, journals, generalia, IT-based information systems, etc.). What constitutes an acquisitions budget in terms of expenditure headings will vary depending upon the academic structure and the relative emphasis on different kinds of activity (teaching versus research; small group work versus lecture theatre format) and modes of library support (short loan provision versus multiple copy acquisition; on-site holding versus document delivery; hard-copy versus online access).

The management of the acquisitions budget includes both the monitoring of the effectiveness of the spend (the extent to which the money is being spent wisely in the best interests of the institution and its members) and of accounts covering all relevant budgetary headings (the extent to which the money made available has been spent and on what). An essential aspect of the management of the budget is, of course, the efficiency of the spending – not too little and not too much. Most academic librarians have traditionally expected to spend just below or just above their non-payroll allocations, even though funds might be carried forward and despite the fact that the desired result might only be achieved through last minute buying or suspension of purchases for long periods of time.[8]

Operating costs

The other major element in the academic library budget covers operating costs. What constitutes operating cost expenditure will also vary from library to library. In British universities, for example, recurrent spending on major equipment installations (notably computers) has not been a charge on the library's non-payroll grant. Nor, indeed, has it been funded from university allocations as such, but from special 'equipment grant' funds made available specifically and directly by central government agency. This situation is likely to change in the future, however, with IT spend becoming a part of the mainstream budgetary process.

A simple, if crude, way of defining the operating cost budget in an academic library would be to say 'what is left over after the acquisitions budget and the payroll costs (if devolved to the library in any budgetary/planning sense) have been calculated'. Typical budgetary subheadings might include: telephones, stationery, postage, photocopying, binding of materials, hospitality. Much will depend on the policy of the individual institution with regard to accountability for 'general' non-payroll costs such as postage. The operating cost budget is an area often overlooked by library resource managers in the past.[9] However, as Martin[10] points out, it is often this area of spend which is the most crucial in terms of effective resource management. Libraries cannot otherwise function in any of their operations, whether it be the processing and cataloguing of stock or the provision of services, the development of collections or the creation of information systems.[11] Telephone calls have to be made, mail posted, books bound, hospitality extended and so on. Money has to be set aside for the associated costs.

Equipment and technology spend

In UK academic libraries at least, spending on major equipment purchase and maintenance has been seen as a separate expenditure head. As long as technology is an aid to providing operational services, then the technological resource could be seen as another operating cost. While librarians might complain that there are insufficient resources available to fund library automation programmes, in practice, academic libraries have been 'raiding' their acquisitions and other budgets for many years in order to pay the maintenance costs of their computer systems or the subscriptions to external databases whether for cataloguing or other purposes.

What is not yet clear is the way in which IT-based spend, for example on CD-ROM purchases or network usage of databases and databanks for which a subscription must be paid, will typically be funded within academic libraries.[12] Nor is it clear how the technology itself will be funded, or how the expenditure will be distributed amongst the traditional, subject-based expenditure heads in the way that book and journal spend is normally allocated. Additionally, there remain, at the time of writing, major questions to be asked about the relative cost-benefits of different types of 'library' provision. Is remote provision actually more cost-effective than on-site supply and provision?

Physical space

Payroll, materials budgets, operating costs and equipment spend are not the only resources required to run an academic library. There remains also the question of the library or information centre as a building – a physical location where collections are stored and from which services are provided. While librarians have had relative freedom to arrange the buildings which they occupy, they have not had the concomitant budgetary control or responsibility. Without major capital resources, it is often difficult if not impossible to rearrange and certainly to replace or extend existing premises. The constraints imposed by existing and perhaps inappropriate space can be a major blockage to effective resource management. As an example, one might consider the adaptation of old library buildings to the housing of latest-generation computer technology for general student use.

Budgetary devolution

The devolving of budgets to, and within, institutions of higher education has led to the development of cost centres, each of which will typically have a total budget covering both payroll and non-payroll spend and possibly other resource heads such as space. Librarians who manage such a cost centre have, at least in theory, a greater degree of control over the total resource. In essence, the library budget consists of a single figure to cover all expenditure, whether on staff, materials or other operating costs, and it is the librarian's responsibility to determine how to allocate the total amount made available.[13] In practice, historical allocations and political pressure (as for example to spend more on acquisitions and less on staff), coupled with a restriction on the hiring and firing of staff mean that the librarian does not normally have an entirely free hand. Indeed, in many institutions where budgetary devolution is practised, there is still a central control on the way in which the budgets of individual cost centres are allocated, with central permission to vary spending between different headings also being required in many cases.

The prospect of real budgetary devolution, while causing problems for the academic librarian, does at least allow a greater freedom of manoeuvre than with a centrally managed resource allocation process, though there is perhaps a limit to the extent to which costs can be disaggregated in this respect.[14] Certainly, the development of resource management systems within the library stands a much better chance of practical success through actual application where the librarian has full internal budgetary control.

At institutional level, there has long been an expectation that funding of central services such as the library is a local matter. In terms of the actual funding of both capital and recurrent expenditure, this trend is likely to continue and, indeed, to broaden. In Britain, for example, the concept of 'top-slicing' funds before they are distributed to individual institutions in order to finance university hardware procurement is set to be abandoned. Local, as opposed to central, top-sliced funding has in any case been the norm in the former polytechnics.[15] Where central funding initiatives have been launched emphasis has been placed on the maximizing of investment in existing and likely future resources and enforced an increasing degree of standardization on local developments. Academic and administrative computing are two areas which have been particularly influenced by central funding initiatives and planning directives in Britain.[16]

The greater the degree of budgetary devolution to the individual institution from central government agencies, the more support services will be reliant on local goodwill, which is not necessarily an easy commodity to acquire, for their budget. The greater the degree of devolution within the organization, the more the support services will be reliant on the specific goodwill of the other cost centres within the institution. Devolution militates against central initiatives and central/general units like the academic library. Support services exist to serve the whole of the academic community and their approach should be driven by campus-wide strategies. Writing of UK universities' approach to campus-wide initiatives in the field of information technology developments, Breaks[17] sums up the major difficulty which any senior manager of a central academic service faces, given the organizational structure prevalent in academic institutions:

> an effective [central] strategy means a loss of individual and departmental freedom in the interests of the wider community. It also means handing over significant decision-making powers to the academic 'servants' [including, no doubt, the senior library staff] of the university.

The library budget itself can be devolved to academic units, the rationale for this move being that the decision-making is thus put in the hands of those who earn the money, and in whose interests the resources should be deployed. A number of the former UK polytechnics in particular have experimented with this approach, to good effect, not least because the academic departments have regarded the library budget as their money and were prepared to augment it with additional funds. However, this can also result in a virement *away* from spending on the library if and when the academic unit has insufficient resources to pay for what it regards as more essential acquisitions (for example laboratory materials and equipment). This could play havoc with those areas of library activity which require a degree of continuation in their funding, such as journal subscriptions.[18]

Virement: the ability to choose

Academic library managers who are also cost centre managers are likely to have a much greater control over, and responsibility for, payroll costs than are their counterparts in the more traditional, centralized institutions. Some may control only temporary or part-time staffing budgets, or payroll costs relating directly to income-generating activities where related salary and wage expenditure is met from the income generated and is not part of the central library budget, whether for payroll or non-payroll spend. What has yet to happen in most academic libraries, even in those that enjoy a high degree of budgetary devolution and autonomy, is the integration of all the various expenditure heads and income streams into a financial and resource management model which is more than simply a tool for managing spending or accounting for funds allocated.[19]

However, UK academic librarians have long had the word *virement* in their resource management vocabulary. Literally meaning 'the ability to choose', *virement* has been a useful tool for librarians, not only as a means of making scarce resources 'go further' but as a way of engendering flexible approaches towards resource management at a time of funding cutbacks. Staff reductions have released funds for computers and cancelled journal subscriptions have allowed increases in the interlibrary loans budgets. Where the library has been able to keep the revenue from the sale of goods and services (most notably photocopying) income has paid for staff, stationery and a host of other expenditure heads which can less easily be justified from centrally-allocated funds.

Payroll: non-payroll ratios

Too often, however, the virement has been one way: out of the payroll and into the acquisitions budget. For many years, a crude but widespread performance indicator of university libraries has been the payroll:non-payroll ratio.[20] The more spent on staff, the less spent on books and, more importantly in a research environment, journals. High staff spend has often been equated with a kind of inefficiency, though this has often been an uninitiated person's view. However, it has to be said that in a time of decreasing resources, it is appropriate for librarians, and their parent institutions, to take a long, hard look at the amount and nature of the payroll spend, not simply in relation to the budget overall, but also in relation to the aims, objectives and effectiveness of the library and the contribution it makes to the parent organization's wellbeing.[21]

Total accountability

The drive towards ever greater accountability in many countries' higher education systems is resulting in *all* aspects of a budget being devolved to cost centres, together with responsibility for the effective control and exploitation of the resources which form part of that budget. In addition to payroll costs, academic librarians are increasingly being asked to manage maintenance, equipment and furniture costs and are even being charged internally for the space which their library buildings occupy as part of the philosophy of budgetary devolution and accountability.[22] It could, of course, be argued that where an academic institution practices budgetary devolution to the point where all costs are recharged, then the internal market (i.e. campus users) will become more volatile and less captive. Faced with a diminishing library service for which internal charges are levied, academic units could well take their business elsewhere if they feel that a better deal could be struck as a result.

Degree of transparency

The degree of openness or transparency in the allocation and management of resources will be determined by a combination of factors, including the management style of the senior library staff, the politics of the parent institution, the aims and objectives of the resource allocation process and the time available for construction and implementation of any planning models. In any system which sets a premium on accountability and 'value for money' in its operation, an open approach to resource allocation and exploitation is important. Indeed, in Britain, for example, institutions of higher education, including their libraries, are *required* to report on the nature and use of the resources at their disposal, as are the central bodies which in large part fund them.[23]

Transparency in the allocation process brings difficulties as well as advantages. The more open the process and the more consensual the style, the harder it will be to take tough decisions – decisions which are likely to result in major shifts in resources. The open, consensual approach is likely to lead to the introduction of 'objective' measures such as the use of formulae (discussed in detail later in this book).[24] The objectivity which the application of 'scientific' or 'economic' models gives tends to be cosmetic, however.[25] Allen and Tat put objective allocation mechanisms neatly into context:

> An objectively based budget allocation is no more than a mechanism that can be used by the librarian to exercise some increased control over the selection process, and to point to the areas of probable greatest need. To achieve the most effective acquisitions programme the librarian must first, or concurrently, establish the purpose the collection should serve, e.g. long-term support for research, current student learning, etc., – determine the priorities between different purposes, and undertake studies of user needs and the actual uses and levels of use of specific books. Then a budget formula can help to maintain a rational programme to build a relevant collection.[26]

While they refer to the allocation of *acquisitions* funds, the comments are equally applicable to other elements of the library budget, and the non-payroll and IT budgets in particular. It must also be said that a transparent allocation process, if supported by those who will lose as well as gain, can take much of the 'pain' out of the annual budgetary round, whether at institutional or library-specific level. A general acceptance of both process and results, coupled with a clear underlying rationale for the allocation of resources, can both speed and ease the resource manager's position considerably, even if in the final analysis the strict application of the allocation mechanism is tempered by the judgement of the library staff.[27]

Capital spend and life-cycle costing

While much of the library resource manager's disposable budget is used to acquire material on a regular, recurring basis, the stock (including electronic sources) thus amassed, and the infrastructure required to support it, constitutes a form of capital resource, requiring ongoing maintenance. In this context, Enright in particular proposed the development of life-cycle costing techniques to the management of library collections in order to ensure that 'maintenance obligations do not become such as to limit the scope for current acquisitions and equally that the scale of acquisitions is not such as to impose impossibly expensive maintenance liabilities which may weaken the library's ability to make its crucial contribution to university needs in the future'.[28]

Enright continues:

> The adoption of a life-cycle costing model should enable the academic librarian to demonstrate the real and genuine requirements of the library in terms of space, services and staff to achieve a balanced operation, together with the scale of any mismatch between the level of recurrent resources received and the obligations and responsibilities which the institution the library services expects it to discharge...
>
> ... the costs of owning physical assets can be substantially hidden because of the time scale over which costs are incurred . . . The visibility of life-cycle costs can be compared to that part of an iceberg as seen from the sea. Just as the destructive force of an iceberg is a function of its total mass, so the visible costs of physical assets obscure the force and power of underlying costs that propel its owner towards or away from prosperity, and, it could be added, survival.[29]

As space and budget problems become more severe, more academic libraries will be forced to consider storage and weeding as alternatives to new construction. Storage and weeding save space, but impose costs that may offset the potential savings. This is one obvious area where life-cycle costing is likely to be of great benefit.[30]

Blockages to effective resource management

Chapter 1 and the earlier parts of this chapter referred to a number of macro-level constraints upon the library resource manager, including institutional culture, approach and overall funding position. Such constraints may be perceived as blockages to effective resource management.

In addition, librarians' own attitudes can be a blockage to effective resource management. Professional attitudes can be misdirected: rather than take harsh decisions, library managers continue to maintain services in the face of substantial resource cuts without major re-examination of either role or financial management, simply because it is deemed to be the 'done thing' to provide certain services and unprofessional to consider doing otherwise. Protecting the library is often seen as the role of the senior library staff, even though good resource management would, in some cases at least, dictate more radical approaches to long-term problems.

As Webster points out, libraries can be the victims of their own success.

> Because of enhanced user education and service programmes, expectations created within the university may go unmet as financial pressures rise... the very technology and co-operative ventures that could help alleviate tight money problems are not possible because of initially high investment requirements.[31]

They are also victims of their size within the institution. They are 'big spenders' requiring large amounts of recurrent and capital funding, and in times of financial restraint parent institutions will be reluctant to concentrate hard-pressed budgets on support services, especially if there is no hard evidence that the institution is suffering unduly as a result of lack of investment.

A major difficulty for academic librarians is the lack of a definitive correlation between good library provision and effective teaching or research. There is a long tradition of saying – and even believing – that the library is a 'good thing' , but if there is any evidence for this, it is only the negative kind which indicates what happens if you do not have a good library rather than what happens if you do.[32] This negative evidence is not necessarily convincing to hard-nosed academics fighting for funds as positive evidence would be.

Problems or blockages arise when academic librarians try to make comparisons between their own and other institutions. Not only is there no single and standard way of collecting resource management data – allocations, activities, unit costs, productivity in given areas, perceived benefits to the different parent institutions – in many countries, but even where comparative data is collected between different library systems, it is often so general or unreliable as to be meaningless[33]. In many institutions, such comparative data is in any case greeted with cynicism when presented by the academic library staff. This may be because it represents 'lies, damn lies and statistics', data which has been manipulated by the librarian (whether consciously or unconsciously) to show good or bad differences, or which is regarded as unreliable and incomplete because of the reasons stated.

Institutional politics

There can be very few academic institutions, whatever the context or the environment in which they operate, which do not have a political dimension to them. Organizational politics have to be taken into account – and, indeed, used to advantage in any approach to resource management within the library. Typically, academic institutions operate a form of 'participatory governance'. Pierce and Andrew comment:

> The costs of participative management are generally high. In the 'participative' organised anarchy that is the university, loyalty to institutional objectives is often lacking and decisions are frequently made in an adversarial environment where compromise is dictated more by the necessity to secure votes than by the need to either benefit the whole or to develop sound innovation. Resources flow to the most politically astute, and the university often turns in on itself – particularly when a small group of faculty or deans becomes all-powerful.[34]

There is nothing new about the 'political game' which librarians in academic institutions have to play. As early as 1968, it was recommended that librarians should sharpen their political as well as their management skills as the 'boom' years of the 1960s came to an end.[35] As Lovecy has pointed out,[36] much of a senior resource manager's work has to be carried out in a political context. Success comes from 'the art of making possible – the art which can bring an idea to practical fruition. It is an art of compromise, cunning and cajolery; rarely, if it is to be successful, one of confrontation'. The successful manager has to be credible in terms of 'delivering the goods', however defined and at whatever cost quoted or agreed.[37]

Service-level agreements

In this context, many public sector organizations have developed service-level agreements which define the level and nature of service to be provided within a given resourcing level. The definitions thus produced can also form the basis of a more detailed assessment of performance of the service than would otherwise be the case. It is possible to measure effectiveness, at least in terms of what the service (as described and defined in the service-level agreement) set out to do in the first place. An SLA can also protect the library resource manager from being put under undue pressure to support additional activities or to develop new services within existing baselines when it is patently obvious that either additional resources are required or another activity will have to cease or be done differently in order to release the required resources. As with other similar resource management tools, there is a political element to the development and use of service-level agreements within academic institutions. However well-written the agreement, it has to be set into the local political context.[38]

Economic modelling

The development of new forms of (primarily electronic) provision has led to the formulation of various economic 'models' in library and information work. Recent initiatives have concentrated on the creation of models of book loan and document supply which allow both library and document supply service managers to take rational decisions on the best and most cost-effective provision of materials. The UK higher education library scene is changing rapidly as the Internet develops and as publishers and providers move from paper-based to electronic publications, as the e-Lib programme projects turn into widely-applicable products and as the traditional on-site library provision breaks down in the face of reducing resources, increasing costs and a greater and more divergent demand from users. The lack of recent comprehensive models in this area has been exposed by Friend.[39]

Experience from the MA/HEM (Methodology for Access/Holdings: Economic Modelling) project shows that pricing policies are one of the key determinants of the economic model selected (both by library managers and end-users) and how different forms of access to materials are perceived. Every service or 'good' has both a price and a value. The price is determined not simply on the basis of the cost (both direct and indirect) of providing the service but, as importantly, on the perceptions of the provider as to 'what the market will stand', and on what desired profit or surplus is to be made from the provision. The value is the user's perception of not only the price paid for the service or 'good' provided, but also the quality of the service. This involves not just the straight price paid, but also its speed, timeliness, and value to the person requiring the service, information, knowledge or other 'good'.[40]

This requires the development of a matrix of costs, prices, requirements, values, priority needs and of economic models and market profiles. This will allow the development of effective pricing policies and service marketing strategies amongst those who provide, or intend to provide, document delivery services, whether for returnable or non-returnable items. Only when such policies and strategies are achieved will a user community be able to take greatest and most cost-effective advantage of the technologies and services now being developed. Choice will be informed by sound economics and scarce resources will be better managed.[41]

Summary

Resource management in the majority of academic libraries is, then, a subtle blend of art and science, of objective and subjective decision making, blending accounting with politics and academic strategy. It is important for academic librarians to ensure that resources are managed – and seen to be managed – efficiently and effectively: no easy task given the competing claims of the various factions and the many pressures both internal and external. But it is the art of the possible in an often difficult if not impossible situation – a situation in which the academic library is only a subsystem in a much larger operation. National, regional and institutional systems will all need to be taken into account. Reference will have to be made to the broader political climate in which institutions of higher education have to operate. The financial position also has a crucial impact upon any resource management models developed. So does the academic environment. Effective resource management is also based on a number of factors: some environmental, some strategic and some infrastructural. These themes will be explored during the course of this book, in relation to types of library, types of resource and approaches to resource management.

References

1 Webster, D., 'Issues in the financial management of libraries', *Journal of library administration*, 3 (3/4), 1982, 16.
2 But see, for example, The Polytechnics and Colleges Funding Council/Universities Funding Council, *Capital funding and estate man-*

agement in higher education, [London], The Councils, 1992.

3   See, for example, Hayes, S., 'What does it really cost to run your library?, *Journal of library administration*, **1** (2), 1980, 1–10.

4   See, for example, Baker, D., 'Resource allocation in university libraries', *Journal of documentation*, **48** (1), 1992, 1–19.

5   See, for example, Joint Information Systems Committee [of the Higher Education Funding Councils] *Guidelines for developing an Information Strategy*, Bristol, The Committee, 1995. See also: Joint Information Systems Committee, *Five-year strategy, 1996–2001*. Bristol, JISC, 1996; Joint Information Systems Committee, *Electronic libraries programme*, 3rd ed. Bristol, HEFCE, 1996

6   For the UK position, see Universities Statistical Record, *University statistics, v3: finance*, Cheltenham, USR, annual, especially table 8. Table 11 deals with library spend.

7   See, for example, Lee, S. (ed.), *Acquisitions, budgets and material costs: issues and approaches*, New York, Haworth Press, 1988; Lee, S. (ed.), *Budgets for acquisitions: strategies for serials, monographs, and electronic formats*, New York, Haworth Press, 1991; Lee, S. (ed.), *Library material costs and access to information*, New York, Haworth Press, 1990.

8   See Johnson, E., 'Financial planning needs of publicly-supported academic libraries in the 1980s: politics as usual', *Journal of library administration*, **3** (3/4), 1982, 23–36 for a listing of the traditional budgetary concerns of academic library managers.

9   Hayes, S., 'Budgeting for and controlling the cost of other in library expenditures: the distant relative in the budgetary process', *Journal of library administration*, **3** (3/4), 1982, 121–31.

10 See, for example, Martin, M., *Budgetary control in academic libraries*, Greenwich, JAI Press, 1978.

11 'Operational costs in acquisitions', *The acquisitions librarian*, **4**, 1990.

12 See, for example, Baker, D., 'Resource allocation in university libraries', *Journal of documentation*, **48** (1), 1992; Beltran, A. B., ' Funding computer-assisted reference in academic research libraries', *Journal of academic librarianship*, **13** (1), 1987, 4–7; Lambert, J., 'Managing CD-ROM services in academic libraries', *Journal of librarianship and information science*, **26** (1), 1994, 23–8.

13 Revill, D., 'Cost centres and academic libraries', *British journal of academic librarianship*, **4** (1), 27–48, 1989.

14 Fletcher, J., 'Financial management systems', in Line, M., *Academic*

library management, London, Library Association, 1990, 220.

15 Breaks, M., 'Information systems strategies', *British journal of academic librarianship,* **6** (2), 1991, 67.

16 See for example the discussion of information systems strategies relating to UK universities in Breaks, M., 'Information systems strategies', *British journal of academic librarianship* **6** (2), 1991, 66.

17 Breaks, M., *op. cit.,* 70.

18 McCartney, N., 'Functions and objectives: polytechnic library', in Line., M., *op. cit.,* 32.

19 See, for example, Yavarkovsky, J., 'Planning and finance: a strategic level model of the university library', *Journal of library administration,* **33** (4), 1982, 37–54.

20 For the UK, the Universities Statistical Record, *University statistics v3: finance,* table 11 provides the raw data.

21 See, for example, The Joint Funding Councils' Libraries Review Group: *Report* [The Follett Report]. Bristol, The Councils, 1993, paras 117 ff.

22 The Polytechnics & Colleges Funding Council/ Universities Funding Council, *Capital funding and estate management in higher education,* Bristol, The Councils, 1992.

23 See, for example The UK Department of Education and Science, *Departmental report: the Government expenditure plans,* London, HMSO, annual.

24 Goehner, D. M., 'Allocating by formula: the rationale from an institutional perspective', *Collection management,* **5** (3/4), 161–74, 1983; Shirk, G.M., 'Allocation formulas for budgetary library materials: science or procedure?' *Collection management,* **6** (3/4), 37–47, 1984; Lester, D.W., 'Twenty years after Clapp-Jordan: a review of academic library funding formulas', in Spyers-Duran, P. and Mann, T.W., *Financing information services,* Westport, Conn, Greenwood, 1985, 79–90; American Library Association, *Guide to budget allocation for information resources,* Chicago, The Association, 1991.

25 See, for example, Council of Polytechnic Librarians [COPOL], *Working papers on bookfund allocation,* ed. D. Revill, Oxford, COPOL, 1985; Pierce, T., 'An empirical approach to the allocation of the university library book budget', *Collection management,* **2** (1), 1978, 39–58; Raffel, J., 'From economic to political analysis of library decision making', *College and research libraries,* **35** (6), 1974, 412–23; Shirk, G., 'Allocation formulas for budgeting library materials: science or procedure? *Collection management,* **6** (3/4), 1984, 37–47; Miller, E.P., and O'Neill, A.L., 'Journal dese-

lection and costing', *Library acquisitions: practice and theory*, **14** (8), 1990, 173–8; Enright, B., 'Concepts of stock', in Line, *op. cit.*, 43.

26   Allen, G. G. and Tat, L. C., 'An objective budget allocation procedure for academic library acquisitions', *Libri*, **37** (3), 1987, 220. See also: Goehner, D.M., 'Allocating by formula: the rationale from an institutional perspective, *Collection management*, **5** (3/4), 1983, 161–73; Genaway, D., 'Administering the allocated acquisitions budget: achieving a balanced matrix', *Acquisitions librarian*, **2**, 1989, 145–68; Genaway, D., 'Can formulas work?' *Library acquisitions: practice and theory*, **10** (4), 1986, 285–313; Schad, J.G., 'Fairness in book fund allocation', *College and research libraries*, **48** (6), 1987, 479–86; Sellen, M., 'Book budget formula allocations: a review essay', *Collection management*, **9** (4), 1987, 13–24.

27   See, for example, University of East Anglia, *Librarian's Annual Reports*, 1988–, during which time a detailed formula allocation process was introduced. See also *Serials*, **5** (1), March 1992 – a special issue devoted to budgeting in different kinds of library and *The acquisitions librarian*, **2**, 1989 – a special issue devoted to managing the acquisitions budget.

28   Enright, *op. cit.*, 47.

29   Enright, *op. cit.*, 47.

30   Lawrence, G. S., 'A cost model for storage and weeding programs', *College and research libraries*, **42** (2), 139–47, 1981. See also Council on Library Resources, *Economics of academic libraries*, Washington, American Council on Education, 1975.

31   Webster, *op. cit.*, 15.

32   See, for example, Erens, B., *Research libraries in transition: academic perceptions of recent developments in university and polytechnic libraries*, London, British Library, 1991 (LIR Report no. 82); Finch, H. and North, C., *The research process: the library's contribution in times of restraint*, London, British Library, 1991 (BL Research Paper no. 95); Pocklington, K. and Finch, H., *Research collections under constraint: the effect on researchers*, London, British Library, 1987 (BL Research Paper no. 36).

33   See, for example, Reid, M. and Bengtson, B., 'Report on technical services costs: a pre-conference to the 1986 ALA Annual Conference', *Library acquisitions: practice and theory*, **10** (4), 1986, 231–6.

34   *op. cit.*, 36–7.

35   Munn, Robert F., 'The bottomless pit, or the academic library, as viewed from the administration building', *College and research libraries*, **50** (6), 635–7, 1989. Reprinted from the January 1968 issue of the same journal,

51–4.

36 Lovecy, I., 'From dream to reality: the politics of an IT strategy', *British journal of academic librarianship*, **6** (2), 1992, 85–6.

37 Lovecy, *op. cit.*

38 See, for example, *Service level agreements: a compendium*, London, Chartered Institute of Public Finance and Accountancy, 1991; *The management of support service costs: a guide to service level agreements and accounting for overheads in local government: consultative manual*, London, Chartered Institute of Public Finance and Accountancy, 1990; Revill, D. and Ford, G., *Working papers on service level agreements*, [Brighton], SCONUL, 1994.

39 Friend, F., 'Economic models for academic libraries', *Publications of Essen University Library*, 20, 30–8, 1996. But see also Bookstein, A., 'An economic model of library service', *Library quarterly* **51** (4), 410–28, 1981.

40 Royan, B. and Brown, S., 'A decision making support tool for information acquisition: MA/HEM', *Vine*, 103, 1996; Baker, D., 'Counting the cost: the economics of electronic publishing', *Information Europe: EBLIDA magazine*, **2**, 14–16, 1996.

41 See, for example, Gollop, M., 'Estimating non-market costs in providing information services: developing an economic model', *Vine*, 103, 1996.

3

'Old' Universities

BERNARD NAYLOR

What is an 'old' university?

In 1992, there was a sea change in British higher education. Two of the most prominent features of the change were the abolition of the Council for National Academic Awards (CNAA), and the abolition of the distinction between 'the universities' funded through the Universities Funding Council (UFC), and 'the polytechnics', funded through the Polytechnics and Colleges Funding Council (PCFC). Since that date, UK higher education institutions have received state funding mainly through a new system, subdivided on a regional basis, as represented by the Higher Education Funding Council for England (HEFCE), the Scottish Higher Education Funding Council (SHEFC), the Higher Education Funding Council for Wales (HEFCW) and the Department of Education for Northern Ireland (DENI). With the abolition of the CNAA, institutions divided sharply into two groups, the first consisting of those which had the right to validate and award their own degrees, and the second consisting of those which had to submit their degree courses to validation by one of the bodies in the first group.

The significance of this distinction, between validating and validated institutions, is acknowledged by all of them. The larger validated institutions, in particular, usually manifest a keen ambition to achieve validating status and they sometimes exhibit, in their publicity, an apparent wish to emphasize that, in spite of not possessing validating powers, they are nevertheless mature and substantial institutions in their own right. Still, the term 'new' universities is also in everyday use, in the 1990s, to mean those institutions which used to be polytechnics, used to be funded by the PCFC, and used to award degrees validated by the CNAA. Granted that they now receive their funds from the same source as the 'old' universities and have an identical right to validate degrees, there is still a feeling that there is a difference between them and the former client institutions of the UFC.

This idea that some older universities are 'more equal' than others of more recent foundation is not new. It seems to repeat itself with every reform or development of the higher education system. New College, Oxford, founded in 1379, was so called to differentiate it from older Oxford colleges. In the 1820s, University College, London, was a 'new' institution founded explicitly to contrast with the two older English institutions of Oxford and Cambridge. In the 1880s, when a number of the newly founded provincial city institutions first sought government funding, they were seen as a 'new' group, contrasting with Cambridge, Oxford, London and Durham. In the 1950s, when a number of university colleges were deemed mature enough to award their own degrees rather than continuing to offer degrees validated by the University of London, this was seen as marking their admission, as a 'new' group, to the 'universities club'. In the 1960s, when several universities were founded from scratch under the auspices of the then University Grants Committee or UGC (which was funding all the existing universities), they were styled the 'new' universities. There was also a debate at the time, in the UK Standing Conference of National and University Libraries (SCONUL), as to whether these 'new' universities should be seen as qualified for admission to membership. (It went in their favour).

We can therefore expect that the 1990s distinction between 'old' universities and 'new' universities will gradually diminish in significance. In any continuing pecking order, 'new' universities and 'old' universities will increasingly intermingle, just as some of the 'new' universities of the 60s intake have now progressed to a point where they are, by many criteria, the equal or superior of some older foundations. The most important and enduring difference will continue to be the possession (or not) of the power to validate degrees. If, at some future date, a number of currently non-validating institutions should suddenly all be given validating powers, they too will probably for a time be regarded as the 'new' universities, and, by their succession to this title, they will probably confirm the assimilation of the 1992 crop of 'new' universities (the former polytechnics) into the overall category of 'old' universities.

With membership of the group of 'old' universities being periodically redefined over time, there is obviously some risk in trying to describe any particular environment and culture as characteristic of all members of the group. Nevertheless, it can be argued that the practice of resource management in the libraries of the 'old' universities has developed in ways which show signs not only of the origins of the group but also of the ways in which membership of the group itself has been redefined from time to time.

Democratic constitutions and traditions of learning

The pre-1992 universities have inherited, grown up with or developed a tradition of, democratic patterns of governance. The strongest expression of this is probably to be found in the conduct of the business of the Senate or Academic Board, 'the supreme body in matters academic'. Senates may well draw their membership from the whole range of teaching staff, from the most junior to the most senior. Senior administrators will be 'in attendance' and the heads of major academic support services such as the Library are likely to be *ex officio* members also. Senate will claim the right to discuss and comment on any matters it regards as relevant to the institution's academic mission. Those with experience of a Senate can probably confirm that the concept of 'matters relevant to the institution's academic mission' is often interpreted very generously.

There may well be some measure of illusion or self-deception in the assumptions some Senators make about the significance of the body on which they serve. There are undoubtedly some 'old' universities where central groups have achieved such a concentration of authority that Senate's role is effectively no more than symbolic. It may continue to debate the university's business, but might as well not do so, almost, for all the consequence there is in what it says. There will also undoubtedly be 'new' universities where the Senate has demonstrated in practice the influence which open debate in a broadly constituted body of academics can have on the conduct of the university's affairs. Still, in the case of the 'old' universities, the power of any central managing group is likely to be seen by Senators as a challenge (sometimes all too successful) to the authority of the body in which the ultimate destinies of an academic institution ought to be determined. In the 'new' universities, by contrast, the Senate is more likely to be challenging a well established tradition of central managerialism.

At some risk of over-simplifying the situation, it could be said that the 'old' universities are implicitly hoping to demonstrate that, while they may be more cumbersome and slower in reaching decisions, the democratic structures which are their inheritance will ultimately prove their superior value by the quality of the decisions they reach and by the degree of engagement and commitment they achieve from those who contribute, directly or indirectly, to reaching them.

An outstanding feature, therefore, of the environment in which the libraries of the 'old' universities operate can be suspicion of the concept of management itself. The present writer has had the experience of being asked by a senior teacher colleague whether he regarded himself as 'a manager' and being chided for answering in the affirmative, on the grounds that this represented a sell-out to a new, intrusive and unwelcome spirit which was fundamentally inimical to the model by which universities should conduct their affairs. In the library, this preferred model would manifest itself, at least among the academically and professionally qualified staff, by a management style which would impose the loosest possible rein on what was seen, not least by the library staff themselves, as a microcosm of the academic community, which needed this hands-off style if it was to achieve its fullest potential.

There is no doubt that increasing pressures on resources, and increasing pressures from within and from outside the university have borne down on this historic preference for a relaxed approach to management. However, as the more detailed exposition which follows will illustrate, there are traces of it almost wherever one looks, which show themselves in a measure of tension and ambiguity about management itself and whether increasingly tight and effective management should be seen as the unmixed blessing it would undoubtedly represent in most areas of enterprise outside the universities.

This tradition of practice is also supported in some measure by a long-standing academic tradition of increasing suspicion of academic disciplines, the nearer they approach to the pragmatic practices and requirements of the outside world. The struggle of engineering to establish its academic *bona fides* is a commonplace of the history of universities. In the twentieth century, the struggle of 'library science' or 'library management' to achieve academic respectability is a similar albeit minor theme. The 'new' universities of the 1990s are regarded, sometimes in a patronising way by some of their 'old' university peers, as pioneering courses which tread closer and closer to the boundaries of academic respectability, and may well cross them at times. It is no accident that there are more schools of librarianship (or whatever the present-day preferred terminology may be) in the 'new' universities sector than in the 'old'.

Whose library is it, anyway?

I am sometimes asked in conversation by teacher colleagues: 'How is *your* library getting on?' I usually begin my reply by saying: 'It is not *my* library. It is *your* library. I merely look after it on your behalf.' Despite the form of their question, the feeling of teaching staff that it is their library is a very real one in the 'old' universities and can have a significant impact on the management of the library's resources. Research studies carried out in academic libraries have conclusively demonstrated how wide the user constituency typically is for the literature of any particular discipline. It is always wider and often much wider than the number of people formally committed to that discipline as teachers or students. The day-to-day experience of librarians confirms the validity of this research finding. Nevertheless, the concept of *our* books and of *our* periodicals is commonplace in the parlance of university teachers. At its most assertive, it presents itself as a challenge to the right and duty of library staff to manage the resources of the library to the optimal benefit of all users.

Historically, the teachers may well have some right on their side. In the oldest universities (Cambridge and Oxford), the university library's status as a separate department is so clearly confirmed by history that any statement of ownership by the teachers sounds as though it is uttered on behalf of the whole university in respect of the whole library, rather than about some subject part of the collections. In many newer 'old' universities, however, the library may well owe its origins, in whole or in part, to collections which grew up in the teaching departments, subject to the total or partial control of the head of the department. In many such universities, there is a complex history, full of territorial rivalries, personal ambition, opportunities for aggrandisement, occasional altruism, and at times a care for the good use of resources, which has seen library collections originally established in and by departments come under the control of the Librarian. Sometimes they are relocated to a more central position as well, but, when they are not, traditional mindsets have been known to die hard, and librarians with political sensitivity will know that *de iure* control may need to be tempered by *de facto* acknowledgment of where real power in the university may lie. When it comes to the management of the library's resources, rational arguments and the political facts of life may sometimes prove hard to reconcile.

There is no doubt that the 'new' universities of the sixties, which now form part of the 'old' universities constituency, have had an effect on this situation. For them, central administrative control of library provision was a dominant feature from the start, and there was also a clear preference for physically centralized provision too. Increasingly since those times, whether it be in the allocation of money for buildings or the demand for statistical information, the funding bodies, whether UGC, UFC or HEFCE etc, have shown an increasing expectation that the libraries of a university will be centrally managed, and that library resource management will therefore be subject to overall central authority. Nevertheless, the practical experience of librarians is that, on the ground, things can be rather different, and the political climate of the institution can be a very important factor.

A question of scale

One of the factors which encouraged heads of teaching departments to relinquish control of the departmental library was the question of scale. Most of the institutions which achieved university status before 1960 were very small by present day standards, often with fewer than 1000 students. Nor, for many years, did they expect to grow. It was in the 1960s that many such institutions embarked on growth which saw them increase in size by a factor of four, five or six over the next twenty-five years. The new foundations of the sixties also started small, but, from the beginning, expected to grow to a much larger size than that which many of their predecessors had been pegged back to for so long.

By the mid-1980s, many of the nineteenth and twentieth century foundations had several faculties, any one of which was larger than the whole university of just thirty years previously. The problems of such growth were not much different from those faced by growing businesses or industrial enterprises. Whole new structures and patterns of management had to be considered. However, the most prominent large scale universities were not very useful as models. Cambridge, London and Oxford all had collegiate structures which broke their larger numbers down into smaller administrative units. These administrative units, like the smaller universities, were capable of being managed in a very 'hands on' way by their senior people because the scale was so small. It made reasonable sense to assume that 'the centre' could look after the mundane questions of staffing, capital allocations, equipment provision, heating and lighting and so on, thereby freeing other staff, teachers particularly but also those in services such as the library, to concentrate on the 'real' task of teaching students, conducting research or serving users.

The growth in the size and complexity of universities was accompanied by a corresponding growth in libraries. Not surprisingly, the introduction of resource management arrangements appropriate to this increased scale did not always keep pace. Universities have also varied in the importance they have attached to the development of 'scaled up' management arrangements. This means that, in practice, the responsibility for resource management which any librarian may have to take up on succeeding to office can vary quite significantly from one institution to another.

If we take, as an example, the major investment represented by a new automated library management system, universities will differ greatly in the amount of responsibility they assign to the Librarian. In one institution, the Librarian may have considerable freedom of action, subject to the practical constraint that the cost of the system will be recovered as an annual charge against the ordinary level of resource allocated to the library. In another, the Librarian's responsibility may be to recommend a purchase to the university authority, but not in the expectation that the financial implications of the preferred deal will be charged in full against the library's own resources.

A value-for-money debate may then be expected at the highest university level, where the resource consequences of the decision will have to be managed.

A question of scope

More surprisingly, the Librarian may find that the central university has retained more authority over the staffing establishment, or certain administrative costs, than it has over the money allocated for buying books, periodicals, and electronic services. The restructuring of library services in a period of rapid technological change may cry out for flexibility in the management of various elements of provision, such as staff and materials. The prevailing resource management arrangements may forbid this, and any proposal for change may be viewed with suspicion.

Higher education is a staff-intensive activity. A very high percentage of any university's expenditure will be on staff. Even the growth of the information technology spend has not affected this very much. In this respect, university libraries are not typical of their institutions, staff expenditure being more commonly in the forty to sixty range as a percentage of total library spend, depending on the precise characteristics of the institution and the library. The other major element of expenditure has always been on books, periodicals and binding. More recently, libraries have experienced rapidly growing equipment needs, especially to meet the demands generated by information technology developments.

Although staff expenditure in libraries is low, by comparison with that in teaching departments, it is staff expenditure, above all, which has constantly been subjected to greatest pressure from the university centre. By comparison, expenditure on books and periodicals tends to be regarded much less critically. Even in the age of the Internet, this is still largely true. In any period of retrenchment, a suspicion often surfaces, in the university at large, that the library will take 'the soft option' and cut expenditure on books and periodicals rather than reduce staff. If additional resources become available, the expectation of the university community is all too often that they can be spent on books and periodicals with no allowance needing to be made for additional and corresponding staff provision. It is almost as though there is an assumption that books can acquire and catalogue themselves and place themselves on shelves without human intervention.

This could perhaps be seen as a hangover from the earlier period when the staffing levels of all university activities including the library were seen as something the centre could take care off, leaving the library staff free for the task of delivering services. Continued to the present day, it introduces a particular tension into the management of library resources. As has already been suggested, there is no good reason to assume that today's distribution of library resource as between staff, printed materials, electronic services and other lesser areas of provision is optimal for all time. However, in any review of expenditure, the Librarian is likely to have to contend with an assumption on the part of the centre that transferring resources *from* one of the other areas into staffing has got to be more suspect than any transfer the other way.

This, in its turn, might be explained as evidence of caution about incurring expenditure which could have recurrent implications. However, the experience of library staff is that there is not the same caution about channelling money into additional periodical subscriptions, even though they also have serious implications for recurrent spend. The problem may rather be inspired by a lack of trust in the hard-headedness of library staff, and whether, in the end, they have the courage to align the deployment of resources with the real needs of the institution. For the librarian, it tends to emerge as a genuine political constraint on identifying and advocating the policies which are really best for the institution, especially if they involve more staff expenditure.

However, there are also more hopeful trends. Despite the territorial claims of teaching departments, there has clearly been a trend in the 'old' universities in favour of the centralization of library management. This could not possibly have come about without central support. The modern library is quintessentially a resource shared by all and there is much more support for this, even in the 'old' universities, than there was 30 or 40 years ago. This trend is strongly supported by recent developments at the level of the funding authorities. Following the Follett report, institutions have been called on to formulate 'information strategies'. A bit more precision as to what is meant by the term 'information strategies' would not go amiss. Still, institutions do recognize in the call a demand that they take a more strategic view of library provision. It no longer appears to be a matter which can safely be left to work itself out through a power struggle between the librarian and some people in departments who have a poor grasp of the complex questions of resource deployment with which the librarians of the late twentieth century have to grapple.

The demand for accountability

'Old' universities, whatever their vintage, will remember the time when the resourcing model was opaque. In those days, the funding authority would make an allocation to each university with only the most general indication as to what provision they were expected to make with it. Sometimes, the truth might only emerge with a subsequent reduced grant, containing an implicit penalty for the institution which, in using its allocation, had not met the funding authority's expectations. Today's regime is very different. Institutions now know exactly the basis for the allocation they have received, in terms of students to be funded at various levels in various disciplines, and in terms of reward for research performance. The claims of teaching departments about *their* books and *their* periodicals may have weakened over the years. More recently, their concept of *their* money has sharpened massively. Even though the funding authorities have made it clear that there is no requirement to make the basis for the allocation the basis for distribution within the institution, the pressure to do so is very strong.

Within each 'per student' unit of resource, an unquantified element for library provision is assumed to be included. Herein lies a stimulus for reviving the teaching departments' assumption that they should have more say in management of the library resource, since, according to the funding authority's model, it amounts to a slice (more emotively, a top-slice) from what has been allocated to the university on account of the teaching departments' student load.

There is another point of view from which to look at this. As universities have become larger, they have come to recognize that devolving more responsibility is imperative if resources are to be managed properly. As a first step, obvious elements of budget such as staff are devolved. Then there is a growing appreciation of the good sense, wherever possible, of placing the responsibility for spending where its implications can be most keenly felt. Heating costs may be especially hard to devolve, but it is a simple enough illustration to say that only the person feeling the cold can decide whether the discomfort is so great that extra spending on more warmth is worthwhile.

Universities further down this road are now devolving the cost of space down to individual budgetary units. On the face of it, it must be seen as salutary for space no longer to feature as a 'free good', and for budgetary units to be compelled to decide whether they prefer to dispense with some space, and thereby save money which can be allocated to meet equipment needs. A system of charging the library for space is particularly hard to handle, considering that the need for library space, whether for shelves or for study places, is most often driven by the demands of the teaching departments. If the cost of space is devolved back to its source in the teaching departments, this is at a cost to the library in terms of flexibility in the overall management of resources.

Somewhere down the same road, there is the question of fund-raising by the librarian. If responsibility for the expenditure side of the library accounts is devolved, then why not some responsibility for the income side? This could seem like an entirely understandable and commendable response to financial stringency. The more money the library can raise, the less it is dependent on an allocation from the university. However, it is reasonable to ask how far it is legitimate for a library to have an increasing proportion of its resources which is, as it were, 'semi-detached' from the university community it is meant to serve. For some other administrative service departments, it seems of very doubtful legitimacy. For the library, it does at least pose questions about mission.

Where is this process of devolving responsibility to end? Is the librarian the best judge of which library needs are most worth meeting? If the need is not for a changed distribution of resource within the library, but rather for the award of additional resource to the library, taken from elsewhere, who is to decide that that need has been proven? Is it the librarian who manages the service, or the teacher, who has responsibility for the students' education and for his or her own research? Calling in the university to mediate between the two parties takes the situation back in time, to the 'bad old days' before devolution began, and calls into question the whole of the process. For the 'old' universities, there is such a complex accumulation of old attitudes and new imperatives surrounding such questions, that the librarian's management of the library's resources is bound to be affected.

Pressures on the periphery

The development of information technology has imposed major new resource demands on all higher education libraries. The libraries of the 'old' universities are no exception, and in that fundamental respect they are not different from their 'new' university peers. What has to be noted is not the difficulty of evaluating the need, nor principally the difficulty of meeting it financially, given present financial constraints. Those problems are shared by everyone. There is an additional problem in drawing the boundaries between the library's need and the needs of adjacent departments (especially the computing service) in ways which can readily be managed. However, the 'old' universities have seen so much change in recent years in the approach to devolving responsibility and, in consequence, in basic patterns of management, changes which have aroused a lot of debate, and been charged with such a weight, albeit now, perforce, a diminishing weight, of past history.

This is one situation in which 'convergence' of the two services (to use current terminology) might be seen, in the 'old' universities, as a welcome solution to an otherwise intractable problem of resource allocation and management. The evidence is still inconclusive as to whether this actually resolves the problem or whether it simply imposes a requirement to settle it within the boundaries of one department or cost centre, rather than across two. And how does that sit with the institutional imperative to take a more strategic view of such matters?

Commitment to research

With the recent completion (at the end of 1996) of the fourth Research Assessment Exercise, there has been additional reinforcement of one major difference between the 'new' universities and the 'old'. Somewhere in the middle of any resulting league table, there will be a degree of intermingling of 'new' and 'old' in the research pecking order. The principal message is still overwhelmingly clear. Research excellence is very heavily concentrated in the 'old' university constituency.

In the new framework of assigning managerial responsibility, resources for research provision pose particular questions. Resources received on account of teaching are assigned under subject headings which correspond to teaching departments. But, in the end, they are about supporting the student experience. Some students undoubtedly make little or no use of the library, and the academic performance of some of those seems none the worse for that. But then, students sometimes skip lectures or even fail to submit assignments. There is plenty of countervailing evidence that, for many students, library use is a major and integral part of the learning experience, and also that, often enough, it does not take the particular form which the teachers themselves might recommend. Texts which are recommended may not be consulted, while others which are not recommended appear to perform usefully in place of them. So libraries have grounds for claiming that, while teaching departments are the bases for computing the allocations from the funding authorities, when it comes to earning the allocations for teaching, the libraries certainly do their share.

It is not quite so simple in the matter of research. There the award is for the research carried out by the members of the teaching departments. It is much more difficult for the library to claim to have superior insight than the researchers have as to what provision is needed. And yet, provision for research is not always identical with provision for the existing community of research. There are long-established traditional responsibilities, which need continuing support, and long-term future needs, and both of them may extend beyond the existing research community of the university, and may need further resourcing.

Summary

Universities which are 'old' by present-day nomenclature are, nonetheless, heavily affected by present day pressures and trends. What they bring into today's complex scenario is a tangled legacy of attitudes and outlooks. These cannot necessarily be clearly defined, partly because some of the 'old' universities are older than others.

The older 'old' universities have a different heritage which they have no doubt shared to some extent with their more recently acquired 'old' university peers. And attitudes and outlooks have rubbed off the other way too. The first task of a newly appointed librarian, it has often been said, is to try to understand as closely as possible the peculiar mix of attitudes which make up the culture of the particular institution he or she must serve. In the end, resource management is a political exercise in which the librarian must participate.

4

New Universities

COLIN HARRIS

The 'new' universities

The SCONUL conference of 1986, in Reading, was attended by a number of German university librarians. One of the British speakers, a founder member of CURL (the Consortium of University Research Libraries) and the librarian of a leading CURL library, at one point offered to assist the German guests' understanding of the British university system by offering an analogy: 'The British university system, like the Football League, has four divisions'. The fourth division comprised the dozen 'technological' universities, those that had until relatively recently been the Colleges of Advanced Technology. They were the 'new universities' of their time. Precisely which universities were in the third and second divisions, and indeed in the first division, could be the subject of very heated discussion indeed, but they would include the 'Robbins' universities – the new universities of their time, those provincial former 'university colleges' that had for decades awarded external degrees of the University of London and then became universities in their own right in the 1950s – the new universities of their time! (The categorization of British universities is itself a fascinating industry. A recent paper in *Higher education review*[1] reviews a number of categorizations, ranging from thirteen categories to twenty. Indeed, Peter Scott's categories include not only 'new universities' but also 'old new universities'.)

All of these 'new universities of their time' do not include what we currently call the 'new universities', which were then polytechnics; they became universities as a result of the Further and Higher

Education Act, 1992.

The polytechnics were created from the end of the 1960s onwards, largely as a result of the redesignation of former colleges of technology, commerce and art that had been engaged in advanced work (i.e. higher education level) or as a result of mergers of such colleges. Such mergers continued through the 1970s and 1980s, particularly to incorporate a large number of former colleges of education (which had earlier been known as teacher training colleges). The resulting institutions are in some cases very complex indeed, often with sites spread over very wide geographical areas, and often with a variety of traditions and cultures, some of which were and still are very hard to change. While this complexity is generally acknowledged, what is not often realized in consideration of new universities is how far back their roots go. For example, the first components of what is now the Manchester Metropolitan University started life in the 1820s and 1830s, and the way in which that university came about was very complex indeed.[2]

Management structures and styles

It seems to be part of the received wisdom of university management that new universities are more 'managerial' than are old universities, which are generally viewed as more 'collegial'.(There is an interesting discussion of this issue in Dopson and McNay, 1996.[3]) There are two principal reasons for this: the first is to do with the manner in which senior offices are filled and held. Old universities have regarded and treated the senior positions of Pro-Vice-Chancellor, Dean and Head of Department as temporary posts, filled normally but not exclusively by existing professors, perhaps partly (particularly in the case of Head of Department) on a rotation basis. Further Education and the polytechnics had no such posts: all positions were filled on a full-time, permanent, dedicated basis.

The fact that managers are appointed on a permanent rather than temporary basis does not itself produce 'managerialism'. But the second way in which the old and the new differed is in the mechanism of collegial management: the committee. In new universities, many of the functions performed in old universities by committees are performed by the managers. Committees exist in new universities, of course, but are principally concerned with academic programmes or with accountability at a high level. Following the Jarratt Report on efficiency in universities in 1985 (Committee of Vice-Chancellors and Principals, 1985) committee structures in old universities were rationalized; many disappeared, the frequency of meetings was reduced and business streamlined. In some cases, university senates were reduced in size, with entitlement to membership narrowed. Lee Harvey and Peter Knight take a sinister view of the 'new managerialism':

> The rise of managerialism involves a shift towards a more formalized management structure and control at the institutional level which is reflected in more direct management of the higher education system by the government.[4]

They go on to comment on its origins and spread:

> In Britain, this managerialist tendency first appeared in the former polytechnic sector. Following the incorporation of the polytechnics, there was a centralising of control and an erosion of the contribution of academics to institutional policy making.... This has subsequently spread into the traditional university sector.

Other factors are of as great or greater significance. For example, perhaps of more interest than the differences between old and new universities are the similarities: they virtually all have permanent, dedicated posts of Vice-Chancellor (or equivalent), Registrar (or equivalent), Finance Director (or equivalent), Personnel Director (or equivalent), Estates and Buildings Director (or equivalent), Librarian, Computing Services Director, Educational or Media Services Director (the latter three increasingly commonly merged in some way at the top level). So a large part of the enterprise, whether in old or new universities, is run by full-time, permanent, dedicated officers. It is no doubt the case that, even where committees exist to oversee some of these areas, their actual task is to rubber-stamp the deliberations, decisions and deeds of the permanent officers, particularly the more senior ones. It seems that every British university has a 'Monday meeting' of the very senior staff, to decide the policy that committees will later believe themselves to be deciding.

The other obviously significant factor is to do with the character of individual players (and, of necessity, with relationships between and among them). And character refers to more than simply 'personality';

for example, anyone who has worked for more than one Vice Chancellor will know that two Vice Chancellors can be like chalk and cheese, in their levels of being informed and connected, their competence (for example in simple things like chairing meetings), their professional respect for others, their 'collegiality', and so on. The mark that a Vice-Chancellor, a Registrar, a Finance Director can make on the way in which a university is run can be as fundamental as the organizational chart.

Research in new universities

Perhaps the defining feature of new universities, reflecting the explicit assumptions behind their creation as polytechnics, is that they are predominantly teaching institutions. Research was very slow to develop in polytechnics, although some developed further and faster than others. Regarding polytechnics, two factors contributed to a preoccupation with the development of teaching. The first was that they were created to be teaching institutions; the second was that, unlike the universities, they were not in a position to be self-regulating in respect of their academic affairs. Courses had to be approved by an external agency, the Council for National Academic Awards, which had the power to withhold approval and to require changes not only to the academic structure and content of courses but also to an institution's policy and practice in respect, for example, of library or other infrastructural support.

The effect of these pressures was to make polytechnics much more explicitly concerned with the development of courses, including their methods of delivery and support. Curriculum or course development, involvement in the development of teaching as well as, or as opposed to, research, was a possible criterion for promotion of a lecturer in a polytechnic long before it was possible in old universities. This emphasis was reflected too in the development of library and other educational support. Modern educational technology (technology both as machinery and as techniques), for example was, in general, much more visible in polytechnics than in universities. Similar concerns were reflected in the development of library services; in the absence of large collections and the absence of the will to build large collections, there was more concern for the exploitation of stock, the linking of library provision and use to the educational (i.e. teaching) mission, etc. So user education, information services, collection management, etc. were much more typical of a polytechnic library's programme than of a university's.

Research developed later; some polytechnics, now the new universities, developed substantial programmes of research, but, as the results of various Research Assessment Exercises show, their performance in general has been substantially inferior to that of old universities (within which, of course, there are huge variations).

At the time of writing, three factors threaten to diminish further the significance of research in the new universities. First, the results of the 1996 Research Assessment Exercise, like earlier exercises, show the amount and quality of research in new universities to be, on the whole, much inferior to that in old universities. Seven grades were used in that exercise (1, 2, 3b, 3a, 4, 5, 5*); not one new university received a single 5*; grade 5 is very rare in new universities, and most did not receive a single grade 4. Overall, the system performed better than in previous exercises, and new universities performed better, but the differential remains.

The second factor is the funding of research that will reflect achievements in the Research Assessment Exercise. Contrary to earlier statements of policy, it has been decided that the 5* grade will be rewarded at a higher level than grade 5. (Earlier the policy was that 5* would simply be an acknowledgement of outstanding quality, with no additional financial reward.) There is no additional funding for research; in order to reward best departments at the previous level, departments with lower grades will suffer. Grades 1 and 2 will attract no funding for research, although a small amount will be set aside to provide some support for development in Grade 2 departments in new universities only. It seems likely that new universities will wish to take stock of the importance of research, of the effort that is expended on it and of the financial rewards that the present model delivers.

The third factor is the 'Harris Report' on postgraduate education,[5] named after the Chairman of the group that produced it, Martin Harris, Vice-Chancellor of the University of Manchester. The report recommends that postgraduate research should take place only in departments that secured a Grade 3 or better in the last Research Assessment Exercise.

The contribution of research to the funding of new universities, both through the Funding Councils' grants and directly through grants from research councils and other bodies, is clear. But the way in which resources are deployed in support of research and teaching is not clear. Overall, old universities show a higher per capita spend per student than do new universities, and (or but) the percentage of the university's budget devoted to the library is frequently lower. The latter point is explained by the presence in the budgets of old universities of much larger amounts for research. The former point, that the per capita spend per student is higher, is explained by the fact that, in general in old universities, the spend is intended to support a much greater research activity as well as students. To compare spending across the spectrum of institutions in which research may account for from 5% of the budget to upwards of 50% of the budget in terms of spending per student is very misleading.

As early as 1987, the Advisory Board for the Research Councils had proposed (in respect of the old universities) that there should be three types of university: R (research universities), T (universities whose function was primarily teaching) and X (universities which would have a selective research mission). Nothing was done explicitly to create this hierarchy. Instead, the polytechnics became part of the university system, maintaining their teaching role, and Research Assessment Exercises combined with market forces produced the RTX system. The 'Russell Group' has emerged as the elite group of research universities (and they lobby for the position to be formalized), the new universities, although with pockets of good quality, are plainly inferior on the whole to old universities in terms of research performance and earnings, and the rest are left to compete for places in the league tables.

Resource management in new universities

In recent years, the body responsible for disbursing the higher education budget among universities (the University Grants Committee, then the Universities Funding Council, then the Higher Education Funding Councils for England, Wales and Scotland) has made more explicit the mechanisms – essentially the formula – by which the grants to individual institutions were determined. One of the consequences of this was that individual departments in universities could see much more clearly how their work contributed to the university's income. Inevitably, the pressure grew for the distribution of funds within the university to be more transparent, explicitly reflecting departments' numbers of students in different disciplines (funding for courses in different groups of disciplines varies), numbers on undergraduate or postgraduate courses, Research Assessment Grade, research income, etc. In many universities a more transparent resource model has been introduced, frequently coupled with an increase in devolved responsibility for budgets. On the whole, it is probably true to say that such a model is less prevalent in new universities than in old, and that new universities' finances are increasingly 'managed' from the centre.

One of the consequences of this is that institutions with devolved budgets are less likely to be in a position to undertake major centrally funded projects, unless there is a top-slicing mechanism, but, once devolution has begun, the new budget holders are likely to resist strongly any moves to top-slice 'their' funds. Following the Follett Report, for example, one old university was offered funds towards an extension of the library building on the normal condition that the funds were matched in some degree by the university itself. A number of millions of pounds were needed, but, the devolution mechanism having distributed resources to faculties, it would only be possible to raise the matching funding by persuading budget holders to contribute. The chances of this happening were so slim that the university turned down the offer of funding and went without its library extension. Meanwhile, its new university neighbour, with its central management of resources, achieved its library extension.

It is probably true to say, therefore, that the process of submitting proposed budgets for consideration by the centre is more prevalent in new universities, where resource allocation is less likely to be determined by formula, and more likely to involve judgement and prioritization by senior university management.

A recent report by Angluin and Scapens suggests that not only are transparency of resource allocation and management as 'command and control' linked (inversely) but also that academic staff morale is likely to be affected by the transparency of resource allocation: 'It is the universities with high-quality information systems, transparent resource allocation and devolved budgets which are perceived as "fair"'.[6]

It is probably now the case that a distinction cannot readily be made between practice in old universities and new. Burgess,[8] quoted by Williams,[7]

> made a distinction between an 'autonomous tradition', 'aloof, academic, conservative and exclusive', and a 'service tradition', 'responsive, vocational, innovating and open.

Burgess related the first model to British universities and the second to polytechnics and colleges:

> In terms of this analysis there has been a considerable shift since 1981 towards the service tradition by both universities and non-university institutions, which in some respects, is paradoxical, since all polytechnics and major colleges are now autonomous. A likely explanation is that both universities and non-university institutions are now in a market environment ...[9]

This is accounted for by the changing basis of funding of universities:

> general grants to universities, with little detailed accountability for their use, were replaced by a system where virtually all funds received are deemed to be for specific services rendered. Polytechnics and colleges, which at the beginning of the 1980s, were for the most part subject to line-by-line budgets and administered according to local authority procedures, are now autonomous and funded for teaching in a way that is similar in all essentials to universities; and they have the imminent prospect of being called universities and funded as such.[10]

That prospect came to pass, of course, and Williams believes that the ways in which institutions receive their funds have a strong influence upon subsequent resource allocation and management within the institution. But it seems likely that it is not possible to characterize resource management in new universities as significantly and generally different from that in old universities. Differences exist, of course, but it is likely that a range of practice will be found in each group.

Some of the differences will be explained by the different legacies of the two groups. For example, in managing human resources, only the old universities have to cope with tenure, and then only in respect of those academic staff whose positions have not changed in recent years. In practice, this has not been significant; the management of cuts in staffing and the use of redundancy has not been significantly different between the sectors.

References

1   Tight, Malcolm, 'University typologies re-examined', *Higher education review*, **29** (1), Autumn 1996, 57–77.

2   Fowler, Alan and Wyke, Terry, *Many arts, many skills: the origins of the Manchester Metropolitan University*, Manchester, The Manchester Metropolitan University Press, 1993.

3   Dopson, Sue and McNay, Ian, 'Organizational culture', in Warner, David and Palfreyman, David, *Higher education management: the key elements*, Buckingham, Society for Research into Higher Education and the Open University Press, 1996, 16–32.

4   Harvey, Lee and Knight, Peter T., *Transforming higher education*. Buckingham, Society for Research into Higher Education and the Open University Press, 1996, 69.

5   Higher Education Funding Council for England, *Review of postgraduate education*, 2 vols., Bristol, Higher Education Funding Council for HEFCE, the Committee of Vice-Chancellors and Principals and the Standing Conference of Principals, 1996.

6   Angluin, David and Scapens, Robert, 'Accountancy called to book in quest for value', *Times Higher Education Supplement*, No. 1272, 21 March 1997, 12.

7   Williams, Gareth, *Changing patterns of finance in higher education*, Buckingham, Society for Research into Higher Education and the Open University Press, 1992.

8   Burgess, T., 'Autonomous and service traditions', in Wagner, L. (ed.) *Agenda for institutional change in higher education*, Leverhulme Programme of Study into the Future of Higher Education, 3. Research into Higher Education Monographs, 45. London: Society for Research into Higher Education. (Quoted in Williams, G.), 1982.

9   Williams, *op. cit.*, 140–1.

10   Williams, *op. cit.*, 141.

Further reading

Committee of Vice Chancellors and Principals, *Report of the Steering Committee on Efficiency Studies in Universities*, (Chairman: A. Jarratt). London, Committee of Vice-Chancellors and Principals, 1985.

Higher Education Funding Council for England (etc.), *The 1996 Research Assessment Exercise: the outcome*, Bristol, HEFCE, 1996.

Scott, Peter, *The meaning of mass higher education*, Buckingham, Open University Press, 1995.

5

Colleges of Higher Education

JULIE PARRY

Introduction

'Colleges range from the large multidisciplinary institutions to smaller monotechnics, from the purposefully secular to the profoundly denominational, and from the peaceful provincial to the uncompromisingly metropolitan.'[1] Martin Gaskell neatly sums up the range and diversity of the colleges of higher education in the UK. These are not universities, nor are they further education colleges, although they may share many characteristics with both. Outside the colleges themselves, the lack of understanding about what they are and what they do seems fairly widespread. It is the aim of this chapter to clarify the role and ethos of the higher education colleges by adopting one of them, Bath College of Higher Education, as the subject of a case study.

In 1996 the Higher Education Funding Council for England (HEFCE) funded 48 colleges of higher education, in addition to the universities and the institutions belonging to the University of London. Some of these colleges have their own degree awarding powers while others have chosen to award the degrees of nearby universities. All have a commitment to quality and are subject to exactly the same quality assurance procedures as universities. In addition to well-established strengths in teaching, a number of colleges now also demonstrate an increasingly high research profile.

Some of the 'monotechnic' colleges have long and proud histories as providers of specialized education. For example, those with sound reputations for teaching in the arts include Norwich School of Art, the Royal Northern College of Music and Rose Bruford College (drama). Other specialized subjects include careers guidance at the College of Guidance Studies and agricultural studies at Writtle College and Harper Adams Agricultural College. The church colleges, such as St Martin's College, Lancaster and Westminster College, Oxford account for approximately a third of the institutions in the sector.

Unifying themes

The Standing Conference of Principals has identified a number of unifying themes in 'Quality and diversity', its response to the National Committee of Inquiry into Higher Education chaired by Sir Ron Dearing.[2]

- **Access** the colleges have a well-established record of welcoming a broad base of applicants including part-time and non-traditional students;
- **Excellence** in certain areas such as Art and Design, Primary Teacher Education, Agriculture and Theatre Studies, the colleges offer centres of national, and sometimes international excellence;
- **Ethos** the colleges have a tradition of support to their students – this takes a particular form in the church colleges but is a feature of the college sector more generally;
- **Growth** the colleges have contributed fully to the development of new cross-discipline studies and professionally-related areas and to the general expansion of student numbers;
- **Efficiency** colleges tend to have low unit costs, short lines of management, and a flexible approach to student needs which enables them to offer particular value for money.

In size, the colleges range from the College of Guidance Studies with 130 students to Southampton Institute with over 13,000 students. The range of subjects offered in the multidisciplinary colleges often reflects the specialisms of their founding institutions. The education of teachers, from initial teacher training to continuing professional development, features in many of the colleges.

Convergence

Many of the colleges have been prime movers in establishing converged services. Terminology differs but the types of service commonly found in different combinations include libraries, information technology, media production and reprographics. Converged services may be the responsibility of a single manager who may or may not be a librarian. In some colleges different services operate closely together but under separate managers. A service that is converged, whether at a structural or operational level, offers great potential in terms of quality and there are significant opportunities for income generation. At the same time, the challenges for resource managers should not be underestimated. A failure to recognize or agree mutually supportive aims and objectives can cause endless difficulties. For example, computer managers are quite rightly concerned about security of information and need to protect networks from unauthorized access. On the other hand, the priority of librarians is to enable users to access information and to exploit as wide a range of sources as possible. An institutionally agreed information strategy is obviously invaluable in enabling each party to achieve its respective aims without undermining the activities of the other.

The development of customer-oriented services often requires explicit standards of behaviour and appropriate training. Librarians, computer technicians and reprographics staff may struggle to find common ground as they learn to work together to meet user needs. As well as establishing mutually supportive goals at strategic and policy levels, managers of these particular human resources need to consider such thorny questions as: Who will be responsible for routine maintenance of equipment? Should IT staff and library staff have to adhere to the same dress code? Who should train library users to use the Internet?

Bath College of Higher Education

The diversity already identified within this sector makes it difficult to generalize about the factors which influence resource management in colleges of higher education. Therefore, one institution has been selected for a more in-depth examination. Bath College of Higher Education (BCHE) is a multidisciplinary institution with approximately 2,500 full-time equivalent (FTE) students and over 300 staff. The college boasts a number of unique features (and challenges), particularly relating to its location and accommodation. On the other hand, many of the demands facing this college are exactly the same as those being faced by fellow institutions in the sector and, indeed, by many universities and further education colleges. Resource managers in other HE colleges may recognize some similarities with their own organizations but in many respects there will be significant differences. Library and information staff in universities and colleges of further education may also note certain similarities with their own institutions.

It is not the aim of this case study to provide a blueprint for good practice, although there are many examples of good practice in the college. As in many other institutions, solutions to problems are often pragmatic. However, the strength of sharing experiences lies in enabling others to compare the effectiveness of their own procedures, to learn new ideas and to reject concepts that would clearly be inappropriate under different circumstances.

The management of library resources at BCHE is closely bound up with the management of resources at institutional level. To provide a specific example, all IT equipment purchased must meet the requirements laid down in the IT standards policy and must be approved by the IT manager. Computer Services will not undertake the installation or maintenance of any equipment which has not been through this procedure. Clearly, this has an impact on the planning and management of all computer systems. Therefore, as well as setting resource management in the general context of college libraries, this chapter will also consider how BCHE's management, structure and operating procedures specifically influence the management of its library resources.

The present college was formed in 1983 as a result of mergers between Bath College of Education (which specialized in home economics), Newton Park College of Education (formerly a teacher training college) and Bath Academy of Art. Students are drawn from all over the United Kingdom and there are significant numbers of international students, particularly from Japan. Various academic initiatives also attract students from Europe and the United States.

The college awards its own degrees up to taught Masters' level and provides research supervision for MPhil and PhD degrees awarded by the University of the West of England, Bristol. There are four faculties: Art and Music; Education and Human Sciences; Humanities; and Applied Sciences. Art subjects are taught at the Sion Hill campus in Bath while all other subjects are based at the Newton Park campus, some 8 km away. With the exception of Art and Design, all undergraduate courses are modularized. A number of postgraduate courses are offered, ranging from Education (PGCE) to Health Studies and Irish Studies to Visual Communication.

Library and Information Services

Unlike many of its sister institutions, the college has largely rejected a converged model for its libraries, IT, reprographics and media production. The first three are operated as separate, central services while the production of media, such as sound and image recordings, is undertaken by faculty technicians. The print room which produces in-house, print-based material charges for its services but computer services are centrally funded and not cross-charged. There is an element of operational convergence in that the Library and Information Services (LIS) staffing establishment includes an IT Officer who teaches IT skills and is responsible for a suite of computer rooms. These house a variety of hardware and software which is available on open access to students as well as being used for teaching purposes.

There is a library at each campus, each offering a range of standard academic library services. Both libraries benefit from committed staff, efficient systems and sound, basic collections. However, opening hours, workflows and the teaching of information handling skills are all constrained to a certain extent by low staffing levels. The OLIB library computer system was purchased in 1996 to enable the library to make its catalogue available via the World Wide Web. This Oracle-based system was chosen to allow connectivity with other college systems. The ability to download student records has removed the necessity to employ temporary staff to key in membership data at the beginning of each academic year. Both libraries have suites of networked computers which are in great demand by students for word-processing, spreadsheet work and Internet access. A limited number of students have e-mail accounts.

It is the relentless growth in the availability and sophistication of

IT that perhaps puts the most strain on Library and Information Services. Effective service delivery relies on achieving the right balance between human and technical resources. However, the appointment of new staff represents a long-term financial commitment in which costs increase over time. Computer equipment, on the other hand, depreciates in value and can be retired from service without incurring further costs (although hardly anyone would ever voluntarily give up or down-grade their computer). The need for providing adequate technical support may be underestimated and the capacity of library staff to take on more and more IT support may be overestimated. At BCHE, library staff are hard pressed to deliver core library services so IT support is provided by computer technicians. Unfortunately, during 1996 the level of technician support actually dwindled as demand rose. Funding cuts in higher education at this time had a particularly serious effect on staffing in smaller institutions. Thus, the involvement of library staff in IT support is not simply a matter of providing the necessary training or motivation. Re-aligning or extending responsibilities may not be a viable option if it results in a concomitant drop in the quality of other services.

Management of LIS

During 1996, a team structure was implemented in Library and Information Services with the aim of clarifying working relationships and increasing flexibility. Previously, individual staff held sole responsibility for key areas of work and backlogs would pile up if that person were away from work for any reason. The teams now have responsibility for whole processes and team leaders aim to ensure that work flows evenly. With a total staff of 25 people divided into five teams, each unit is rather smaller than the ideal but the structure is clear and communication relatively easy.

The Director of Library and Information Services has overall responsibility for the libraries and for student computer facilities. She also heads the LIS management team which is comprised of the four most senior members of staff and meets every four weeks to discuss matters relating to policy and the management of the service. Three other teams are each led by a qualified librarian with management responsibilities. A 'flexible team', consisting of library shelvers and temporary staff, is led by a senior member of support staff. Each team holds regular team briefings and notes from meetings are circulated to all staff. The aim of the meetings is to provide a short but regular opportunity for every member of staff to contribute to discussions about the running of the service.

Library and Information Services: the college context

The work of Library and Information Services is inextricably bound up with the systems, structures and academic work of the college. Therefore, the defining characteristics of the college naturally have a significant effect on the way in which LIS organizes its operations. The key features of the college which have an impact on resource management include its size and accommodation; management systems and procedures; quality assurance procedures and strategic planning. These and other matters will be explored in more detail in this chapter.

Size

Bath College of Higher Education is a medium-sized college in the HE sector. However, in comparison with many universities, it is a small institution. There are many benefits in being small. Generally, it is easier for people to get to know each other on a small campus and students can benefit from a more supportive atmosphere than may be possible in large, impersonal surroundings. Libraries in small institutions are unable to benefit from the economies of scale enjoyed by larger organizations. The bookfund per capita may be as generous as in some large universities but, overall, the total amount available is much less. This can result in a lack of flexibility and difficulty in funding developments and initiatives. There can be few, if any, university libraries that would contemplate providing a service without a subscription to BIDS (Bath ISI Data Services). However, the subscription rate for an institution with under three thousand students is exactly the same as for one with thirteen thousand students. The impact of such a commitment is proportionately greater on a smaller bookfund and can make quite a dent in a budget which is already tightly stretched.

The staffing of small libraries is an issue for many multi-site institutions, both universities and colleges. Despite the fact that smaller institutions have fewer staff, libraries are still required to open for a significant number of hours each day. Simply running a circulation desk and an enquiry service for 45 hours a week with the full-time equivalent of only 2.87 staff (as is the case at the Sion Hill campus) puts a strain on human resources. Carefully worked out timetables are the key but unexpected staff absence through illness can involve staff time in rejigging the schedule. Planned absence is easier to cope with but team briefing meetings, the building block of effective team management, can still require planning and goodwill to enable staff to miss timetabled desk duties in order to take part.

Accommodation

The college's location and its accommodation may be seen both as strengths and weaknesses. The Newton Park Campus is situated about 8 kilometres West of Bath and occupies land which is leased from the Duchy of Cornwall. The Sion Hill/Somerset Place campus is close to the centre of Bath and is accommodated in a large, modern building and a Georgian crescent. Accommodation which is not purpose-built can provide many interesting challenges for the resource manager. The Sion Hill Library is long and thin, running at first floor level through six Georgian terraced houses. Access is, therefore, limited to users who can negotiate their way upstairs. The layout of the library is dictated by the physical nature of the building and there is little scope for flexibility.

Putting a computer network into a Georgian terrace demands a careful approach. A close eye may need to be kept on external contractors, particularly if they are aiming for speed rather than the preservation of original architectural features. Knowledge about floor loadings is particularly important in order to prevent structural damage by the injudicious placing of shelves. Experience has shown that emergencies such as flooding can and do happen so it is sensible to have a disaster-plan ready. Insurance companies need detailed information, including value, about stock and equipment for which claims are made. In such cases, detailed catalogue entries and equipment inventories are invaluable.

BCHE's other campus at Newton Park boasts a refurbished library which was extended and re-equipped in 1995. Here too, the nature of the accommodation has been dictated by the shape of existing buildings and the constraints imposed by various planning authorities. As a result, the library occupies a network of separate rooms but a careful approach to interior decoration has ensured that the overall effect is coherent. One advantage of this arrangement is the designation of separate areas for different types of use such as group study, quiet study and silent study. This gives library users plenty of choice although, in the absence of closed-circuit television, there is a potential security risk. In addition, there is plenty of scope for flexibility as the study rooms have been equipped with trunking which will enable them to be networked and turned into additional IT space if required. BCHE is not unique in its surroundings and there are many other institutions which face similar challenges in trying to deliver twentieth century services in buildings which may date back one or two centuries.

Management and committee structure

The Board of Governors has formal responsibility for the work of the College. The most senior members of the College are the Director and three Assistant Directors. Together with the four Deans of Faculty, they comprise the Director's Corporate Team. Membership of the Academic Board consists of the above, other senior managers and representatives from each faculty as well as the Students' Union. Some of the work of the Academic Board is carried out by sub-committees which address resource management (Academic Planning and Resource Committee) and quality (Academic Quality and Standards Committee). Management of the faculties and the central services is largely devolved to the deans and heads of service.

The role of LIS in the decision-making process

The Director of Library and Information Services is a member of the Academic Board and its two principal sub-committees, APRC and AQSC. Participation in the College's decision-making process is seen as essential, particularly as there are resource implications inherent in almost every decision that is taken. For example, the process for approving new programmes of study requires that a satisfactory commentary on library resources must be provided by the Director of Library and Information Services. This is not a hollow exercise and it is not unknown for approval for a new course to be withheld until it has been confirmed that appropriate library resources will be available.

Strategy

The College operates its strategic planning process on a cycle which develops a new plan every three years with annual updates. The overall plan is informed by the strategic plans developed within the faculties and departments, including LIS. By utilizing the team structure and system of briefing meetings within LIS to discuss service developments, staff at all levels are able to contribute to the strategic plans of the service and the wider institution.

During 1996 the College made a successful bid to the Joint Information Systems Committee (JISC) to participate in a pilot project for producing an information strategy. Together with five UK universities, the College received a small amount of funding and the help of a consultant to enable a working party to develop the strategy, following guidelines published by JISC. The project was led by one of the Assistant Directors and the Director of LIS was heavily involved. The emphasis on 'information' rather than 'information technology' was welcomed, as was a strong focus on teaching and learning, as stressed in the JISC guidelines.

Involvement in projects such as this may seem to take managers away from day-to-day tasks and could even be dismissed as irrelevant by some. However, in the long-term there are many advantages to be gained. Firstly, any links between the library and the project will encourage a fresh look at relevant aspects of the service. Secondly, the involvement of library staff sends out a strong, positive message that LIS staff are willing and able to play an active role in the life of the institution. Thirdly, any activity that raises the profile of the service is worth doing. In the ever-present battle for resources, the service that fares well is the one which constantly evaluates and promotes itself and has a high standing within the organization.

Financial management

The College has rigorous financial procedures which provide clear guidelines within which resource managers must operate. The systems are well documented and present no technical difficulties. However, complying with these requirements represents a significant investment in time, particularly where the guidelines do not necessarily match the needs of running a library service. For example, any item or book costing more than a fixed amount is automatically registered as an 'asset' and listed in the College inventory. Therefore, in addition to the standard library procedures for acquiring, checking and withdrawing stock must be added the annual process of checking expensive items against the centrally maintained assets register. No resource manager is in the position to ignore institutional regulations, particularly those of a financial nature, but such activities can place a significant burden on the staff who have to carry out the necessary administrative work.

The College's revenue budget is allocated to faculties and central services according to an agreed formula. The library bookfund is the amount which is left after top-slicing recurring costs such as maintenance contracts and non-book items from the LIS revenue budget. The bookfund itself is allocated on the basis of a formula based on FTE student numbers. Over many years different weightings were applied to various subjects to take account of factors such as high library dependency (Humanities); diversity of collections (Music) and high cost of journals (Science). However, the weightings tended to cancel each other out and persuasive arguments could be made by articulate academics in favour of almost any subject. Therefore, following extensive consultation in 1996 all weightings were abandoned and the budget is now allocated according to student numbers only. However, a small proportion of the bookfund is top-sliced for pump-priming new courses. The identification of resource needs is a requirement of the approval process for new programmes of study. Those proposing new courses are encouraged to specify costs for building up areas of library stock and these are taken into account when the bookfund is allocated.

Income generation is now a necessity for many services. At BCHE all student photocopying and laser printing facilities are run by Library and Information Services. Income from the sale of photocopy cards pays for maintenance contracts, consumable materials and new equipment. Although profits are ploughed back into the ongoing project there is perhaps scope for using some of this income to pay for staff to carry out routine tasks such as adding toner and keeping supplies of paper topped up. This would free up valuable time currently spent by other library staff on keeping the machines running.

Staff management

Most institutions now have well-established policies relating to the appointment and management of staff. At BCHE, staff recruitment guidelines aim to ensure that legal and ethical issues are handled effectively. All new staff follow a structured induction programme and must complete a satisfactory period of probation before being confirmed in post. Academic, support and maintenance staff are issued with handbooks that provide information on all aspects of employment from health and safety to inclement weather procedures. An appraisal scheme is in operation for all academic staff and senior managers while support staff take part in an annual training needs assessment exercise.

Quality

Systems for quality assurance are well established in the college. The Academic Quality and Standards Committee is responsible for approving programmes of study, procedures for student assessment, the assurance of standards and the appointment of external examiners. Each of the four faculties has a Faculty Quality Management Sub-committee which provides the AQSC with an overview of the annual monitoring exercises undertaken by each programme of study for which it is responsible. From these documents, the Academic Office collates and passes on extracts which refer to library and information services.

With the exception of the Finance Department, neither Library and Information Services nor any other central services are subject to the same rigorous quality assurance processes as the faculties. The evaluation of library services has often taken second place to major developments and the exigencies of service delivery. However, pressure to consider service level agreements and performance indicators suggests that a more sustained and structured approach to quality assurance is now a pressing need.

University status

There is one issue which is a matter of some concern to many within the college – the question of university status. Many colleges of higher education aspire to the title of university. Some have achieved this through merger while others aim to become universities in their own right. Most manage to include the word in their recruitment literature by referring to themselves as 'University College' or 'University Sector College'. However, to the world at large (including universities) any institution with the word 'college' in its title is very often assumed to offer vocational rather than academic courses.

The quest for a university title represents a good deal more than mere status. It is argued that the word university would more accurately reflect the quality and nature of the academic activities of BCHE and as a result benefit student recruitment. For the library it would open the doors to membership of the Standing Conference on University Libraries (SCONUL) and would help to progress moves towards collaboration with local university libraries.

Future developments

For the future, the aim is to position LIS as a leading player in quality enhancement within the college. Possibilities include developing and delivering an effective learning module which would include information handling and study skills. There is scope for the service to provide a centralized focus for innovation in teaching and learning through staff development programmes and involvement in the production of learning materials. However, careful planning is vital to ensure that systems, staffing and facilities all proceed in tandem. In resource-constrained circumstances projects can easily fail if any one of these factors develops out of step with the others.

Summary

According to the 1996 Quality Audit Report, 'Bath College of Higher Education is a close-knit institution with a well developed sense of community and common purpose. Staff at all levels are committed to helping students achieve success to the limits of their potential and are generous with their time when students seek support'.[3] The college has consistently achieved high scores in teaching quality assessments and has done well in research assessment exercises. Through its contribution to high standards of quality, the library has benefited from resource allocations which are as reasonable as can be expected in an HE college under the financial constraints of the late 1990s.

References

1   Gaskell, M., 'Moving forward', *Managing HE*, **4**, 56-7, 1996.
2   http://www.niss.ac.uk/education/scop/dearing.html, 29th November, 1996.
3   Quality Assurance Group, *Bath College of Higher Education quality audit report*, Birmingham, Higher Education Quality Council, 1996, 23.

Further reading

The Library Association: Colleges of Further and Higher Education Group, *Guidelines for college libraries: recommendations for performance and resourcing*, edited by Kathy Ennis. London, Library Association Publishing, 5th ed., 1995.

6

Total Quality Management

PETER BROPHY

Introduction

It would be as well to begin this chapter by clarifying what TQM (Total Quality Management) is – and what it is not. It is a management and organizational philosophy, a way of life, a corporate culture, a way of doing things, a long-term commitment. It is not a management system or set of techniques or procedures, nor is it a short-term fix. It requires an unflinching commitment to some of the key principles of quality management, principles established after long trial and error in a wide variety of what are generally recognized as the world's best companies. It is hard work. It is not: 'Can I help you?' said in a peculiar accent and with a high pitched emphasis on the word 'you'; a greeting that confirms that the telephonist has been through the company charm school and has a diploma which gives him or her the right to leave you hanging on the line listening to the Boston Pops Orchestra playing Verdi's *Requiem*! No: TQM is a serious matter.

Brophy and Coulling[1] put it this way:

> TQM is a systematic and holistic approach to the management of organisations and there are dangers in taking too analytical an approach to it. Like all the best systems, its whole is greater than the sum of its parts. Neither is it a goal in itself: any manager who thinks that his or her organisation can 'achieve' TQM is seriously deluded! Commitment to TQM must be long term and organisation wide. It will show benefits, but only after months and years of sustained effort. It will be expensive to implement, but will prove economic as savings from turning failures into quality materialise; it will put the

organisation in the firing line, because only 100% customer satisfaction will do. TQM is not for the faint-hearted.

It is helpful to begin an analysis of TQM's role in resource management by stating some of those principles on which quality management is based. There are the basic definitions of quality:

Quality is fitness for purpose

and

Quality is conformance to requirements.

The simple questions 'Whose purpose?', 'Whose requirements?' lead very quickly to a recognition that it is the customer who is at the centre of all this concern. Without customers, or users if you will, the business does not exist. Of course some libraries may still count their customers in terms of posterity but unless some kind of customer shows interest in the product the organization has no purpose and will, sooner or later, die. Indeed it can be argued that understanding what customers want now and what they will want in the future, and then providing it consistently, is all that there is to management. An exaggeration, no doubt, but one which has a kernel of truth. *Customer satisfaction* is all.

There is another underlying feature of quality management which needs to be stressed. TQM acknowledges that

- there is always room for improvement
- all organizations can and do fail
- employees (not least managers) make mistakes
- we could all do better.

Crosby[2] is famous for his work on the 'cost of quality', and from that and other gurus' work has come the recognition that continuous improvement is essential. The organization which is practising TQM thus has twin targets in view: customer satisfaction and continuous improvement.

What is the relevance of all this to library resource management? Simply that unless all the resources at the librarian's disposal are targeted on meeting as many customers' needs as possible, as much of the time as possible, then the service being offered is not all that it should be.

So what, in a nutshell, is TQM? It has been defined, very often differently, by many writers but its essence can be found in the following quotation describing the experience of coming into contact with another public service, a hospital:

> When my father was dying of cancer, he went from one hospital to another, ending up at the Royal Marsden in Sutton. It was a transformation – an utterly different scene. ... I could take you to hospitals where the standard of care may be good clinically, but emotionally it is appalling. When my father died you could not have bought better service. I was a patient, too – my father was dying, therefore I was cared for. When the tea came round, I was offered tea. I was part of the family, part of the enterprise.[3]

This was an experience recounted by Nick Ross in a recent interview. It is a story of TQM in action, whether the nurses, doctors and hospital managers called it that or something else. TQM, then, goes to the heart of the customer experience.

In Brophy and Coulling's book, TQM is seen as encompassing an interlinked framework of 10 elements, illustrated by Fig. 1. Note

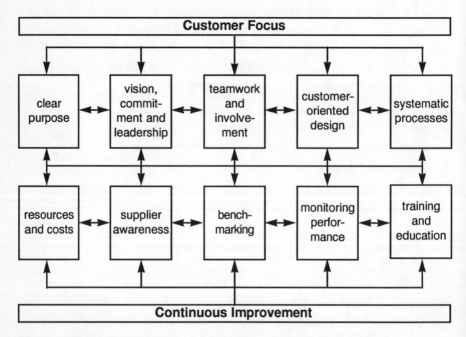

Fig. 1.1 *Customer satisfaction through continuous improvement*

again how customer satisfaction and continuous improvement form the environment in which TQM operates:

In the remainder of this chapter we will look briefly at the contribution that each of these elements of the model has to make.

Clear purpose

Clarity of purpose is necessary to ensure that the whole organization is focused on achieving the same ends. It is the answer to one of management's key questions, 'What business are we in?' There is nothing more wasteful than devoting resources to a service or product which is not what the customer wants, or continuing to assign resources to something which, while perfectly valid in its time, is no longer an adequate contribution to achieving what should be the real purpose of the organization. There are many ways of establishing purpose, of which the process of developing a meaningful mission statement is one. What is essential, however, is that the purpose is understood and 'owned' by all employees so that all are pushing in the same direction.

Vision, commitment and leadership

It is through shared vision, wholehearted commitment and clear leadership that purpose is turned into appropriate action. Vision is necessary both to set out – in broad terms – how the purpose is to be achieved and to give a unifying inspiration to the work of each individual. Leaders have a responsibility to articulate and communicate the vision. They must give their staff and the users of their services a sense of where the organization will be in two, three, five, ten or even twenty years' time. What *is* the future of academic libraries? Of this library? Arriving at the vision is a shared enterprise and involves that most difficult of management skills, listening.

Teamwork and involvement

The modern organization can only function effectively through teams of people contributing to the achievement of the corporate goals. Leadership thus involves enabling, supporting and facilitating staff at all levels to maximize their contributions to the organization. Teamwork has many advantages:

- • It enables problems to be tackled by more than one person at a time, so that the resource applied to a problem or service can be tailored to meet the load that it places on the organization.
- • It allows a mix of skills and abilities to be brought to bear, so that specialists with different backgrounds and expertise can use their particular skills to best effect.
- • It can help to break down sectional and departmental barriers (although new barriers *between* teams must not be allowed to develop) and so overcome some of the problems which occur at the interfaces within the 'quality chain', i.e. the sequence of steps from initial inputs to delivered service which all must be as effective and efficient as possible if quality service is to be achieved.

But teams are also the natural, human way of working. We are social animals and staff encouraged to work in teams will tend to be better motivated and more content than those having to cope with a task on their own. 'A happy staff is an effective staff' may be hackneyed, but it is true – as is its converse.

Customer-oriented design

It has been argued that the whole of the quality management approach can be summed up in the two steps, 'Right design; Right execution'.[4] The design of a product or service must incorporate the customers' requirements at the earliest stages, since an incorrect design cannot, by definition, provide quality. The connection with effective resource management is obvious.

In industry the importance of good design is more obvious than in services. At a basic level there is the need to ensure that the product will actually work – so a manufacturer of 3¼ inch floppy disks needs to get the dimensions right! Moreover there are often legislative requirements to be complied with. For example, electrical connectors must meet the relevant health and safety legislation or they cannot legally be offered for sale. On top of that, competitive pressures in the market place mean that in order to generate sales a product must be both functional and aesthetically appealing. Good design takes account of all these factors while ensuring that the product can be manufactured at a cost which allows the organization to make a profit.

Such considerations are just as relevant to services, even though they are often hidden. It is useful when designing or reviewing services to ask some 'design-related' questions, such as:

- does this service produce a result that meets the customer's implicit or explicit design tolerances?
- if there were relevant 'health and safety' legislation would it pass muster? (e.g. do I get eye strain trying to decipher the printout?)
- is the service functionally and aesthetically pleasing? (which might include cleanliness of premises or layout of printed results)
- is this the most efficient design for this service?

Systematic processes

It is amazing how often managers think that their organizations have clear procedures when in fact they do not. Libraries are by no means immune to this. At one level it is epitomized by the staff manual each copy of which is subtly different, each annotated with different pencilled comments about 'what we really do'; at another it is the pristine manual which no-one ever consults because 'we all know how best to do it'; at another it is the lack of any agreed procedures, so one member of staff tolerates noisy behaviour ('most of the students seem to like it that way') while another insists on silence ('this is a LIBRARY!'). Or the problem may be exemplified by:

- a process designed to do something which has changed radically, while the process has only been adapted instead of redesigned;
- a continuing process which has lost its meaning (why count users coming through the door when most use electronic networks to gain access to the Library?);
- processes for which no, or inadequate, records are kept so that if something goes wrong it is impossible to find out who was at fault or how the error occurred – and so the process cannot be changed to prevent a repetition of the error.

One way to avoid these problems is to adopt a systematic approach such as that provided by the ISO9000 standard, and to seek external accreditation so that an experienced auditor comes in at regular intervals to check that the procedures in place do not contain any 'holes'. The organization retains total control over its procedures, and can change them whenever it wishes, but benefits from a certified approach which ensures consistency and completeness. While full accreditation to ISO9000 is not everyone's cup of tea, the approach is itself valuable and can be used effectively within the overarching context of TQM. The two are certainly not in conflict.

Resources and costs

Since this volume as a whole is very much concerned with resource and costing issues, relatively little need be said here about the general concepts of resource control, costing, and so on. However, a number of comments on the question of costs, seen from a TQM standpoint, are relevant. The issue is really one of reducing the cost of quality, which is really the cost of quality *failures* and of their prevention, so as to ensure that all available resources are being targeted on the delivery of quality services to the external customer or end user. This cost can best be thought of as leakage of resources away from service delivery, rather like the leakage from a mains service pipe reducing the water available at the tap in your house. Reducing those costs can only produce a net gain to the organization.

The literature of quality management provides some guidance on the types of quality cost which can be considered. Typically, these are:

- *The cost of prevention* which is the cost of all the processes and actions taken to prevent mistakes and failures happening. For example, a considerable amount of staff training will be concerned with preventing error, and as such comes under the heading of a cost of quality: it does not add directly to the delivery of the service. Preventative action is an important part of quality management, since one of the ground rules of TQM is that action is taken to improve processes rather than 'firefighting' errors and failures. But important as preventative management is, it does not directly add value to the end product.
- *The cost of assessment, audit and appraisal* involves the costs incurred in checking to ensure that quality standards are being met. In UK higher education it sometimes feels as if 99% of our costs are attributable to satisfying one body or another that stan-

dards are adequate! But even if such assessments are kept to the minimum and even if they are extremely valuable in suggesting improvements and sharing good practice, again they do not add directly to the service and so are a quality cost.

- *The cost of internal failure* consists of everything done *before* delivery to the customer which results in wasted work. A simple example would be a catalogue record which had to be amended before it could be added to the live database. The time spent on that task is again a quality cost.

- *The costs of external failure* tend to receive most attention because they consist of the costs incurred when the customer is dissatisfied with a product or service. Car manufacturers offer the obvious example with well-known examples of high warranty costs. It is worth thinking about the equivalent in libraries and information services, as when a book borrowed is found to be inadequate and another is needed. What were the costs, both to the library and the user, of acquiring and making available the first volume?

- *The costs of exceeding customer requirements* should not be neglected. If customers are happy with black and white photocopies there is no point in sending round colour copies: all that is achieved is an additional cost.

- *The cost of lost opportunities* is again more obvious in the industrial and private sectors, where if a potential customer is turned away then the loss of potential business has an obvious cost. Academic libraries, overwhelmed with demand, may be grateful for a few 'lost' customers! But would they really be happy if all their research users were to find that they could get a better service elsewhere?

Supplier awareness

The idea of supplier awareness has again come from industry and commerce, but deserves consideration, especially as most libraries and information services have a curious (i.e. largely non-existent) relationship with their ultimate suppliers, authors and publishers. It follows that the relationship with our actual suppliers is rather crucial. One lesson from other sectors is that the emphasis within a TQM culture has shifted from encouraging competition *between* suppliers towards developing partnerships *with* suppliers. In some industries it has been recognized that confrontational relationships with suppliers can be a fast track towards the destruction of the basis on which quality can be developed, in exactly the same way as confrontation between staff and departments inside the organization. (It is odd that most people instinctively accept the latter but are less convinced that the lesson applies to the external world.) The satisfaction of the final customer is in the interest of both the organization and its suppliers, and a partnership offers the way to move quality forward ultimately minimizing costs.

Benchmarking

Benchmarking is a vital technique that enables an organization to check its performance against its 'competitors' and so to find out whether it really is 'the best in the business'. This process of comparison is really no more than the systematic sharing of good practice and good ideas with the ultimate aim of becoming the organization against which everyone else wants to benchmark.

Camp[5] suggests that there are four different types of benchmarking:

- *Internal benchmarking* is often used within large organizations to compare the performance of one division or department against others.
- *Competitive benchmarking* is used to seek out information on equivalent organizations' activities in order to establish how they deliver quality products or services. In industrial or commercial organizations this information can be difficult to obtain, hence 'industrial espionage'. In a public service setting, such as that in which most libraries and information services operate, information may be shared much more readily.
- *Functional benchmarking* involves a deliberate decision to examine an organization in a dissimilar field to see how a particular function is carried out elsewhere. Some libraries have looked in detail at customer service in organizations like Marks & Spencer to find out how they achieve quality in this area.
- *Generic benchmarking* goes beyond specific functions and tries to

establish how other companies, which may or may not be in a totally different industry, carry out their business. It requires a broad view, but it might, for example, be used to identify how the concept of 'flat' management structures can be applied in practice. Much of Peters and Waterman's work, for example, is really concerned with generic benchmarking.[6]

Monitoring performance

A great deal has been written about library performance measurement, and a variety of approaches are in place, most notably the work of ISO TC46/SC8, that of IFLA and, in the UK academic sector, the recent work which has been undertaken under the title of *The effective academic library*. A more general overview is that provided by Goodall.[7] Within the context of TQM, performance monitoring provides much of the basic information needed to monitor quality on an ongoing basis. The use of service level agreements and performance indicators as tools in resource management is described in the next chapter.

Training and education

It is noticeable that many companies are signing up to the 'Investors in People' scheme, which requires companies to commit a stated percentage of their staff's time to staff development. This is but one indicator of the importance now being attached to training as a vital contributor to the delivery of quality services. Since an academic institution may spend up to 70% of its resources on staff, it is surprising that training of university staff has not been given greater prominence in the past.

One current concept, which fits well with the overall philosophy of TQM, is that of the 'learning organization' or 'learning company'. It has even been suggested that the implementation of TQM is in fact identical to the establishment of a learning organization.[8] To quote Brophy and Coulling again:[9]

The idea behind this concept is that organisations need to go beyond the training of individuals, to encompass the whole company as a 'learning entity'. In other words, the organisation itself should be capable of learning, of adapting and changing in response to internal and external stimuli, through facilitating the learning of individuals, teams, sections, departments, and ultimately the whole enterprise. Of course organisations themselves cannot think or feel, so what is being suggested is the organisation of individual learning in a systematic way that enables the total contribution to be brought to bear on the company's activities in a planned, yet dynamic fashion. The Learning Company concept encompasses a wide view of 'customers' ... that is, all the stakeholders who have an interest in it and its activities.

Summary

In conclusion, it is important to reiterate that the contribution to resource management that TQM can make does not lie so much in its individual techniques but rather in its holistic view of management and of the organization, built on the twin peaks of an enveloping commitment to customer satisfaction and continuous improvement.

References

1 Brophy, P. and Coulling, K., *Quality management for information and library managers*, Aldershot, Gower, 1996, 71.

2 See, for example, Crosby, P. B., *Running things: the art of making things happen*, New York, McGraw-Hill, 1986.

3 Howell, J. Maxwell, R. and Ross, N., 'Priorities for healthcare: who sets them?', *RSA journal*, **CXLII** (5454), 1994, 35–49.

4 Plummer, R., 'Design objectives' in *Gower handbook of quality management*, ed. D. Lock. Aldershot, Gower, 1990, 103–16.

5 Camp, R. C., *Benchmarking*, Milwaukee, USA, Quality Press, 1989.

6 See, for example, Peters, T. and Waterman, R. J., *In search of excellence: lessons from America's best run companies*, New York, Warner Bros, 1982.

7 Goodall, D. L. 'Performance measurement: an historical perspective' *Journal of librarianship*, **20** (2), 1988, 128–44.

8 Hammond, V. and Wille, E., 'The learning organization', in Prior, J. ed. *Gower handbook of training and development* 2nd ed. Aldershot, Gower, 1994.

9 Brophy, P. and Coulling, K., *op. cit.*, 85–6.

7

Service Level Agreements and Performance Indicators

Jean Steward

Introduction

In December 1993, the Report of the Joint Funding Councils'
Libraries Review Group, chaired by Sir Brian Follett assessed the
problems facing the academic library sector and found that:

> Over the last decade, libraries have faced new and changed demands as a
> result, in particular, of substantial growth in student numbers, rapid inflation
> in the costs of printed materials, and the added opportunities – and costs – to
> which information technology (IT) has given rise. The scale of these devel-
> opments has been such that funding has not kept pace with them.[1]

The scenario is one that has been challenging university librarians
since the 1980s and in response managers have had to become more
strategic in their approach, more focused in their service provision,
more imaginative in the techniques they have employed and more
responsive to the needs of an increasingly demanding public.
Universities are recognizing the need to develop clear strategies for
meeting their information needs, and the Follett Report emphasized
the need for institutions to have 'a clear statement of aims and the
methods by which they are to be met ... available for managers and
users of the library'.[2] The Report recognized that the information
strategy to be adopted will vary widely from institution to institution, depending upon the nature and individual strategic objectives
of each university, but stated that:

> Whatever the approach taken, the strategy should pay particular attention to
> defining the needs of the various groups of library users, to the performance

measures and indicators which the institution believes are appropriate, to quality assurance and assessment, and to the management of staff and physical resources.[3]

The use of service level agreements (SLAs) supported by performance measures is one option open to libraries which can assist with the development and implementation of an information strategy. An SLA is not a substitute for an information strategy and does not in itself provide a library service appropriate to a university or college for the 1990s and beyond. It can however serve as a framework for a rigorous analysis of service provision and a means of communicating and agreeing that provision with the institution and of then assessing its effectiveness. This chapter reviews the usefulness and the advantages and disadvantages of service level agreements and the associated performance indicators.

Service level agreements

Libraries and librarians have always had a strong service ethos, but this has not always been focused on user needs or expectations. Users are becoming more demanding and their expectations are increasing to the point where, as Yohe describes:

> They expect that all information is immediately accessible to them; that they can have whatever information they want, whenever they want it, wherever they want it and however they want it . . . They expect effective help in using these resources . . . They do not want to 'learn' how to use these resources, only to 'know' how . . . If support is required, they expect to make a single contact, which will result in instant, on-site response by a person who has full knowledge[4]

The charter movement, emanating from the British Government's Citizen's Charter published in 1991 has reenforced this expectation of perfection and users are increasingly strident in their demands for services and resources. Service level agreements can play an important role in managing these expectations in a time of diminishing resources and in developing a mutual understanding of the nature and extent of the services which can be provided. Management culture and organizational change have ensured that mission statements and definitions of service objectives are common practice for organizations: the library manager needs to think strategically about the effective use of limited resources to ensure that these are utilized in the most cost-effective and efficient way to support its organizational objectives. The library must be clear about the services it will provide with the funding it is granted and the users to whom these services will be made available.

A service level agreement is a contract: 'the means by which two parties communicate to each other their commitments in relation to the resourcing and provision of services to a given level, over a given period'.[5] In SCONUL's *Library profiles 1993/94*,[6] 19 out of 96 respondents had a published service level agreement/charter, seven of which were internal to the library, while 12 had been formally approved by the institution. The number of such agreements is growing, but no more recent figures have been published. There is no one style which can or should be adopted for such an agreement. In December 1994 SCONUL published *Working papers on Service Level Agreements*,[7] which gives examples of the range of approaches adopted by universities in the UK. These range from service level statements (often the precursor to a full agreement, in which the library staff codify current service provision prior to discussing this with their users) to documents which have been negotiated with the university or a department and which define service standards and requirements for both the library and the users and which describe the mechanisms which will be used to monitor performance.

The key elements of a service level agreement are, as the name implies, twofold: service level and agreement. To define *service level*, an SLA will:

* describe the nature and level of library services which will be provided, as a core service from centrally provided funds
* codify the detail of the services to be provided explicitly
* provide realistic and measurable targets which users may expect the library service to meet
* describe the performance measures and indicators which will be used to judge the service
* may also describe additional 'premium' services which may be provided for a charge to be met either from end users or from departmental budgets.

As an *agreement*, the SLA will:

- define the group or groups of users to whom these services will be delivered
- form a contract between two sectors within the organization (the library and a faculty or department) or between the library and the organization as a whole
- define the obligations on the users or the other party to the contract, as well as the obligations on the library.

It may also define the remedies offered to users if service standards are not met.

SLAs are therefore used as internal documents within an organization. Where funding is provided by the traditional method of a block grant from the centre to the library to provide services for the university community it is often sufficient to create one agreement with the whole organization. As noted above the first stage is often for the library staff to consider and codify the service elements which it offers and to agree internally on what these should be. This in itself may be a difficult process. Although most libraries will have a mission statement and most library staff when first asked believe that they have a clear understanding of the services, there are often different perceptions about the nature and purpose of specific services. The act of writing a service description will raise a variety of questions: are all services available at all times the library is open, or are there different levels of service in 'office hours' and in the evenings and weekends? What level of reference service is available after 5.00 p.m.? Can undergraduates expect to find a copy of every item on every reading list in library stock? How many copies of a core text should be provided for a course with 200 students, if they are all expected to read it within one week? How quickly should a new purchase be processed? Is it reasonable to hold items in processing for one week so that a new books display service can be offered each Monday? How much time should be spent helping a reader print from a CD-ROM? Should additional induction sessions be run in the evenings when part-time students attend seminars? Should library staff insist that all faculty notify the library about requests for course materials to be placed in the short loan collection before the start of the teaching period? What sanctions should be imposed if they do not? The creation of a service level statement will provide an opportunity for staff to test the assumptions which have underpinned the services provided in a rigorous manner, and will generate debate, clarify objectives and often lead to changes in attitude and in practice.

Testing assumptions and clarifying objectives must be user-based if a service level statement is to become a contractual agreement with the university and with users. Consultation will be vital throughout the process. Feedback and information may be obtained through analysis of complaints and suggestions, questionnaires, user focus groups, attendance at meetings of student associations, school boards, liaison and other contact between individual members of library staff and users. The approaches used must be acceptable to users if they are to be effective and should not be too intrusive. As Clark notes:

> What is clear is that the challenge facing the information manager today is composed of four key issues – understanding the clients' needs, having an appropriate information collection system, understanding the business the clients are in, its strategic and tactical intent, and providing information in a fast, integrated fashion to those whose availability is limited and whose attention span is short[8]

It is the process of establishing a dialogue with users which can result in a mutually acceptable statement of the obligations on the library service and the library users which is of key importance rather than the document itself. Similarly the last stage will be to agree formally the service level statement with the university – normally through approval by Library Committee, School or Faculty Boards and/or Senate. There may often be tension between the users, who are interested in service quality and quantity, and the organization, which may be more concerned with cost effective use of limited resources. A service level agreement must be realistic and affordable to be achievable and it is the process of formal approval which will ensure that any document is firmly based on the possible and not just the desirable. The challenge is to achieve the best which is possible:

> To be effective the information services must further the parent organiza-

tions's ends. Knowledge of these ends provides the key to prioritization. In trying to manage more tasks on fewer resources, priorities are critical. Information managers cannot do everything, so they must make sure that they do what makes a difference.[9]

The process of implementing a Service Level Agreement allows library staff to work with the organization to define those services which will make a difference.

The traditional block grant to the library service has normally meant that the library provides a core or base service equally to all parts of the university. Funding models are however becoming increasingly complex, and as well as being accountable centrally to the university and to external auditors, university libraries are becoming accountable to individual departments or faculties. Teaching quality assessment considers library provision for each specific subject area separately. University resource allocation models increasingly define a clear relationship between faculty-based income and library expenditure. Some universities no longer fund the library out of a central resource pool, but expect the library service to negotiate with each faculty for resources to provide the services which the faculty require. In this context, service level agreements will need to be developed with each sector of the university and will need to be based on a much clearer understanding of the individual costs of service and stock provision. When the acquisitions budget for the library is allocated by this method negotiation skills are key, and the tensions between faculty wishes and user demands, between conflicting needs for research and teaching support are complex. The library staff may need to negotiate on behalf of students at a time when university funding is increasingly dependent upon research income. If the whole library budget is devolved the situation is more complex. Who will pay for evening opening of the library? Will a faculty decline to pay that element if it does not undertake evening teaching? Will lawyers argue that as they pay for law stock only members of the School of Law should be allowed to use those items? Service level agreements must be used to define a core level of service which all members of the institution can expect as well as providing accountability for expenditure of funds at departmental level. The challenges are likely to increase over the next few years.

SLAs are also increasingly used where there is a need for an external contract between a university library or information service and an outside organization. Relationships within the higher education sector are becoming increasingly complex, with course franchising and validation arrangements between institutions and closer links between universities and colleges of higher and further education – Suffolk College for example became a University College of the University of East Anglia from Summer 1996 and a Service Level Agreement between the libraries of the two previously independent organizations will be necessary to describe the relationship and interplay of library service provision between them. Another prime example is nursing courses, where the pre- and post-registration teaching of nurses has been contracted to the higher education sector. Nursing libraries in hospitals which supported both 'trainee' nurses and the information needs of professional staff have been transferred to university ownership. Multidisciplinary hospital libraries must now be funded jointly by the NHS sector and by the university which was awarded a teaching contract. Again this has led to a clear need for a contract or Service Level Agreement which describes the range and level of services which the university library and the trust(s) will provide.

There are both advantages and disadvantages to the use of service level agreements. On the 'plus' side, an SLA:

- provides an opportunity to examine rigorously the nature and level of service which the library provides
- develops a dialogue with users on their needs and required levels of service provision
- helps to manage user expectations by developing a mutual understanding of what can be achieved with finite resources
- provides a basis for medium term planning
- provides an open and agreed set of measures by which performance will be assessed
- defines the obligations on users of the service as well as on the library.

On the 'minus' side, however, a service level agreement may:

- set a maximum level of service provision targets rather than a minimum which should be exceeded where possible
- inhibit flexibility – by setting a pattern for a period of time which cannot be reviewed until that time period is complete
- prevent long term change – for example where a new or different service is not immediately agreeable to the community it may be difficult to introduce
- absorb too much library staff time, and thus preclude time on other more important activities or developments
- become an end in itself rather than a means to an end.

The use of service level agreements is a matter of judgement – it is a tool which can assist the strategic manager to define and agree the library service which is most appropriate and cost-effective for the university in meeting its individual aims and objectives. It is a tool which is suited to the social, political and economic climate of the 1990s; whether it will survive and how it will evolve in the next century remains to be seen.

Performance indicators

Whether or not service level agreements continue to be used in future, performance indicators are almost certainly here to stay. The literature on performance indicators is vast and as yet there is still no definite national or international agreement within the profession about the indicators which are appropriate to measure library performance. SCONUL's *Library profiles 1993–94* included the question: What principal performance indicators are used by the library? The answer was 'responses to this question are too varied to permit useful categorisation'.[10] In 1995 DG XIII-E3 published *Library performance indicators and library management tools*, stating that 'prompt dissemination of the report will be of immediate benefit to the many libraries in Europe now in need of information and guidance in the area'[11] whilst stating in the Executive Summary that 'The report goes some way to meeting the need in this area, but further work is recommended'. There is still some way to go.

There is however consensus that it is important to measure performance, as summarized by Bloor:

The gathering and analysis of performance data can provide a basis for setting priorities and allocating resources. Monitoring performance can give a guide as to how well the library is meeting its objectives, charting progress towards specific goals and identifying any problem areas. The ability to demonstrate that certain levels of performance are being achieved can be useful when justifying the allocation of resources, or arguing for more.[12]

There is also consensus in the literature about some of the principles that should underpin the use of performance indicators. They should:

- not be an end in themselves, but should be used as practical tools to support decision making and library management
- be measures that are appropriate to the particular objectives of the library
- be simple to collect, use existing data and information and be affordable
- be within an agreed framework to allow comparisons with and benchmarking against similar organizations
- be understood and accepted by users, and be made publicly available
- facilitate internal and external audit and quality assessment.

There are tensions between these principles – and particularly between the need to develop indicators which are appropriate measures of individual library performance against stated objectives and the need to allow national collation and external comparators. There are added difficulties in creating meaningful measures of quality of performance as well as quantity of product. It is relatively easy, if time consuming, to measure inputs – quantities of finance, staff, buildings, equipment and stock, population served – and to devise performance indicators which show the relationships between these measures: *per capita* spend, number of volumes *per capita*, etc. It is harder to measure outputs, i.e., what the library provides for the population it serves. There are no widely accepted measures of outcomes, i.e., the effects on the users of the services the library provides. There are too many variables to be able to relate the quality of library services specifically to the grades achieved by students, the value of a piece of academic research or the employment prospects of a graduate.

Performance measurement must be an integral part of a service level agreement. SLAs include specific commitments to provide particular services at particular times and to particular levels. They often include time or other standards which must be met. For example, an SLA may state that new books will be processed within a set number of days or weeks, that faults will be reported within a set number of hours or that queues will not exceed a set length before an additional service point is opened. They also include a commitment to measuring whether the standards are met. The monitoring of the specific standards quoted in the agreement may not be easy, particularly where they cannot be automatically derived from an automated library system, and will require discipline by the library staff to ensure that statistics are recorded and collated. New mechanisms may also be required to publish the results. This may be done within the Annual Report of the librarian or by regular reports to Library Committee or its equivalent. Information produced in this way is not readily available to most library users and further approaches will be needed if the results are to be open to the university community at large. Regular information in library newsletters, on library web pages and on noticeboards will be required. Successes and failures to meet targets will be public and the library service will have to live with the consequences!

Service Level Agreements describe a range of services and while some are easy to measure others are not. It is usually the more important elements of the SLA which are the hardest to measure. For example the provision of books, journals and other library materials is at the heart of almost all university libraries. The University of East Anglia Library's SLA includes a section on collection development which starts by saying:

> The Library will provide as appropriate a collection of print and non-print materials for the University's teaching and research as resources allow.[13]

The section continues with more specific requirements, which can be monitored and measured more easily, but it is this first statement which is the prime objective of our collection development policy, and it is on our ability to deliver this that our service will and should be judged. A similar statement will be present in every other library SLA. It is not easy to provide indicators of the *quality* of these collections, it is easy to measure the *quantity*, the quantity added each year in each subject. It is possible to measure the percentage of items on reading lists which are in stock, although this may take considerable staff resources to achieve. It is possible to assess 'fill rates' – the level of users' ability to find the items they require on particular visits to the library. Conspectus techniques may be used to evaluate the relative strengths or weaknesses of collections in particular subjects. Faculty and students can be surveyed and asked for individual opinions on the quality and quantity of materials available to support their teaching, learning and research. Teaching quality assessors have their own, sometimes idiosyncratic, methods of evaluating stock during visits on site. No single technique can provide an assessment of the collection. The results would be debatable and open to different interpretation even if all of them could be used, and the costs involved in undertaking them all on a regular basis would in itself be open to challenge as a misuse of scarce resources.

This example of just one key element of a service level agreement epitomizes the problems faced in agreeing and implementing performance indicators. A report by the Joint Funding Councils' Ad-hoc Group on Performance Indicators for Libraries, *The effective academic library: a framework for evaluating the performance of UK academic libraries* proposes a framework with five elements upon which 'overall library effectiveness should be measured and proposes specific performance indicators which could be used in these five areas'.[14] They are:

- integration – between the mission and aims and objectives of the institution and the library
- quality – user satisfaction with overall service provision and specific key services
- delivery – of specific objectives and volume of output
- efficiency – relating service provision to resource inputs
- economy – numeric indicators to provide a control or context in which the other indicators may be judged.

The report aims to suggest a range a performance indicators which can be applied relatively cheaply and easily in all university libraries, using a mixture of techniques: statistical data collected manually or derived from the library's automated systems, user surveys and satisfaction reports and insitutional documentary evidence. The range of data indicates the 'soft' nature of some of the measures which need to be applied. The report also states that this is the recommended base level to be used to provide an overall assessment of the effectiveness of the library service, and that 'more detailed indicators can have substantial relevance and benefit'.[15] More detailed indicators will be needed to monitor a service level agreement and the framework provided in the report could be applied to sections or 'key deliverables' within an SLA and comparable indicators designed.

The creation of an SLA involves discussion and agreement between the library staff, library users and the institution. Similar discussion and agreement will be needed on the performance indicators which should be used to assess that agreement. Unless these are accepted by all three parties, the effort involved in the collection, collation and presentation of the performance measures will have been wasted in part or in total. There is no model SLA which can be applied in all universities and equally there is no set of performance indicators which can be used to monitor an SLA. As we move towards the 21st century good library management remains an art and not a science. The judgement factor and the differences between individual libraries will continue – 'vive la difference'!

References

1   Joint Funding Councils' Libraries Review Group. *Report: a report for the HEFCE, SHEFC, HEFCW and DENI*, Chairman: Sir Brian Follett, 1993, 5.

2   Ibid., 28

3   Ibid., 28

4   Yohe, J. Michael, 'Information technology support services: crisis or opportunity?' in *Cause/Effect*, **19**, (3), Fall 1996. http://cause-www. niss.ac.uk/information-resources/ir-library/html/cem9633.html. 1.

5   Ashcroft, Margaret, *Provision of library and information services to nursing professionals, 'NURLIS' phase II: management guidelines* for English National Board of Nursing, Midwifery and Health Visiting, Stamford, Capital Planning Information Ltd, 1993, III:5.

6   SCONUL. *Library profiles, 1993–94*, London, Sconul, 1995.

7   Revill, Don and Ford, Geoff, eds., *Working papers on service level agree-ments*, Brighton, SCONUL, 1994.

8   Clark, Pamela, 'Client aspirations and relationships: issues for the infor-mation manager', in *New roles, new skills, new people*, (Key issues in the information business, 5), Hatfield, University of Hertfordshire Press, 1995, 18.

9   MacLachlan, Liz, 'How to manage more or less: the management chal-lenges of the new world', in *New roles, new skills, new people*, (Key issues in the information business, 5), Hatfield, University of Hertfordshire Press, 1995, 62.

10 SCONUL, *Library profiles, 1993–94*, London, SCONUL, 1995.

11 Ward, Suzanne *et al.*, *Library performance indicators and library manage-ment tools*, Luxembourg, European Commission, Directorate-General XIII, 1995, 6.

12 Bloor, Ian, *Performance indicators and decision support systems for libraries*, (British Library Research Paper, 93), Boston Spa, British Library Research and Development Department, 1991, 3.

13 University of East Anglia Library, *Service level agreement 1996*, [unpub-lished], 13.

14 Joint Funding Councils' Ad-hoc Group on Performance Indicators for Libraries, *The effective academic library: a framework for evaluating the per-formance of UK academic libraries. A consultative report to the HEFCE, SHEFC, HEFCW and DENI*, Chair: Kevin Ellard, Bristol, HEFCE Publications, 1995.

15 *Ibid.*, 7.

8

Costing of Materials, Operations and Services

JOHN HUTCHINS

Introduction

The estimation and calculation of costs are central to library management and in particular to the allocation of resources in library budgets. This chapter can only outline what is involved. For greater depth see Roberts, and for valuable articles examining the costing of particular operations and services see the collection edited by Roberts. For library costing within wider economic contexts and the information market see the monograph by Kingma.[1]

Three broad categories of costs may be identified:

- materials: costs associated with the acquisition and maintenance of published materials (i.e. the library stock, its selection, purchase, cataloguing, binding);
- operations: costs associated with the exploitation of the library (i.e. circulation, shelving, enquiry service) and external resources (i.e. access to other libraries and databases, interlibrary loans);
- overheads: costs of administering the library buildings (i.e. janitors, cleaners, heating, lighting), purchasing and maintaining equipment and furniture, and the general administration of library staff and services.

The distribution of budgets within and between these cost categories is highly dependent on broad policy decisions which may lie outside the remit of the librarian and library staff. For example, a 'reference library' will have no staff for circulation (borrowing and return of stock) but may well have staff to collect books for users and to return them to the shelves after use. A library with short opening hours may have lower staff and overhead costs than a library with long opening hours. Borrowing conditions and opening hours are often decided at an administrative level higher than the library. On the other hand, policy decisions within the library can also affect broad-level budget distributions:

- buying catalogue data from external sources may lead to lower staffing levels than required if all materials are catalogued at the local level;
- an automated circulation system may involve fewer staff than a manual system;
- the concentration of interlibrary loans from a single source may well be cheaper than borrowing from a variety of different sources; and so forth.

Why costing?

Whatever the local conditions may be that determine the broad allocation of resources, it is important that the librarian has at least a good overall idea of the costs of providing services, acquiring materials and maintaining equipment, etc. within the local circumstances, ideally with detailed costing of certain essential components. Answers can therefore be given, as needed, about the costs of providing new services (e.g. to new sets of users, for new courses) and of changing existing services (e.g. new opening hours). Specific costs are often needed:

- how much is spent on books per student
- how much does it cost to do each circulation transaction, to shelve a book, to stay open an extra hour
- what are the full comparative costs of print purchases against CD-ROM acquisitions (materials, staffing, equipment)?

As well as the monitoring of expenditure (whether staff or materials or equipment), costing has to include data on usage. The costs of circulation transactions must be calculated on the basis of staff salaries, staffing levels and hours, and overheads in relation to the numbers of transactions performed. Likewise, the budgeting for expenditure on acquisitions must take into account how effectively materials have been used.

In the costing of most library activities a distinction must always be maintained between capital costs and recurrent costs. For the continuation of existing services and for the estimation (or allocation) of purchases in current subject areas, it is generally only recurrent costs that are relevant. However, whenever there are new services and new areas of material expenditure, there will probably have to be some capital costs:

- for building up the library collection in a new field
- for cataloguing the stock acquired, in additional shelves, etc.

If additional staff are needed only during the setting up of a new collection then they may also be regarded as 'capital' costs. Extra staff are, however, usually appointed to cope with anticipated future expansion on a recurrent basis.

Staffing costs

The aim of costing the activities of library staff is to determine the contribution of the staffing component to the overall costs of each library activity. Some activities are wholly (or almost wholly) made up of staff costs. An obvious example is the general administration of the library. This includes:

- the salaries of the chief librarian and of his/her deputy or deputies
- the salaries of the general library office secretaries
- the proportion of salary time devoted by other library staff to general administration (e.g. at meetings).

However, there are in addition some overheads in the costs of stationery, telephone charges, computer equipment, and part of the costs of heating and lighting offices.

Another example of a library activity made up almost entirely of staff salaries is the information (enquiry) service, with relatively small additional overhead, material and equipment costs. At the other extreme is the acquisition of books. The salaries of the staff doing the ordering and initial accessioning of new books is generally only a small fraction of the total budget for acquisitions. Most money is expended on actual purchases. Likewise for periodicals, the bulk of the costs goes on subscriptions; the staff costs of ordering, accessioning, and shelving the journal issues as received are relatively small in comparison.

Since most library staff are engaged in a variety of activities when at work, it is often not possible to assign the salary of any one member of staff to any single activity. For example, in a single day the same individual may:

- assist at the circulation desk
- shelve books
- answer general enquiries
- relieve janitors during breaks
- help in the acquisitions department.

Similarly, a particular service point may be staffed by individuals from a wide range of different departments during the same day.

The collection and analysis of staffing times and salaries will involve the detailed survey and observation of the operations of each library service, and cannot be undertaken lightly or too frequently. To ensure consistency, it is preferable for the survey to be done by a single individual or a small team. Observation can be intrusive; and, for some staff, it may arouse suspicions if the survey is done only by senior staff. A more expensive alternative is the employment of external consultants, but it has the merit of more transparent objectivity, both for the library staff and for any non-library recipients of results.

Most difficult to determine is the amount of detail required for the survey. The identification of major functions and tasks in each service area is simple, but more detailed breakdowns may be necessary. It may not be difficult to arrive at costings for circulation activities as a whole, and this may be sufficient in discussions about extending opening hours. However, the costings of individual activities, for example book reservations and recalls, require much greater detail. These costings may be essential in discussions of the extension or discontinuation of specific services to particular categories of users. There are similar considerations in the costing of cataloguing processes. The overall costs may easily be calculated, and this may be sufficient, but the costs of cataloguing books in different subject areas, or the different costs of cataloguing new acquisitions and of adding extra copies of books, will demand finer detail. In both these cases, staff will probably have to keep records for a period of some weeks.

Materials costing

The recurrent costs of materials are relatively easy to establish. It does not generally involve the distribution of the expenditure to more than one service area (unlike the distribution of individual staff expenditure). In particular, items of equipment are intended for specific purposes in individual departments. The costs of using such equipment per transaction or operation can be easily calculated.

An important question, however, is whether capital costs (e.g. the purchase of new equipment) should be spread over a number of years and included in the overall expenditure of a particular activity. The decision will depend on the objective of the costings: if it is to calculate the total cost of a department or service over a period of years, then capital costs must be included. If it is to contribute toward the estimated costs of extending a service to new users (e.g. a new student course), then it may be more reasonable to include only recurrent costs.

Overheads costing

Expenditure by the library on general administration and on heating, lighting, cleaning, etc. cannot be attributed to particular services such as cataloguing, circulation or acquisitions. However, they ought not to be excluded from the costings of any services. In the past, librarians have often underestimated true costs by omitting such overheads, usually because they do not appear on library budgets. But overheads cannot easily be distributed to particular activities – an exception might be the costs of storage (shelving). In most cases, overheads must be added pro rata, e.g. distributed equally to each transaction, to each student, to each book catalogued, each periodical issue added to stock, etc.

Costing services by user category

Using the methods sketched above, it is possible to calculate the current costs of each library service and of each individual activity within the library. It will then be possible for the librarian to calculate:

- how much it costs to lend a book (the proportion of staff costs, of materials, of equipment, and of overheads);
- how much it costs to select, order and purchase a new book (the staff costs and the purchase price, the stationery and the overheads);
- how much it costs to acquire an additional copy of a book;
- how much it costs to add a new periodical issue to stock;
- how much it costs to shelve a new book or periodical part;
- how much it costs to reshelve an item which has been borrowed.

Similarly, for other operations, it is also possible to calculate how much is expended per student, per member of the academic staff, per member of library staff, etc.

However, the librarian must also know how much is expended on different categories of student or of academic staff. More detailed analysis is required in which the costs of each activity are further broken down by user category. Such analysis may be easy enough for circulation, since relevant loan figures are generally available. It is more difficult for enquiry services, where user categories are often not identifiable. In the case of book purchases, individual items are not generally categorizable as items for students (undergraduates) as opposed to purchases for research purposes. In-library periodical usage is virtually impossible to itemize according to user categories.

For books and periodicals, analyses by academic department or faculty may be easier. Periodical titles are generally bought for specific departments, and so are most books. The processes of selection, ordering, acquisition and cataloguing are generally the same whatever the subject matter of the item purchased, and staff expenditure will therefore be uniform for all items. Differences in costs from one academic department to another are primarily a reflection of the variability of prices from one subject field to another.

Costing extensions of services

With calculations of current costs there is a basis for the estimation of future expenditure. The library will know about salary increments, price inflation, costs of equipment maintenance, etc. and forward budgeting can take them into account.

However, this assumes a static level of service and no new demands. The extension of services for increased student numbers or, in particular, for new courses, are not simple projections from current practice. It may be that larger numbers of users or larger numbers of books acquired can be dealt with by the existing levels of staff – hence, average costs for transactions and processes would be reduced. However, this implies that present staffing levels are underused. A continual rise in users cannot be sustained indefinitely. At some point additional staff have to be appointed, and therefore average costs of transactions and processes will rise again.

Is it possible to estimate the staffing costs involved in the extension of services? This entails the identification of a minimal level of service and staffing for each library activity, which in turn entails the establishment of the number of transactions or processes performed by the 'average' competent member of library staff. The problem is that such a measure is nearly impossible to calculate. Experienced staff can deal with much higher numbers than newly appointed staff, but to place the minimal staffing of a service at a level which will work only if the most experienced staff are employed, would be unrealistic; it would only need a few absences for sickness and a few resignations for the whole service to collapse. However, to use the actual averages of current staff implies that no overall improvement in efficiency is possible and that therefore any increase of service in a particular area of activity can be met only by an increase of staff. The alternative is to look at the levels in other libraries, but these are determined by local circumstances and different situations. Comparisons of throughput can be meaningless. Politically, the librarian cannot ask for more staff for every increase; the best way forward is to emphasize increased 'productivity' over a period of time and to ask for staff increases when levels have risen well above previous averages.

Costing new services

Similar, and in some respects, even greater, difficulties arise with the introduction of new services, for example to support a new subject area in teaching or research. There are not only staffing implications from the rise in user numbers and acquisitions. New subjects may make higher demands on staff time, on average, than existing subjects precisely because they are unfamiliar subjects. An allowance for unfamiliarity as well as for increased workloads has to be made; but its size can only be estimated.

Expenditure on materials must also be budgeted. The librarian will be asked how much is required to provide basic collections in new subject areas, and what the future recurrent level of budgeting will be. Such requests may come from the senior university authorities or from an external institution sponsoring or funding the new initiative.

For example, in recent years degree courses for nurses have been funded by health authorities. For the initial stocking collection it is possible to make estimates on the basis of other libraries' collections and the recommendations of relevant bodies, e.g. the Law Society. These can give estimates of materials expenditure, but the librarian must add to them all the staffing costs and overheads involved, including:

- cataloguing
- classification
- labelling
- shelving.

For the recurrent budget it is almost impossible to make estimates until the specific demands of students, researchers and teachers are known (e.g. the areas of specialization, the methods of teaching). Yet, of course, the teachers and researchers will want to know from the beginning how many journal subscriptions can be afforded, what their book allocation will be, and the funding bodies will also want to know the level of their future commitment. (The actual amount involved will be the result of negotiation among the parties – which may or may not involve the librarian.) All the librarian can do, in most cases, is to assume that the new subject area will be similar to some other subject already in the collection. The likely demands of a new course in counselling, for example, might be guessed from experience with current courses in social work and psychology. In this respect, if present recurrent budgets are derived from a formula, it may be possible to estimate how the formula allocation may turn out for the new subject area – assuming that enough data is available to make the calculation. However, initial allocations (whether by formula or not) will be provisional, and subject to change in future years.

Costing 'holdings' versus 'access'

In the costings mentioned above, another factor complicates future projections. No library can ever be self-sufficient, even when it has strong collections of teaching and research materials. It must provide means of discovering, locating and obtaining materials outside its own collections. With the relative decline of funding for universities and libraries, the impetus towards an 'access' policy becomes greater. The development of electronic transmission of data and texts suggests that ultimately (perhaps in the not too distant future) most information required for research purposes will be obtained from external sources, and that researchers will no longer regard their local library as a major information source. There will be a similar tendency as far as teaching is concerned, with online access to external resources of many kinds (including interactive multimedia learning aids) playing an increasing role in undergraduate and postgraduate courses.

Although the local library may no longer be the principal resource in the future, it will be one of the most important, and it will have to continue to purchase materials (print and electronic based) for its users. At the same time, it will be expected to be the principal channel for users in accessing external resources. This scenario entails a different allocation of financial resources, with much less for the purchase of materials (particularly print), much more for expenditure on online services, much more for the supporting equipment, and more on the staffing assistance for users. At the extreme may be envisaged the almost total disappearance of the printed research journal, with:

• expenditure on subscriptions diverted to on-demand purchase of

electronic articles;
- a considerable reduction in the duplication of heavily used textbooks, with expenditure devoted to the provision of online electronic extracts of books;
- a concomitant reduction in the borrowing of textbooks by students;
- a considerable increase in the use of interlibrary services (less for actual borrowing, and more for electronic copies of articles);
- an increase in demands on library staff for assistance to users in locating and exploiting materials in electronic forms and in exploring telecommunication networks.

For the present, however, libraries must continue to provide the traditional services and to purchase materials at current levels (if not greater, given the ever growing amount of publication). At the same time, they must provide the new 'access' services. Where the new services or publication formats are alternatives, then the librarian needs comparative costs.

As far as interlibrary loans are concerned, there is usually little doubt that a once-only request for a specific item is more cheaply obtained from another library than purchased (plus the costs of cataloguing, shelving, etc.)

However, when the same item is required more than once, when does it become cheaper to purchase than to borrow? Calculations are possible in the case of journals, since the costs of subscriptions, of staff expenditure, and of shelving can be established. If these costs over a given time scale (e.g. the estimated half-life of a journal's use) are less than the costs of obtaining the items from elsewhere over the same period – assuming the level of demand for articles from the journal can be extrapolated with confidence – then purchase is the cheapest option. Other factors may also be included: at present on-site availability has the advantage of immediacy for the user. Borrowing from elsewhere has a cost in waiting times for lecturers or students. The more urgent the demand the higher the cost, and the salaries of professors are higher than the grants of students. Whether such costs should be included when considering purchase against borrowing is an open question; they are not strictly library costs, since the salaries come from the university. Fortunately perhaps, the situation may change in the future when, with electronic delivery, 'borrowing' from elsewhere also becomes virtually immediate.

In considering the purchase and access to materials in different formats (print, CD-ROM, online services), the librarian should take into account the relative costs of acquisition, recurrent fees or subscriptions, equipment and its maintenance, shelving, storage, and staffing (both one-off and recurrent), and of course, the effects on usage (and there are now software programs available to assist librarians in these choices.) It is known that bibliographic information on CD-ROM is far more accessible and attractive to users than in traditional print form – although, what the level of usage is likely to be is difficult to estimate in advance of purchase. For a useful survey comparing usage of CD-ROMs, online services, and hardcopy versions of various resources in a variety of libraries see East.[2]

In the case of online services, where materials (articles or bibliographic data) are purchased as required, the estimation of future library expenditure is even more complex. The library may be prepared to charge users the full costs of obtaining full-text articles, although it can be argued that this would not be done if the article were available locally and the user had not wanted a personal copy. But, the library is probably less prepared to charge users for bibliographic information. This would be regarded as a general service function of the library and not attributable to specific user interests (see next chapter). Since the on-demand use of online services cannot be known in advance, the library must adopt a different approach to the allocation of financial resources.

Indeed, there is a much wider question with the development of electronic resources. Increasingly, researchers, lecturers and students have access to these resources at their own desks. They do not see the library as having any role, even if subscription by the library has made access possible (e.g. the BIDS – Bath Information and Data Service). Will the costs of access and the retrieval and purchase of data be borne by departments, by the university as a whole, by the lecturers personally, or by the library? And how will expenditure be controlled? If the library is to have this responsibility it will have to have some means of allocating financial resources and monitoring their expenditure.

Budgeting allocations

The allocation of library resources to staff expenditure and overheads (as broadly defined above) is determined to a large extent by local demand and is thus based on experience and historical precedent within the library itself. But the allocation of resources to purchases has often been a matter of negotiation between the librarian and departments. In the past, current allocations were based on past expenditure. Powerful departmental voices could obtain more purchasing power than weaker members of the university. Traditional areas of expenditure (in particular, journal subscriptions) tended to be favoured over newer formats (e.g. CD-ROM) and newer services (online electronic resources). With reduced budgets and with the greater flexibility demanded by new developments, it is clear that librarians must attempt to be more equitable in the allocation of financial resources for materials of all kinds. In recent years, more and more librarians are turning to allocation formulae, discussed later in this book.

References

1 Kingma, B. R., *The economics of information: a guide to economic and cost-benefit analysis for information professionals*, Englewood, Col., Libraries Unlimited, 1996; Roberts, S. A., ed., *Costing and the economics of library and information services*, (Aslib Reader Series, vol. 5) London, Aslib, 1994; Roberts, S. A., *Cost management for library and information services*, London, Butterworths, 1995.

2 East, H., *Balancing the books: resourcing electronic information services in academic and public libraries*, (British Library R&D Report 6057.) London, British Library, 1991.

9

Allocating Funds for Purchasing Resources: The Main Factors

John Hutchins

Introduction

This chapter will outline the issues involved in the acquisition of materials, whether they are purchases or loans, printed or electronic, for the support of the teaching and research functions of an academic library. It excludes the funding and budgeting for library staff, equipment, furniture, and operational support (which has been treated in chapter eight). The focus is therefore on the selection and purchasing of books, periodicals, CD-ROMs, online services, and interlibrary loans, concentrating on the factors which need to be considered in the allocation of resources and in the development of formulae for the distribution of funds. The literature on this topic is large; for valuable introductions and surveys see Packer (1988), Rein et al. (1993), Revill (1985), Schad (1992), and Sellen (1989).[1]

Access versus holdings

The first major issue is fundamental and influences the overall distribution of library budgets between staffing and acquisitions. It is the choice between access and holdings, i.e. in what circumstances and to what extent should the library anticipate demand by purchase ('just-in-case') and when should it wait until demand appears – to be satisfied by borrowing or acquiring from elsewhere ('just-in-time'). It is generally agreed that certain demands can and must be anticipated, primarily the needs of students for course materials, basic textbooks and essential periodicals. These must be available immediately when required. They cannot be borrowed from elsewhere, they must be purchased. At the other extreme, many research materials (monographs, conference proceedings, primary documents, research periodicals) answer the one-off needs of researchers, which could not have been anticipated, even if full knowledge of current research activity in the university was accessible by library staff and which would not have been purchased even if ample funds had been available.

In these two cases clear decisions can be made: undergraduate textbooks must be held in library stock (often, of course, in multiple copies), advanced research material must be obtained by interlibrary loan. However, there remains a large body of potential purchases which lie in between, where decisions have to be made about whether to acquire or to borrow. In the past, librarians could make judgements based primarily on their familiarity with past usage and likely future demands. Today, financial considerations play a more central role. Material which in the past might have been purchased for anticipated future needs is now no longer acquired, and increasing reliance is made upon the collections of other libraries, principally the British Library, since all other academic libraries are making similar reductions in their acquisitions for potential future needs.

However, there is a further factor: the increased access to information about published materials that has been made possible by online bibliographic sources. Both researchers and students are becoming more aware of materials not available in their local libraries (or even in any British library) and are wanting to make use of them. The demands for these materials, via the traditional interlibrary loan service or via electronic downloading of documents, is necessitating the increase of library funds to support these 'access' tools at the expense of acquisitions for local 'holding'. Few libraries have been able to maintain previous levels of acquisitions as well as to increase budgets for electronic resources.

Books versus periodicals

Acquisitions budgets have always created concern for librarians and library users about whether there is the 'right' balance between books and periodicals. Library Committees often ask whether a library 'of this type' should have 50%, 60%, 70% or some other percentage of periodicals. It is recognized that in different subjects different emphases are given to books and to journals. The traditional distinction is one between the humanities and the natural and applied sciences, the former preferring books and the latter preferring journals. However, it has long been recognized that not all sciences place equal weight on journals. A most useful study by Devin and Kellogg (1990)[2] compares the percentages of citations to journals and books in a wide range of subjects.

However, attempts to establish a percentage for any particular subject are unlikely to be effective unless account is taken of the research demands and teaching methods within the local institution. Some teaching methods place greater demands on the periodical literature than others. In universities where teaching is predominantly in seminars and small groups, libraries are likely to experience more students doing individual projects than in universities where teaching is primarily delivered to large groups in lectures. In general, project work is more likely to require access to 'research' material in journals.

The most realistic attitude to take on this question is to allow the proportion for each individual subject to be determined by actual local demand – which means monitoring local usage and interlibrary loan requests as well as listening and responding to the users themselves.

In practice, increases of periodical subscriptions have been greater than those for books. Over time, the balance within a particular subject may go so far towards periodicals that the whole budget may be devoted to journals. In these circumstances the answer is not necessarily to impose an upper threshold (and thus cuts in subscriptions) but to review the teaching and research requirements as a whole.

An alternative often adopted is to designate a separate fund for all periodicals in all subjects. Then a threshold for the library as a whole can be imposed. However, balancing the conflicting demands of different subjects and of teaching vs research within the global budget for periodicals remains problematic.

Print versus electronic

In some respects this is just a variant of the books/periodicals question. There is no point in trying to impose a 'balance' or percentage limit on purchases of electronic information sources (whether CD-

ROM, subscriptions to national databases, charges for using online databases). What matters is whether the resources are satisfying actual needs.

But, is this the whole answer? Some electronic resources are ephemeral; some are not purchased and 'held' locally, but are charged for on demand. By contrast, printed resources are available at no extra cost to the library 'forever' (or at least until discarded).

An attraction of CD-ROMs is that they are physical additions to library collections. Librarians have little difficulty treating their acquisitions as direct alternatives to the purchase of printed volumes. Some bibliographies and CD-ROMs might be acquired in addition to already available hard copy versions and decisions would be made in the same way on usage criteria, as in the case of providing multiple copies of heavily used textbooks (see below).

Where the electronic resources are not purchased but paid for as required (as in online resources) then the library must designate a budget for the purpose. As yet, few libraries distribute this budget among individual subjects or departments; most have a global sum. But in principle, there is no reason for not budgeting for this usage in the same way as for book and periodical acquisitions.

General versus subject

How much of the acquisitions budget should be devolved to subject allocations and how much to general funds? Certain areas of library collections are regarded by librarians (and normally accepted by users) as of 'general' (not subject-oriented) interest. They would include general dictionaries and encyclopedias, general directories and biographical information, library catalogues (e.g. the British Library catalogue), and general bibliographic resources (national bibliographies). By extension, other parts of the collection might also be included: bibliographies covering a wide range of subjects (e.g. Science Citation Index, MLA Bibliography), the whole of a 'quick reference' collection even if it contains information on specific subjects (e.g. business data, directories of social services), and in particular the collection of government publications.

In some cases, the notion of 'general' may go further. There may be a reference collection comprising not only the types of material listed above but also textbooks and standard editions of 'important' authors and such collections might also be regarded as 'general'. In other cases, an Undergraduate Library of textbooks or a Short Loan collection of books in great demand might also be treated as 'general' collections.

These differences reflect local traditions and may be the result of past political arguments. If, for example, 'subject' allocations are wholly under the control of academic departments and past experience makes the librarian distrust the way some funds are being spent, then the librarian may well be inclined to increase the proportion of the budget allocated for 'general' purposes.

Clearly, no hard and fast percentages can be suggested in this area. But whatever the proportion allocated to 'general' funds, the library will find itself increasingly asked to justify expenditure in this area – and this is a question of monitoring usage. With less money overall, it will also be asked to clarify the dividing lines between 'subject' and 'general' materials.

Research versus teaching

In the past, librarians argued with a good deal of justification that it was not possible to divide expenditure between research and teaching needs. It is obvious that particular books may be read by both research students and undergraduate students; that a journal article on a research topic may be required reading for a first degree; and so forth. Individual books are rarely purchased with one particular type of reader in mind. The only exceptions might be the introductory textbooks for first year students – but even then, they are likely to be read by lecturers starting to teach in a subject previously unfamiliar to them. Other exceptions might be some of the most esoteric research journals, but all librarians have been surprised from time to time to find that some third-year student has been assigned a project requiring the reading of articles in such journals.

When considering the division of budgets between teaching and research it is not a question of whether individual items should be purchased from a 'research' or from a 'teaching' allocation (whether within a particular subject or not) but what balance overall should be given to research and teaching demands.

The impetus for such a division comes from the increasing demand for accountability within universities. The global allocations from the Higher Education Funding Councils to UK universities distinguish explicitly between money for research and teaching purposes. The research performance of a university is assessed and compared with those of other universities, at the level of particular subjects or 'cost centres', and these assessments have direct effects on a university's income. Similar assessments of 'teaching quality' are being conducted, with the intention of directing more resources to some universities than to others.

Within universities, relative strengths in research and in teaching are likely to have direct influence on the mechanisms for allocating resources to faculties and departments. In this case universities will either give greater support to subjects or departments with good assessments or assist those with poorer records in order to improve the university's overall rating. Increasingly, their libraries will be expected to reflect these decisions in their expenditure allocations to subjects.

There are two possibilities here. The first possibility is that the university as a whole will earmark specific sums or percentages for library expenditure for each 'cost centre' (subject or department), and probably designate sums separately for research and for teaching. The second possibility is that, even if the library continues to receive a global sum, it will be expected to show how its subject allocations reflect the research and teaching strengths of each 'cost centre'. If its percentages differ from those allocated by the university, then some justification will be required.

The practical implication is that librarians must know in detail the principles (and ideally the mechanisms) of their university's allocations to each 'cost centre' and how research and teaching assessments have influenced the calculations. Universities are being obliged to be more open about how they allocate resources to faculties and departments and some have devised formulae for calculating allocations. To what extent libraries should mirror their university's allocation mechanism will depend on how well they can justify divergences.

Cost centres versus subjects versus departments

In few universities and libraries can 'cost centres' be equated with 'subjects' or 'departments'. National pressures may lead universities to adapt all accounting procedures to nationally agreed 'subject' groups (for research and teaching), and libraries will be expected to follow.

However, librarians know from experience that each part of their collection is used by wide ranges of different departmental interests. It is not just the mathematicians who borrow the books on statistical methods, it is not just the social workers who read the periodicals on social welfare, or the lawyers who look at the law reports, etc. Even so, these facts may continue to surprise the academics who believe that they are the only ones with any interest in 'their' books.

The inclination of librarians, therefore, is to allocate according to subject areas which cut across the narrow definitions of departmental (or faculty) 'subjects'. Where expenditure has typically been controlled by academics and budgets have been devolved to departments, it may well be difficult to do anything other than allocate resources on the basis of staff and student numbers. Where 'subject' expenditure has been controlled by the library, the library will have to show increasingly in the future how its distribution relates to the mechanism adopted by the university for allocating resources to departments.

Student demands and teaching methods

It is a truism, well known to both librarians and teaching staff, that different teaching methods affect the ways students use libraries. In some cases, there is heavy demand for a few titles for just a few weeks (or days) in the year. In other cases, demand for a wide range of titles may be spread over a term or semester. In others, the demand may be for a collection with 'research' depth. In general terms, librarians know from experience the types of teaching method that lead to different kinds of demand.

However, the situation is changing. Students have less money to spend on purchasing their own books than they did in the past; consequently more library books are in heavy demand. More students are studying for each subject in each university, and there is heavier demand for course materials in general. There are more distance-learning students, who cannot reach the library (or the university) as often as those based locally. Here, there is heavy demand for books for longer loan periods.

In the past, librarians could judge demand fairly well without statistics of usage, but now with demands of different kinds from a wider range of students and course types it is essential to monitor demand continuously (which is obviously possible only with computer-based circulation systems), and the results of this monitoring have to influence the allocation of resources.

New subjects and new areas of research activity

The expansion of university teaching and research into areas not previously covered by the library is a recurring problem for all librarians. Despite efforts of rationalization at a national level it is unlikely to disappear. In the past, librarians could make rough estimates of likely set-up and recurrent costs and expect, in most cases, for their estimates to be agreed and the money to be forthcoming from central university funds. Now they will be asked to justify the basis for their calculations and often to account for actual expenditure in some detail. The consequence is that librarians are faced with the need to devise mechanisms to calculate costs in a way which can be seen to be valid.

Special collections of national significance

Nearly all academic libraries have some parts of the collection which have to be treated in a special way: a collection of rare or valuable books; an important donation; an archive; a particular overall strength in some subject area. In many cases, these special collections are resources of national importance. Librarians are obliged to maintain and often build upon these collections. The deployment of resources to these collections is often a matter of local or national negotiation, and the granting of special ear-marked funds. Obviously, no direct guidance can be offered in such cases, since circumstances differ widely.

Preservation versus acquisition

A related issue is the allocation of resources to the preservation of materials. Paperback books are frequently bound on acquisition (or acquired already bound from booksellers), and in most libraries these costs are assigned to the 'subject' or 'departmental' budgets. The same may apply to periodicals, which are regularly bound for preservation; and the costs assigned to the 'subject' budget. However, the costs of binding continue to rise, and the usage of some books and periodicals does not always justify binding. Increasingly, libraries delay binding (particularly of periodicals and research monographs) until wear and tear make it essential. For these purposes, libraries set aside a general fund for binding which will also cover the re-binding of heavily used textbooks.

There is also a more general issue: how much of the library budget should be devoted to the maintenance of the existing stock? As collections grow and age, preservation (repairing and binding) requires a greater demand on resources. At a certain level, expenditure on preservation has significant impact on funds for acquisitions and/or access to non-local resources. Decisions about what to retain – and therefore, what to preserve – are linked to decisions about what parts of the collection continue to have research significance, what parts have national importance, what could be borrowed in future from other libraries or what can be accessed from other locations (including travel by users to other collections). Decisions about preservation are clearly linked to decisions about holdings and access.

Towards a formula

Increasingly, libraries are developing formulae to capture some or most of the factors outlined above. The aim is to achieve a greater transparency in the allocation of funds for the purchase and acquisition of library materials. The next chapter discusses what is involved in this.

References

1 Packer, D., 'Acquisitions allocations: equity, politics, and formulas', *Journal of academic librarianship,* **14** (5), 1988, 276-86, ; Rein, L. O., Hurley, F. P., Walsh, J. C. and Wu, A. C., 'Formula-based subject allocation: a practical approach', *Collection management,* **17** (4), 1993, 25-48, ; Revill, D. H. ed., *Working papers on bookfund allocation,* Oxford, Council of Polytechnic Librarians, 1995; Schad, J. G., 'The future of collection development in an era of fiscal stringency: a symposium', *Journal of academic librarianship,* **18** (1), 1992, 4-16, ; Sellen, M., 'Book budget formula allocations: a review essay', *Collection management* **9** (4), 1989, 13-24.
2 Devin, R.B. and Kellogg, M., 'The serial/monograph ratio in research libraries: budgeting in the light of citation studies', *College and research libraries,* **51** (1), 1990, 46-54.

10

Developing a Formula for Library Resource Funding

John Hutchins

The coverage of a formula

In recent years, many libraries have begun to use formulae for calculating the amounts to be allocated to particular 'subjects' or 'departments' for purchasing books, for subscribing to periodicals, and for other library materials and resources – reviews of the literature are given by Packer (1988) and Rein et al. (1993).[1]

The factors to be taken into account have been outlined in the previous chapter. Many formulae cover only the book purchasing component of library acquisitions, but there are strong arguments for a formula to include periodicals and non-print materials. A further obvious extension is the inclusion of the costs of binding books or periodicals. With the increasing acceptance of 'access' instead of local 'holdings' it is also clear that interlibrary loan expenditure should be regarded as an alternative to book and periodical expenditure. Likewise the expenditure on online bibliographic searches can legitimately be seen as complementary to purchases of printed bibliographies.

There are three main reasons for introducing a formula to allocate book and periodical funds. They are not mutually exclusive and are not unproblematic.

1   The first objective is to be more equitable. But the context has to be defined: should the library heed the weightings given by the university to different 'cost centres'? Should it take account of research strengths?

2   The second is to maximize 'benefits' over 'costs'. But whose benefits – the university's (in terms of research output, publication output), the students' (quality of learning, examination results), or the library's (satisfaction of needs, lowering users' frustrations)?

3   A third reason put forward is the improvement of library efficiency – e.g. to maximize the proportion of newly purchased materials which are used or borrowed, and to reduce the amount of materials not used (within reasonable periods).

Consultation within the university about the factors to be included and the structure of the formula is essential for any formula to gain acceptance. In the end, defensibility and accountability can be more important than 'objective' equitability (cf. Packer, and Rein et al. for the 'political' perspectives.)[2]

The content of a formula

Formulae may divide the library budget according to departments (or faculties or schools of study) or according to subjects. It is generally agreed that formulae should cover all monograph literature which can be assigned to subjects taught in the institution, i.e. textbooks for teaching, and research monographs. Publications of general or multidisciplinary interest are frequently excluded. Hence, reference materials (dictionaries, bibliographies) and government publications are generally purchased from a separate allocation. The same may be done for subjects which are not taught in the university but are of wide interest, e.g. religion in an institution with no Theology faculty or department, psychoanalysis where there are no courses in psychology. In some libraries, the 'general' fund may extend further (as indicated above).

It is sometimes argued that periodicals should also be excluded. In essence two reasons are put forward:

• many periodicals are interdisciplinary and cannot (or should not) be assigned to particular subjects or departments;
• the problems of incorporating periodicals without distorting calculations (see below).

The argument for inclusion is that a formula should attempt to cover all allocations, not just a part (perhaps less than half the acquisitions budget.) The question of a separate budget for periodicals will be dealt with below. The following sections survey the parameters and data which may be included in formulae.

Teaching staff and students

The most common factor is size of department, faculty (or 'subject') in terms of:

- number of teachers
- number of students (undergraduate and postgraduate)
- number of non-teaching research workers.

A common alternative to student numbers is the number of student course hours (i.e. the number of courses in the department (or 'subject') multiplied by length in hours and the numbers of students enrolled).

In general, the information is relatively easy to collect. If allocations are based on departments (or faculties), then university data can be used directly. If, however, allocation is by subjects and these do not correspond to departmental divisions, then the library will have to have some basis for redistributing staff and student numbers to its 'subjects'. In the case of academic staff this may involve asking heads of departments (or faculties) – or all staff directly – what subjects they teach or research. There are difficulties in making clear to departments exactly what the library's subjects cover, unless crude results are acceptable.

For student numbers, the university administration may be able to provide figures for enrolments in different course modules, and these may be cumulated to correspond to library subjects. Alternatively, national course codes may be employed where they are available, but in this case the national categories may not match well with local library subjects.

Frequently, formulae include some weightings of staff and student numbers. It is widely assumed that greater 'importance' should be given to teaching staff than to students or to non-teaching (research) staff, to professors than to lecturers, to postgraduate research students than to undergraduate students. These weightings are by their nature subjective, and any which are introduced will have to obtain the approval of the university as a whole if the formula is to be accepted. Nevertheless, there are some common weighting patterns which recur in many formulae:

- teaching staff count four or five times as much as undergraduate students.
- postgraduate research students count twice as much as undergraduates; taught postgraduates are equated with undergraduates.
- non-teaching research staff count half as much as faculty teaching/research staff.

The weighting of some 'subjects' (or departments) greater than others is also practised occasionally. There are various reasons:

- it is argued that in some subjects (the Humanities, for example) library materials are more important for research and for teaching than in others;
- some teaching methods lead to greater demands on library stock than in others (see above), and these are more common in some subjects (or departments) than others;
- the university wishes to foster research in some subjects more than in others.

In the latter case, it may be possible for the library to employ a weighting used by the university in allocating resources to departments or 'cost centres' (although there may be differences between these and the library's 'subjects'). The other weightings are even more subjective and even more disputable than those for staff and students. In both cases, however, it can be argued that if usage is included in the formula (as described in the next section) then weightings for 'library importance' or 'teaching methods' are superfluous.

Needs, demand, usage

Many formulae include data on the actual usage of the library stock in different subjects. Some, indeed, are based exclusively on such data, e.g. at Sussex University Library.[3]

Circulation data can cover books and periodicals actually borrowed. Most libraries now have access to circulation statistics in various forms showing:

- number of times (over a period) each item was borrowed;
- length of time (within a period) each item was borrowed (and hence not on shelves);
- number of items on loan at a particular point in time (repeated at intervals over a period).

If these data are to be used in subject allocations, they must be categorized by subject (perhaps classmark). If they are to be used in departmental allocation then they need to be categorized by department. If the formula includes staff/student numbers, it is also useful to have categorization by type of borrower (undergraduate, staff, etc.)

The analysis of circulation data by subject may additionally include:

1 the calculation of how much (in percentage terms) the borrowing of each subject contributes to the total library borrowings, e.g. of all books borrowed 15% may be from the history collection, and 5% from the music stock, etc.

2 the calculation of how much of the total stock of a subject has been borrowed (over a year or shorter period, or at any one moment), e.g. of all the history books in the library perhaps 55% are borrowed during the year and perhaps 20% at any one time, and of the music stock perhaps the figures are 20% and 7% respectively.

Both types of analysis can be used in a formula. The first calculation can provide percentages for the division of the total budget available for a department (or the library as a whole) into 'subjects'. In the case of a multidisciplinary department the data provides an objective for distribution among different interests. The second calculation (percentage of borrowing within a subject) can be used to give an addi-

tional weighting for subjects within a departmental or library allocation, so that heavily used parts of the collection receive more
resources than less used parts.

There seems to have been no study of which kinds of circulation
data are most useful (i.e. equitable) in allocation formulae. Libraries
appear to adopt the data which are most easily collected. There is,
however, general agreement that data should be cumulated or aver-
aged over a time span at least as long as the normal degree course,
i.e. three years, in order to minimize fluctuations of usage from one
year to another.

Just as staff/student numbers could be weighted according to the
'importance' of library materials in the subject or of 'research performance', it might be argued that usage should also be weighted. The
reasoning might be that the reading of books or journal articles is
more important or valuable in some subjects or departments than it
is in others. However, such weightings will be subjective and are
unlikely to bear critical examination.

All librarians know that circulation data do not reflect true usage
– even a book borrowed is not necessarily read. Some formulae
attempt to include data on in-library use. This is not the place to discuss the problems of gathering and evaluating such data (usually by
extensive sampling)[4] but it may be noticed that most commentators
are agreed that the results indicate a correlation between in-library
use and out-library circulation data to some extent. The proportions
are similar but not identical. The fact that in-library usage may be up
to four times borrowing[5] has an obvious implication for withdrawal
policy, but not necessarily for allocation formulae, where what matters are the relative values and not the absolute values. If in-house
data is available and the results are significantly different from circulation data then some weighting may be worthwhile – how much
will depend on local circumstances.

A more serious objection to the use of circulation data is that it has
limited use and does not reflect real demand. A poor collection will
be poorly used. Some counter-balance is provided by data from interlibrary loans (ILL). The use of materials from other libraries is an
indicator of demand, as borrowings may show deficiencies of the
local collection. This question will be dealt with below.

Literature size

The basic argument for including a factor for literature size in an allocation formula is the observation that the amount of potentially purchasable literature varies markedly from subject to subject. Whatever the size of the department or the level of borrowing, it is argued, a university library ought to acquire a certain proportion of the literature of the subject. It implies that there is a basic 'core' minimum level of purchasing, below which the collection in that subject is no longer adequate for any teaching or study. The argument is applied most often by small departments, which might suffer if the main factor in the allocation formula is staff and student numbers.

The main sources for data on literature sizes are:

- national bibliographies;
- selective lists of recent publications, e.g. *Choice, British Books*;
- databases of books in print, e.g. *Bookbank, Books in Print Plus*;
- statistical data on numbers and prices of academic publications, e.g. those produced by the Library Information and Statistics Unit;[6]
- lists of periodicals in print, e.g. *Ulrich's Periodicals Index*;
- comparative surveys of holdings in large (national) research libraries;
- standard 'core' lists published by subject groups, e.g. the Law Society's lists;
- citation analyses.

Each have their disadvantages or inadequacies, both regarding comprehensiveness and representativeness. It should be noted that what is required for a university library formula is not an estimate of the total published literature, but of the amount of currently published literature which is of academic interest in the local context and which could be purchased.

National bibliographies and lists of 'books in print' and 'periodicals in print' do not distinguish in sufficient detail the level of readership. Selective lists and other library stocks may be better indicators of potential academic purchases, and better still are the statistical data contained in the LISU publications.[7]

However, even when numbers of academic publications are available, it is difficult for an individual library to judge whether all the books in the category would be potential purchases or not. Few libraries aim to cover all aspects of any one subject – specialization is the norm.

Furthermore, academic libraries do not only purchase from English-speaking countries. To estimate the size of a subject's literature, libraries need to know the amount of potential publication in other countries producing English materials (e.g. the Netherlands, Scandinavia, India, etc.) and countries producing publications in languages which the library covers (e.g. French, German, Spanish). In the latter case, libraries are generally interested in foreign literature only in certain subjects (e.g. modern languages, history, development studies); in some subjects only English language materials are required (e.g. law, and most natural sciences). Clearly, the gathering of data for these other potential publication sources is a major task, and in most instances the data are just not available. Furthermore, there will always be the question whether all publications from such sources (even if at an academic level) would really be potential purchases.

Superficially, subject lists would appear to be the best sources. The list of the law publications 'which every academic library should have' is certainly an excellent guide to the size of the literature, although again every library would not want (or need) to cover the full range because the department's (or school's) teaching would be more limited. A major impediment to the use of the Law Society's list is the absence of similar lists for other subjects. The library may be able to estimate how much is needed to purchase what is needed in law, but it would not be able to estimate how much to allocate to another subject for the same level of coverage.

The desirability of lists for other subjects is clear, as long as they cover the same mix of retrospective and current publications and they applied the same criteria of selection. It is doubtful that this could be achieved.

As further sources of data there are citation analyses and the collections of other libraries. Citation analyses are normally undertaken to assess the 'adequacy' of a library's collection for research in particular subject areas. If restricted to citations in publications by members of the institution alone they can also be used as indicators of usage of library stock and of the ILL service. However, for the purposes of estimating literature size they are of doubtful value, primarily because they do not focus on current publications.

Assessing literature sizes from the holdings of other libraries has its own problems. Few libraries are truly comparable in depth or range of coverage over all subjects; relative sizes of collections in other libraries is unlikely to give much guidance for budget allocation purposes. National collections may indicate some maximum sizes in areas where a comprehensive collection policy applies. In theory, analysis of the data in a conspectus of collections should enable librarians to estimate the relative sizes of literatures in different subjects.[8] To my knowledge such an analysis has not been done, but even if it were, it would not indicate the amount of literature currently being published.

Average costs of books and periodicals

The obvious reason for including price data in allocation formulae is the recognition that some subjects are more expensive than others. This is particularly true for periodicals: science journals are notoriously much more expensive than journals in humanities and social sciences. Although librarians may protest at the quasi-monopolistic hold of the publishers, it is a fact of life which cannot be avoided.

For the purpose of an allocation formula what is required are the average costs of books and periodicals in each of the subjects to be covered. Overall average prices, whether national, international, academic, etc., are of no value for this purpose.

Libraries frequently wish to distinguish between their own average expenditures on books and periodicals and the national or international averages for all potential purchases. Figures for local expenditure are generally easily available, since they are needed for internal auditing purposes.

Some of the sources for national and international averages are the same as in the previous section:

* national bibliographies,
* books in print,
* periodicals in print,
* statistics of academic publications.

In addition we can add statistics provided by subscription agencies (e.g. Whitakers and Blackwells).

The same problems enumerated above apply to the sources listed above. The difficulty of extracting data relevant to academic purchasing of books and periodicals (and in the range covered locally), and the lack or inadequacy of data for foreign publications.

The best sources are, in the case of books, the statistics from LISU for UK and US academic publications and, in the case of periodicals, the data provided by Blackwells on average journal subscriptions within broad subject groups. The latter are international in coverage (unlike the data from LISU for books), and thus may not reflect the coverage of the local library. But at least they exist.

In addition to or instead of external average prices, an allocation formula may take into account the actual costs of purchases by the library itself. The main reason for doing so is that external data do not reflect the range and coverage of the potential purchases in particular subjects (or over the library as a whole); and, in particular, there may be no external data for foreign publications in the subject.

However, there are strong reasons for not using local data exclusively. Recent purchasing policy may have distorted averages by the selection of cheaper publications – in some subjects perhaps more than in others. For example, there may have been a preference for paperbacks rather than hardbacks; selection policy (or financial constraints) may have led to an avoidance of expensive research monographs; there may have been above average emphasis on (generally cheaper) emphasis on textbooks for students; and, in the case of periodicals, cuts in subscriptions may have applied to a higher percentage of the more expensive titles than of the cheaper titles.

The effects may have been more marked in some subjects than in others. The effect of a too low average (in local library expenditure) might be that the formula allocates an even lower allocation for a subject than might have otherwise been the case. This effect of the formula could be an encouragement for some to concentrate purchases on expensive items in order to raise the averages used in the formula. The use of external data should rectify such discrepancies from one subject to another.

Historical precedent

The major aim of an allocation formula is to get away from the subjectivity of budgeting based on historical precedent, i.e. in essence, when the sum allotted to each subject is an increase on that of the previous year taking into account inflation and perceived changes in the coverage required (new courses, increased student numbers, etc.) By contrast, a formulaic approach implies that calculations are more objective and to some extent start every time from scratch. (They are rarely, however, completely zero-based since most take into account past usage and past years' average expenditures.)

In practical application, few libraries can ignore the allocations of previous years. The effects of a formula may be substantial changes in allocation levels from one year to another. Academic staff and departments are unlikely to tolerate large fluctuations. Few will quarrel with upward movements, but those seeing a reduction are likely to question the basic premises of the formula. Even if they are convinced of its equitability, dramatic changes are not feasible for practical reasons within the library itself – the cancellation of subscriptions and standing orders take some months to become effective. Consequently, it is often wise to adjust the results of formula allocations so that large changes are introduced gradually.

Even when the use of a formula is well established, there is good reason for not ignoring past allocations. If there are considerable changes from one year to another, then the library will find itself on the defensive in justifying not only the proposed new levels but also the past levels. It will be faced with arguments such as:

- If the formula indicates we (the department or subject) should be getting more now, why have we not been getting this much before? Should we receive a supplement as recompense for past underfunding?
- If the formula indicates that we should be getting less now, why were the past allocations wrong?

Adjustment for historical precedent is particularly important when a formula allocation method is being first implemented. It is safest to devise an initial formula which produces results which are not dramatically different from the historical levels. This is more likely to be accepted. Once the notion of a formula as such has been agreed then it is easier in future years to introduce changes which move allocation levels further away from historical ones. In any case, it is always wise to introduce formulaic allocations as 'guides' to actual allocations, to allow the library staff to make adjustments in the light of representations from academic staff (e.g. for new courses, new research activities). It is simple politics that the library should never be seen as inflexible.

Departmental allocations

The conflict between library 'subjects' and university 'department' interests, mentioned in the previous chapter, is not easily resolved. The problem may well become more acute for librarians as universities allocate their own budgets increasingly according to 'cost centres'. Libraries will have to show equitability of allocations by these criteria.

One option (adopted at the University of East Anglia Library) is for the acquisitions budget as a whole, after deductions for 'general' stock allocations, to be divided first among faculties and departments; then each 'departmental' fund to be divided according to library 'subjects' (using staff and student numbers, average prices, usage patterns, etc.); and the totals for each subject from each department to be added together to give an allocation for each subject as a whole. The Library is then able to manage the expenditure in each subject independently; and there are no departmental allocations as such. At the same time however, members of academic staff can see how much 'their' departments are receiving in comparison with others. The aim is to be both equitable in 'subject' allocations and transparent in 'departmental' accountability.

Special allocations (outside the formula)

The provision of special allocations for 'general' stock (e.g. reference materials, rare books, archives, government publications, etc.) has been mentioned already. Such allocations are usually treated as special 'top-slices' of the book/periodicals budget and would not be included in formula calculations. The level of such allocations is inevitably based on historical precedent, which does not mean that expenditure should be hidden from scrutiny and regular assessment.

The same procedure can be done for acquisitions for short loan collections and/or for multiple copies of textbooks. However, it can also be argued that it should not be done. The demand for multiple copies and short loan books is not spread evenly over all subjects. They may well be concentrated in the social sciences, for example. The provision of what might be seen as an 'arbitrary' amount for such collections could be seen as unjustifiable favouritism of one section of library users. At the very least the library should have statistics available to show where expenditure has gone, e.g. in terms of the subjects of books or their borrowers. A more satisfactory solution might be, where feasible, to incorporate heavy demand in the formula through statistical adjustment (weighting) of the general usage data, although the determination of exactly how the adjustments are to be calculated is not easy and may in the end be 'subjective'.

It is widely agreed that new subjects and new courses require separate treatment. There are considerable problems in the costing for initial stock building, primarily the lack of data on literature size, relevant average prices, and uncertainty about demand (teaching and research) at the local institution. Initially, then, new subjects will be outside any formula allocation. At some stage (politically determined) when the 'new' subject is well established it should be integrated into any formula. The most obvious time is when it reaches its full student complement, when usage and expenditure has stabilized. Any attempt to do so earlier will involve assumptions that may prove untenable in the long term (and thus difficult to retreat from). The problem for a formula is that there is no usage data (out-library or in-library), there is no library data for average prices (only external data may be available), and there are no firm student and staff numbers. It is possible sometimes to use 'dummy' student numbers, but usage is almost impossible to quantify.

Periodicals

In some libraries, it has been the custom to have a separate allocation for all periodical subscriptions. Whatever the reason, there may be difficulties in fixing the amount required for a global periodical allocation: is it to be a fixed percentage of the library budget, or is it to increase with rising subscription costs? It may be just a political compromise. Distribution of funds within a global periodicals budget encounters the same problems as distribution within a book budget. Historical precedent may work for a long time, but eventually (particularly when funds become inadequate) a more 'objective' method will be demanded – given the inflationary increases of subscriptions, this may come very quickly.

It is difficult to see that a formula for periodicals allocations among 'subjects' can avoid taking into account the same factors as for books:

- staff and student numbers,
- usage,
- average prices,
- literature size,
- some provision for special collections and new subjects.

For this reason, it may be better to include periodicals in the overall formula allocation process. There are problems with an integrated formula, primarily because the prices of individual periodical subscriptions are much higher than those of individual books. One approach (adopted at UEA Library) is to use not the actual average prices of books and periodicals but to use an 'average price ratio' which indicates how much the average for an individual subject deviates from the average price for all subjects. For example, if history journals cost on average £75 per annum and chemistry journals £250 p.a., and the average for all periodicals (in the library) is £100, then the ratio for history would be 0.75 and for chemistry 2.5. Likewise for books, the ratio for history might be 0.85 and for chemistry 1.75. As a crude but effective indicator of cost differences in an integrated formula, the ratios for books and periodicals can be added giving, in this example, 1.6 for history, 4.25 for chemistry, and 2.0 for the library as a whole.

Extensions to other acquisitions-related expenditure

Within the context of expenditure on materials, the purchase of books and periodicals is just one item, albeit a major and dominating one. Others, however, are equally part of resource allocation, and some of them are of increasing importance. In most cases, the allocation of funds under these heads will be done by historical precedent and by current demand. In the future, it would seem logically consistent to treat these budgetary heads in the same way as for books and periodicals, i.e. to move towards more 'objective' methods of allocation. Whether the distribution should necessarily use the same 'subjects' or 'departments' as for books and periodicals is an internal matter.

The most obvious extension, and one which many libraries implement already, is the integration of binding costs into formula allocations. Nearly all libraries bind periodicals, for easier handling and for improved preservation. It would seem logical that the costs of binding periodicals should be charged to the 'subject' allocation from which the subscription is paid.

The same comment applies to books. Often, libraries receive books from suppliers already with some form of binding, and this cost will be part of the total price of each individual book. To allocate a separate budget for binding paperback books which are not already bound is not logical. However, the incorporation of such post-purchase binding costs necessitates the gathering of data on how many books purchased in a particular subject are bound and at what average cost.

The initial stocking of non-print materials (microfilm, CD-ROMs, etc.) may have been from special allocations, on the analogy with new subjects and courses (as described above). Ultimately, however, they should be seen as just alternative forms for printed materials and charged to subject allocations in a comparable way (see previous chapter). If they represent the (partial) duplication of printed resources – as with CD-ROM bibliographic databases, then their acquisition may be regarded as akin to that of additional copies of textbooks in heavy demand.

No modern library is self-sufficient and interlibrary loans must be seen as supplements and complements of local collections. It would seem superficially logical to consider the borrowing of a book or journal as equivalent to purchase, and to charge the costs of borrowing to the relevant subject or departmental allocation, to treat it effectively as if an item purchased. The procedure would require accurate costing of the interlibrary loan service (excluding staff costs, since these are not included in acquisition budgets). But the principle would be clear.

However, there are good reasons for caution. It can equally be argued that researchers and students need to borrow books from other libraries because subject (or departmental) allocations have been inadequate in the past and perhaps also the present. To charge borrowings to subject allocations would be doubly unjust, since it would reduce further the amount available for local acquisition. It can be argued that a high level of interlibrary loans indicates that more should go to the subject. This suggests that interlibrary loans should be regarded not just as equivalent to 'purchases' but also as equivalent to 'borrowings' from the local stock. If, in a formula, relatively higher levels of usage contribute to higher expenditure allocations, then relatively higher levels of interlibrary loans should also contribute to higher allocations.

However, the inclusion of ILL data with circulation and in-library use data in a general formula for allocating funds for acquisitions may well be unsatisfactory. Simple addition would seem to be inadequate, since the relatively small number of items in the ILL data will be lost in the much higher figures for the use of the local collection, and in addition this would ignore the different (usually higher) costs associated with ILL materials. Some weighting would clearly have to be attached to ILL borrowing.

In general, it seems better to use ILL data for the development of a separate formula for distributing ILL allocations between departments (or faculties). The ILL budget would be a 'special' allocation within the general library acquisitions budget. As such it would have to be based on a (subjective) judgment of how much is needed (or can be afforded) to meet demands. Within the global ILL fund the allocation to subjects or departments can be based on the numbers of staff and research students (and, optionally, undergraduate students) and on average usage in recent years.

Similar problems are posed with the allocation of funds for the provision of online services for accessing remote databases, whether bibliographic or full-text document resources. Some libraries charge for the 'traditional' bibliographic service undertaken by library staff, others do not. The analogy for not charging is with printed bibliographies. Once bought, users are not charged for consultation. It is argued that, whether a library has acquired the printed version or not, it should not ask users to pay for accessing an electronic version. But some libraries do charge, primarily it would seem in order to keep expenditure within bounds.

As libraries move away from the 'holdings' approach and closer to the concept of 'information resources', it would seem logical to treat any charges for accessing online databases as just another 'purchase' from a subject allocation. Where these charges are annual fees there should be no problem. Where, however, charges are based on actual usage, there will be difficulties in allocating a fixed annual sum, particularly if usage exceeds the allocation and there is no residual sum after book and periodical purchases. In addition, as with interlibrary loans it will be argued that higher use is a response to inadequacy of traditional resources. The need again is for a mechanism which treats such 'access' events as both 'borrowing' and 'purchase' events, with suitable weightings according to relative costs.

Summary

As demands on library resources grow, as new types of materials appear, as different patterns of acquisition and methods of payment are introduced, and in particular as budgets grow tighter, the need for objectivity and equitability in the allocation of resources becomes ever more desirable. The introduction of formulae has been a natural consequence. Once introduced, it is difficult (perhaps impossible) to return to allocations based on historical precedence. Of course, there are sharp divisions about what factors and data are to be included and how formulae are to be constructed. Some plead for 'scientific' formulae not tied to local politics and pressures; others favour pragmatism and wide acceptability, however 'flawed' the resulting formula may be from an objective perspective. No formula can be perfect, it should serve as a guide or framework for expenditure, not as a straight-jacket; above all, it should be flexible and capable of change and revision over time.

References

1   Packer, D., 'Acquisitions allocations: equity, politics, and formulas', *Journal of academic librarianship*, **14** (5), 276–86, 1988; Rein, L. O., Hurley, F. P., Walsh, J. C. and Wu, A. C., 'Formula-based subject allocation: a practical approach', *Collection management*, **17** (4), 25–48, 1993.

2   *op. cit.*

3   Peasgood, A. N., 'Towards demand-led book acquisitions? Experiences

in the University of Sussex Library', *Journal of librarianship* **18** (4), 242–56, 1986.

4   Van House, N. A. et al., *Measuring academic library performance: a practical approach*, Chicago, American Library Association, 1990.

5   Revill, D.H. ed., *Working papers on bookfund allocation*, Oxford, Council of Polytechnic Librarians, 1985.

6   LISU, *Average prices of British [USA] academic books*, Loughborough, Library Information and Statistics Unit, 1987–.

7   As footnote 6.

8   Gwinn, N. E. and Mosher, P. H., 'Coordinating collection development: the RLG Conspectus', *College and research libraries*, **44** (2), 128–40, 1983; Holt, B. G. F. and Hanger, S., *Conspectus in the British Library: a summary of current collecting intensity data as recorded on RLG Conspectus worksheets with completed worksheets on microfiche*, London, The British Library, 1986.

11

Research Collections

KEITH WEBSTER

Introduction

The mission of research libraries is to acquire information, organise it, make it available and preserve it. [1]

If research collections are believed to be distinctive from library collections in general, then the aim of this chapter is to focus on aspects that are peculiar to them. Some topics addressed will take a narrow research library perspective; others will be part of wider library provision, but examined in the extent to which they impinge on research collections.

What constitutes a research library, and what forms a research collection? Authoritative definitions are scarce, but the Anderson Committee (discussed later in this chapter), which investigated the strategy for library provision for researchers, was given a remit which excluded the library needs of those in institutions of higher education who were following undergraduate and taught postgraduate courses. This is accepted here, although it must be noted that as project and dissertation work on these courses grows in complexity, the library resources and collections required will overlap with those provided for higher degree and academic research.

Research libraries can perhaps best be distinguished by:

- the size, range, depth and quality of the collections;
- the considerable holdings of particular concentration and strength over a wide time span and of sufficient importance to

attract scholars well beyond its parent institution;
* the necessary general background stock to support its specialisms.[2]

Research collections are not the exclusive property of large university research libraries: many smaller academic libraries will have some collections of research level, and the challenges facing research libraries also impinge on the wider university library sector. The focus of this volume is academic libraries, but it is important to recognize that the process of academic research is supported by libraries beyond those in our institutions of higher education. In Britain, research bodies such as the Royal Society, the British Academy and the Royal Colleges of Physicians and Surgeons all play a vital role in providing library services, as do many major public libraries.

Libraries have a clearly recognized role in supporting research. Erens[3] reported that 95% of active researchers considered a well-stocked library very or fairly important to their research, whilst fewer than 0.5% felt that a library was not at all important to their research. In texts designed to support the proliferation of Master of Research (MRes) degrees, considerable attention is paid to library skills and the role of the library in supporting the work of successful researchers(see for example, Frank[4]).

This chapter will not focus on resource management techniques which are being covered elsewhere in the volume, nor will it provide extensive detail on any one topic surrounding the management of research collections. Instead, it will highlight the main issues facing the manager of research collections, and provide pointers to more detailed sources of information. The aim of this overview is to provide a picture of research collection management at the end of the twentieth century.

Pressures on research collections

Research libraries world-wide are facing an unprecedented range of pressures and demands: from users, through technological demands, and as a result of changes in the environment in which they operate. It is as a result of these constraints that library managers have developed new approaches and techniques to resource management. It is instructive to examine briefly the nature of challenges facing library managers as an introduction to examining current practice and future trends.

User demands

In the UK, greater emphasis has been placed on research within university departments. Funds are awarded directly as a result of Research Assessment Exercises, a process through which the quality of research is judged on the basis of academics' publications. This has led to increased research activity in universities, and, in turn, greater demand for library services and collections in support of research. At the same time, there has been a rapid growth in the number of students registered for postgraduate degrees: in 1989/90 there were 145,700 postgraduate students in the UK. By 1994/95 this number had increased to 306,200 (source: Education statistics for the United Kingdom).

Technological developments

Access to bibliographic databases, through electronic networks and CD-ROMs, leads to constantly increasing demands for unstocked items, especially journal articles, as researchers can find information quickly and easily about items of potential interest. The impact of electronic publishing is only beginning to be appreciated, but it is interesting to note that in researching this paper, the author found the majority of contemporary material available through the World Wide Web, and in some cases, the documents to which reference has been made are available *only* through that medium.

Environmental changes

All academic libraries have experienced the effects of reduced budgets, book and journal price inflation soaring above the retail price index (RPI) and reduced purchasing power, coupled with rising user expectations. The Library and Information Statistics Unit at Loughborough University reported that the average price of British academic books has increased by nearly 70% during the past ten years and that of USA academic books by over 45%.[5] The average periodical price has soared from an average of £130 in 1990 to just under £240 in 1995.[6]

The inevitable impact of this trend has been the widespread cancellation of serial subscriptions, and reduced book purchasing. The Association of Research Libraries conducts an annual survey of serial cancellation rates; figures for 1996, in line with those for preceding years, show that 57% of participating libraries planned to cancel serials. In an attempt to support serial purchases, almost half of the respondents indicated a reduction in monographic acquisitions.[7] Many libraries were reported to be investigating document delivery for specifically requested articles as an alternative to subscription.

Coupled with these price rises has been a growing trend for more material to be published. The number of books published in the UK increased from 65,000 in 1990 to 97,000 in 1995.[8]

The impact of these trends is beginning to emerge. As early as 1987 a British Library-funded study found that

> there is evidence to suggest that damage is being inflicted upon academic research as a consequence of reduced library finances ... more far reaching consequences of the reducing library budget will only become apparent over the longer term.[9]

Financial constraints inevitably result in a narrowing of library holdings. Cancellations to existing titles coupled with an increase in published material mean that a smaller proportion of new literature is being acquired by libraries. Fragmented library holdings lead to some researchers buying literature directly, bypassing the library, and denying access to the wider library membership. Direct purchase, and the use of inter-library loan and document delivery services has enabled academics, with some effort, to obtain much of the literature required for their research. In updating his earlier work, Erens[10] found that by 1995, 37% of academics reported that they were purchasing more books and journals from their own funds than they had done in 1989. However, purchase by individuals to overcome library cancellations means that the wider scholarly community's ability to keep abreast of developments through browsing literature on library shelves, has been hampered substantially.

In recognition of these and other constraints, the four higher education funding bodies in the UK commissioned a review of library provision, under the chairmanship of Professor Sir Brian Follett, the report of which was published in 1993.[11] Specific mention was made in the Follett report of the pressures facing libraries in supporting research, and a further group, under the direction of Professor Michael Anderson, was founded to examine library provision for researchers.[12] The Anderson Committee identified a number of issues of concern in areas such as legal deposit, access to catalogue records and grey literature, but, more crucially, made recommendations on the development of national or regional strategies for library provision in support of research. It was envisaged that such a strategy could involve national libraries, university research libraries, Research Council libraries, larger public libraries and some libraries funded by learned and professional societies. It was agreed that such a strategy would provide:

(i) the means to locate and to gain access to material with reasonable ease, reasonable speed and at reasonable cost to individuals and individual institutions;

(ii) the long-term preservation of material which is of importance for future research or which may be considered part of the national heritage, while recognizing that the library of long-term preservation may not be the same as the library which originally acquired or provided access to the material;

(iii) a system which is perceived by its users to operate fairly and to the advantage of all. On the one hand, there must not be a sense that some institutions are providing services and receiving nothing in return, or that some are having unreasonable demands put on them by virtue of the importance of the material they hold. On the other hand, there should not be institutions which are 'freeloading' on the system as a whole and entering into research commitments while depending on other institutions to provide for the resulting library and information requirements;

(iv) a system which works with economy and which provides value for money and the most effective use of existing resources, particularly bearing in mind that, with certain exceptions, most acquisitions will be made with public funds;

(v) a system which is not only sustainable and capable of developing and adapting to changing circumstances, but which does not undermine the strengths of the present system; and

(vi) a system that plays to the strengths of the different participants, whose participation is supported by formal and public commitments not just from the librarians but from the senior management of the organizations concerned.[13]

These recommendations have been considered by the Funding Councils, and, if adopted and resourced, will have major implications on the management of research collections in the future. As a precursor to such a strategy being developed, the report went on to recommend that individual institutions should identify in their information strategy how they plan to provide access to library material in areas in which they claim to be active, and that a summary of library support be included in submissions to the Research Assessment Exercise.

Management issues

It is neither feasible nor even desirable to expect each institution itself to provide itself for all the research needs of its staff and users.[14]

All university libraries must attempt to meet the needs of their clientele, although as budgets face continued cutbacks it is increasingly difficult to cater on the library's own shelves for all of these needs. The pressures and opportunities facing today's research libraries have fuelled a tremendous debate on holdings and access. The days when large libraries could hope to hold every volume sought by their readers have long disappeared. Libraries must attempt to serve both as owners of information in traditional formats and as gatekeepers to the huge volume of information available in print and electronic forms.

Librarians should not be talking about access vs. ownership because both are relevant and both will continue to be necessary. What is needed is a way to balance the two and make access a viable partner to complement ownership.[15]

The guiding precept must continue to be that it is in the users' interests that the most heavily used materials are available locally. However, the global collection of materials held by libraries, and stored on computers, will become increasingly important. The research collection will continue to hold items locally except those that are used so infrequently that there is no benefit, either economical or in terms of service to readers accrued from owning them. This presents the major challenge of the access *vs* holdings debate:

> the almost universal policy of shifting . . . holdings to access should have a key corollary: that somewhere there will be holdings and that access will be possible . . . [16]

Those who advocate a move towards access frequently work on the basis that the supply of journal articles is the primary function of libraries, and that the cost of document delivery from external services is negligible. However, the cost of obtaining articles in this way can be high, and only infrequently-needed titles can be covered economically in that way. The financial and economic costs of owning or not owning titles must be calculated. Baker[17] offers insights, and his work has been expanded by the MA/HEM research project which uses a spreadsheet to model the costs and benefits of different forms of access and holdings for information resources.[18]

The introduction of combined database and document delivery services such as Uncover and BIDS presents a further dimension. For the first time, scholars who are willing and able to pay, can order documents from their office or laboratory, without reference to their local library. As pricing structures adjust to the demand for such services, libraries may find a reduced role in document delivery. We may move rapidly from an access *vs* holdings debate to an 'access *vs* bypass' problem.[19]

A further issue is the continued role of the scholarly monograph. Tens of thousands of academic texts are published each year in the UK alone – many in areas such as science and medicine where, although it is accepted that periodicals are more critical, books are still in demand. Document delivery of books can be difficult, and offers only short-term access to an item, unlike the retention copy which is normally supplied in response to a request for a journal article. Trial services, such as the monograph interlending service being piloted by the UK-based Consortium of University Research Libraries (CURL), and the excellent resources of the British Library offer support, but Anderson's observation remains valid: someone, somewhere, has to hold an item before others can gain access.

Should items of interest to a researcher be found within the library of another institution, agreement and mechanics need to be in place to provide access. For a single item, interlending may be one option, but many are rightly reluctant to trust their most precious items to the postal service. In such cases, and in instances where whole collections are to be consulted, direct use by the researcher is the principal solution. Almost all libraries are willing to open their doors to visiting scholars who can demonstrate a need, but the impact of retrospective conversion of card catalogues, amongst other activities, is leading to an increase in the number of visitors to libraries. Current activity in adding records of older materials to online library catalogues means that identification of the location of items is becoming easier, and demand made on libraries by scholars from other institutions will inevitably increase.

The Anderson Report[20] identified three ways through which host libraries could be compensated for the additional expense: top-slicing, block subscriptions and transaction charges. Top-slicing would be unpopular amongst institutions with smaller libraries, where resources that they could not spare would be diverted to larger institutions. Subscriptions would be straightforward to administer, but the basis for negotiation between institutions is difficult to imagine. Transaction charges would be administratively cumbersome, and, possibly difficult to police: if an academic wished to visit another library, would he or she have to seek the permission of his or her own institution's library beforehand? Perhaps an alternative arrangement would be a collaborative approach, similar to those in place in the Manchester area, in the north-east of England and in Scotland. These would not resolve the issue of UK-wide access, but might prove fruitful models for future work. The collaboration between members of CURL offers a more geographically distributed model.

Library collections have for many years contained items in a variety of formats, the distinction normally being made between book and non-book materials. In recent years, this distinction has changed slightly, to differentiate between paper-based and electronic materials. This concept has been adopted here, as the issues facing collection managers can largely be distinguished in that way. The distinction itself, however, brings to the forefront one of the major issues in academic libraries today: how best can libraries marry the technologies of the 19th and 21st centuries to provide an integrated service for users? There is no easy answer, and the issue has been seized by the Electronic Libraries Programme in its call for bids for projects to investigate the hybrid library.[21]

The paper-based collection

Acquisition

It is through judgement and selection that collections are managed most effectively.[22]

The mechanics of the acquisition of library materials have been comprehensively documented elsewhere (for example, Futas[23]) and will not be repeated here. Instead, this section will highlight some of the issues surrounding the costs and management issues of acquisition and retention. We have already seen that the increasing costs of library materials, and reduced purchasing power, reinforce the need for detailed costing information to aid library management.

The cost of library materials is subject to especial scrutiny; in addition to the payment to publishers for the purchase of books and journals, there are costs associated with selection, cataloguing and processing, storage and preservation. One financial technique, piloted by the British Library, to take account of all these factors, is life-cycle costing.[24] In life-cycle costing, the costs associated with every stage of a book or journal's life-span are identified and calculated. For example, the life-cycle cost of the acquisition and retention of a monograph will include the cost of selection, the cost of the item itself, accession and cataloguing costs, initial and ongoing preservation costs and handling and storage costs. A prerequisite for successful costing is adequate management information systems from which data such as accommodation and staff costs can be extracted. The use of life-cycle costing enables the manager to identify the true cost of an acquisition, whether in paper-based or electronic form.

One of the key sentiments of the Anderson report[25] was the need for someone, somewhere, to own an item to ensure long-term access. The main point is to ensure that someone does acquire the item, rather than hoping or assuming that acquisition and retention has taken place. Libraries in the UK are in the fortunate position of being able to rely upon the collective work of the British Library, the national libraries and the other legal deposit libraries, in ensuring that comprehensive collections are developed and preserved. However, there is scope for further work in developing further arrangements for works not covered by legal deposit, such as foreign language monographs, grey literature and non-print materials. Much work was carried out in the 1980s in the preparation of regional and subject-based Library and Information Plans in which participants prepared statements of their collections, and their acquisition and retention policies. This work could be developed, perhaps on a regional basis, where institutions shared their policies, developed collaborative arrangements, and put into place agreements on access to researchers from other institutions.

Retention and preservation

In the creation of knowledge ... preservation comes first, and creation is made possible by preservation, rather than the other way around.[26]

Libraries have for a long time practised retention of stock, in the belief that if you dispose of something today, someone may need it tomorrow. This has been particularly true of research collections. Space constraints and physical deterioration make large-scale retention increasingly problematic. The preparation of surrogate works, in the form of microfilm or digital images offers one solution. Of greater importance is collaborative retention procedures. Libraries must prepare and publish retention policies, in order that libraries of last resort for particular types of materials may be identified.

Once material has been acquired for a library's stock, and a decision has been made that it should be retained, attention must be paid to the role of preservation. It is not acceptable to retain an item, only to find that when it is required it has fallen into such a state of disrepair that it is unusable. Much has been written on the techniques of preservation, and these are documented from a managerial perspective in a key work.[27] Of prime importance to the manager of the research collection is the development of a preservation policy that will help to determine priorities and methods. The policy would address such matters as priorities between types of material and subject areas of the collection, guidelines on storage, handling and disposal, disaster management planning and staff training. Of these, disaster management planning has been developed considerably during the past ten years, and guidelines for library managers were published by the British Library in 1996.[28]

Evaluation and assessment

There has been no co-operative attempt to determine the relative strengths and weaknesses of the country's research collections. An American methodology, Conspectus, was adopted by the British Library and the National Libraries of Scotland and Wales, as well as a number of Scottish Universities. This offered a solid framework for the identification of collection strengths, but fell into abeyance once it became apparent that it would not be adopted by other libraries. Technology is offering some assistance: widespread access to library catalogues through electronic networks is now possible, and effort is being made to convert into electronic format remaining card catalogues. This work is described more fully below. Libraries are also using the World Wide Web to promote their research collections. At the University of Newcastle, for example, the Library's *Guide to special collections* has been converted into electronic form, offering scope for regular updates and promotion to scholars elsewhere. Guides to the collections of CURL member libraries are being produced, offering a showcase for many of the country's finest research collections. However, these efforts are far from comprehensive, and do not highlight collection strengths in the same way as Conspectus could.[29]

The electronic collection

It is

> unlikely that an electronic approach to comprehensive research provision, despite its undoubted attractions, will offer a feasible base for a research strategy at least in the shorter term, even for journals.[30]

Despite these sentiments, technological developments offer two principle opportunities for the research library, firstly the provision of information in electronic format, and secondly the identification of paper-based information through electronic resource discovery tools. It is important that the reality of Anderson's views are borne in mind whilst the library manager explores ways in which technology can aid the management of collections and improve services to the researcher.

Electronic publications

Although the first electronic journal was published in 1976, it has been during the 1990s that the academic community has begun to accept the possibilities of publishing research findings in electronic format. Inevitably, the widespread acceptance of electronic publishing presented a new series of problems for library managers. In an attempt to help institutions to develop solutions and working practices, a national project was established in 1995. The Higher Education Funding Council for England developed a UK Pilot Site Licence Initiative (PSLI) to allow widespread access, on a trial basis, to the electronic journals produced by four publishers (Institute of Physics Publishing, Blackwell Publishers, Blackwell Science and Academic Press). Access to their electronic publications under the scheme, whereby HEFCE pays a lump sum in exchange for access to participating higher education institutions, varies from publisher to publisher. One allows access to all their electronic titles, another permits access only to those titles which are already purchased in paper form by an institution. In addition, each publisher offered discounted rates to subscriptions to their paper-based titles. An evaluation of the scheme showed that almost all institutions participated in the pilot scheme, because they expected to save money and obtain access to a wider selection of journal titles.[31]

Initial findings of the evaluation show savings in paper subscriptions of up to £40,000, and reductions in document supply charges. There are, however, a number of issues which remain to be resolved, and which will require considerable thought in coming years:

1   At present, developments such as the PSLI have been negotiated with individual publishers, and the end-user has to know which publisher is responsible for each title of interest. As titles can move from one publisher to another, this can add to confusion. Some form of seamless access is likely to be required.
2   No standard form of pricing for electronic journals, or for combined packages of print and electronic journals, has been developed.

3   Electronic publications are liable for Value Added Tax, unlike their paper-based counterparts.

4   Access to archives of electronic journals is a further area of uncertainty. For how long will a publisher maintain a back-issue archive, and will access be permitted to those issues which have been paid for should a library cease to subscribe to a title.

In another electronic journal activity, a survey of users of a selection of electronic journals in one subject field (materials science and engineering), was reported in the TULIP project final report. Concerns expressed by end-users included the poor coverage (both in terms of number of titles and the size of back runs) of the electronic archive, and the lack of integration with other information sources, such as bibliographies and library catalogues.

This final point reinforces a major issue: library managers have to exploit the riches of their collections, and meet the needs of their users, without any clear indication as to whether investment in paper-based resources or technical development represents the best long-term investment. In terms of managing the balance between electronic and print resources, an initiative which is attempting to resolve a number of these issues is the Superjournal Project, funded under the Electronic Libraries Programme.[32] This project is building up a body of electronic journals, based on established print publications, to explore the question systematically.

Digitization

The primary concern is balancing the needs of preservation of the unique content and the costs of enhanced access.[33]

Digitization has been promoted as a panacea for many of the ailments facing research libraries. A technology that converts to computerized form the printed pages of monographs and serials must surely alleviate space constraints and provide reliable and flexible surrogates for crumbling stock.

Technology for digitization is undergoing huge development at present, but there are two broad approaches: capturing an image of the original in the manner of a photograph, and scanning the original in such a way that text or images can be edited in software packages such as word-processors. A combination of these techniques allows the layout and presentation as well as the content of the originals to be captured. Searching systems which can be added to digital images can be used to compensate for the poor indexing of earlier materials, particularly journal literature. In digital form, material can be accessed by many users at the same time, in any number of different locations, using commonly available PCs. This overcomes the inherent drawback of the previously accepted form of surrogate books and journals, microfilm. Indeed, one of the major digitization projects in the USA is being developed entirely around a digital archive created from microfilm copies of original items.

There is an abundance of information on digitization, in the form of conference proceedings, journal articles, WWW sites and demonstrator projects. However, many issues remain unresolved: there are problems of lack of commonly agreed standards, concerns about long-term preservation, copyright issues and expensive start-up costs. A number of projects are attempting to resolve these issues, and it is appropriate to draw attention to some of these here, in order that readers may keep abreast of subsequent developments. In a rapidly changing environment, it is impossible to provide concrete guidance as to future developments.

One approach to digitization is JSTOR (Journal STORage), a non-profit venture in New York which uses digitization technology to preserve and make accessible a range of journal literature, while attempting to balance the needs of librarians, scholars and publishers.[34] Funded by the Mellon Foundation, JSTOR scanned five history and five economics journals and made them available through the World Wide Web to readers in a sample group of test libraries. The main aim of JSTOR is to determine the economic feasibility of conversion to digital form where the costs can be shared amongst a number of project partners. It is envisaged that reduced demand for space, reduced library operating costs, and added value to users can all be offset against digitization costs.

A major development in digitization activity in the UK has been the establishment of a National Digitization Centre, capable of handling one million pages each year, at the University of Hertfordshire. This will allow the higher education community to overcome the high start-up costs which would be associated with individual projects, and permit standardization of technical approaches to digitization. A further Joint Information Systems Committee (JISC) project is the Knowledge Gallery, which is aiming to convert into digital form archives of images held in higher education institutions, and make them available to the entire higher education community. JISC has established a Committee on Electronic Information, a working group of which is examining the collection management and collection development policies for digital information at a national level. Five national datacentres have been established to collect electronic data in different subject areas (for example the Arts and Humanities Data Service).

Managers of research collections will have to accept that it is impossible to resource adequately digitization work in isolation. It is through co-operative venture such as those described above that greatest progress will be made.

Resource discovery

Library catalogues form an important tool for identifying the whereabouts of library material, whether in digital or paper-based form. Traditionally, of course, catalogue records were recorded on index cards stored in large wooden cabinets in libraries, and accessible only to those able to visit a library to make use of them. As computerized cataloguing systems have been developed, the role of the traditional card catalogue has been replaced by the online catalogue. However, many original card catalogue records remain available only in that form. There has long been a recognition of the need for resources to be allocated to retrospective conversion programmes to convert the catalogue records into electronic format on OPACs.

To this end, the Follett Implementation Group on IT (FIGIT) commissioned a study in 1995 to examine the justification of funding a national programme for retrospective conversion.[35] This study found that while over 10 million records, representing 2 million individual titles had already been converted, a further 28 million records, representing some 6 million titles remained to be converted, at an estimated cost of £25 million over five years. Some progress towards this target has been made in the humanities field through allocation from the Higher Education Funding Councils' Non-Formula Funding (NFF) of Research Collections in the Humanities.

If funding is made available, it is inevitable that there will be a requirement that libraries whose records have been converted will make their collections accessible to all requiring access from within the higher education sector. Indeed, this has already been demonstrated by conditions attached to funding awarded under the NFF scheme, and is entirely in keeping with the spirit of the Follett and Anderson reports.

Retrospective conversion is only the first stage of the much wider issue of determining where required research materials may be found. At present, a user may have to search a number of different catalogues in a quest for a specific items. Work has started under an eLib project, MODELS (MOving to Distributed Environments for Library Services) to organize access to printed scholarly material through resource discovery tools.[36] The MODELS study has identified two ways of easing resource discovery, either by creating a union catalogue in one database of records from a number of institutions, or by developing an interface which searches a number of physically remote catalogues simultaneously. One notable example of the former approach is COPAC, the catalogue of records of a number of CURL member libraries.[37]

Digital preservation, legal deposit and copyright

The important role of information in digital formats is accepted. However, just as with traditional paper-based resources, attention must be paid to preservation issues. There are uncertainties regarding the long-term preservation of digital media, both in terms of technological developments, and the integrity of digital images over time. The Electronic Libraries Programme (eLib), at a conference in 1995, identified seven priority areas in the field.[38] Other bodies, such as the Commission on Preservation and Access and the Research Libraries Group, have conducted major studies.[39]

One key aspect of the maintenance of an archive of digital publications is legal deposit. In the UK, the legal obligation on publishers to deposit their publications with specified libraries has existed in some form since 1610. The current statutory provisions cover almost all forms of print publications but exclude digital publications. A government consultation paper has set out proposals to extend the scope of legal deposit to include new publication media.[40] However, the proposals for the legal deposit of online publications are such that they will be subject only to voluntary deposit arrangements.

A major issue of debate in electronic libraries has been the question of copyright. Technology offers so much scope for storing, transmitting and delivering publications quickly to users, but copyright legislation prohibits many of these activities, and many copyright laws were prepared before the era of widespread use of electronic information.

> Unless progress is made in this area, the potential of information technology is unlikely to be realised.[41]

Licensing arrangements between publishers and libraries seem to be the main way forward, and several eLib projects have carried out work in this area. JISC have published position papers,[42] as has the International Federation of Library Associations (IFLA)[43] and eLib has carried out a study on the technology of Electronic Copyright Management Systems.

Summary

Against this view of the rapidly changing world of research collections, libraries will continue to acquire great quantities of printed material. Some of this will be digitized, if it is believed to be the most cost-effective method of making it accessible. Co-operative arrangements for acquiring material, and sharing it with other libraries and scholars will flourish.

Large collections of material in digital formats will be made available, and electronic journals will flourish. It is to be hoped that publishers will pass on to librarians responsibilities for maintaining back-files of such titles when the publisher no longer wishes to hold them. Local collections will become more narrowly defined to ensure depth of coverage and expertise of staff. In some small fields, current technological developments, legal changes and licensing and conversion into digital format of published materials will make electronic libraries truly accessible to the end user.

It is the librarian's duty to manage these precious resources to meet responsibilities to both present and future generations of scholars.

References

1 Graham, P., 'Preserving the digital library in *Long term preservation of electronic materials: a JISC/British Library workshop* (British Library R & D Report 6238), London, British Library, 1996, 7.
   <http://ukoln.bath.ac.uk/elib/wk_papers/>

2 Heaney, H., 'The university research library' in S. Corrall (ed.), *Collection development: options for effective management*, London, Taylor Graham, 1988, 18.

3 Erens, B., *Research libraries in transition*, (Library and Information Research report 82), London, British Library, 1991, 26.

4 Frank, S., 'Reviewing the literature: use of library and information systems', in T. Greenfield (ed.), *Research methods: guidance for postgraduates*, London, Arnold 1996, 47–51.

5 Library and Information Statistics Unit, *Average prices of British academic books: July to December 1996*. Loughborough, LISU, 1996.

6 Library and Information Statistics Unit, *Library & information statistics tables for the United Kingdom*. Loughborough, LISU, 1996.

7 Association of Research Libraries, Office of Scholarly Communication, *Cutbacks in library materials purchasing: OSC quick SPEC survey*, Washington, DC, Association of Research Libraries.
   <http://arl.cni.org/scomm/prices.html>

8 Library and Information Statistics Unit, *Library & information statistics tables for the United Kingdom*, Loughborough, LISU, 1996.

9 Pocklington, K. and Finch, H., *Research collections under constraint*, (British Library Research Paper 36), London, British Library, 1987, 3.

10 Erens, B., 'How recent developments in university libraries affect research', *Library management*, **17** (8), 1996, 9.

11 Joint Funding Councils' Libraries Review, *Report*, (The Follett Report), Bristol, Higher Education Funding Council for England, 1993
   <http://www.ukoln.bath.ac.uk/follett/follett_report.html>

12 Joint Funding Councils' Libraries Review, *Report of the group on a national/regional strategy for library provision for researchers*, (The Anderson Report), Bristol, Higher Education Funding Council for England, 1995.
   <http://www.ukoln.bath.ac.uk/elib/wk_papers/anderson.html>

13 *Ibid.*, 6.

14 Joint Funding Councils' Libraries Review, *op. cit.*, 1993, 51.

15 Hoadley, I. B., 'Access vs. ownership: myth or reality', *Library acquisitions: practice and theory*, **17** (2), 1993, 191-5.

16 Anderson, M., 'The Anderson Report: an overview' in P. Wressell, P. & Associates (eds.), *Library service provision for researchers: proceedings of the Anderson report seminar, Cranfield University, 10 and 11 December 1996*, Bruton, LINC, 1997, 1.

17 Baker, D., 'Access versus holdings policy with special reference to the University of East Anglia', *Interlending and document supply*, **20** (4), 1992, 131-7.

18 MA/HEM *Methodology for access/holdings economic modelling. Acquisitions decision support tool user manual*, London, SCONUL, 1996.

19 Cotta-Schonberg, M., 'Collections' in M. B. Line, G. Mackenzie and J. Feather (eds.), *Librarianship & information work worldwide*, East Grinstead, Bowker-Saur, 1994, 165-200.

20 Anderson, M., 'The Anderson Report: an overview' in P. Wressell, P. & Associates (eds.), *Library service provision for researchers: proceedings of the Anderson report seminar, Cranfield University, 10 and 11 December 1996*, Bruton, LINC, 1997, 1–7.

21 Joint Information Systems Committee, *JISC Circular*, 3/97 Electronic Information development programme: eLib phase 3, 1997.
    < http://www.niss.ac.uk/education/jisc/pub97/c3_97.html>

22 Enright, B., Hellinga, L. and Leigh, B., *Selection for survival: a review of acquisition and retention policies*, London, British Library, 1989, 15.

23 Futas, E., *Library acquisition policies and procedures*, 2nd edn, Phoenix, Arizona, Oryx Press, 1984.

24 Enright, B., Hellinga, L. and Leigh, B., *Selection for survival: a review of acquisition and retention policies*, London, British Library, 1989, 77–82.

25 Anderson, M., *op. cit.*

26 Abell, M. D., 'The collections of research libraries' in W. J. Welsh (ed.), *Research libraries – yesterday, today and tomorrow*, Kanazawa, Japan, Kanazawa Institute of Technology, 1993, 39.

27 Feather, J., *Preservation and the management of library collections*, 2nd edn, London, Library Association Publishing, 1996.

28 Matthews, G. and Eden, P., *Disaster management in British libraries: project report with guidelines for library managers*, (Library and Information Research report 109), London, British Library, 1996.

29 Wood, R. J. and Strauch, K. (eds.), *Collection assessment: a look at the RLG Conspectus*, (The Acquisitions Librarian 7), New York, Haworth Press, 1992.

30 Joint Funding Councils' Libraries Review, *op. cit.*, 1995, 10.

31 PSLI Evaluation Team, 'UK Pilot Site Licence Initiative: a progress report', *Serials*, **10** (1), 1997, 18.

32 Superjournal Project. Web pages.
<http://www.superjournal.ac.uk/sj/>

33 Angiletta, A. M., 'On the relationship of academic program and research libraries at the electronic frontier: something old, something new, something borrowed and someone's probably blue' in A. H. Helal and J. W. Weiss (eds.), *Electronic documents and information: from preservation to access, 18th International Essen Symposium, 23-26 October 1995*, Essen, Essen University Library, 1996, 24.

34 JSTOR. Web pages.
<http://www.jsotr.org>

35 Bryant, P., Chapman, A. and Naylor, B., *Retrospective conversion of library catalogues in institutions of higher education in the United Kingdom: a study of the justification for a national programme*, Bath, University of Bath, 1995.

36 Dempsey, L. and Russell, R., *National resource discovery workshop: organising access to printed scholarly material*, Bath, UKOLN, 1996
<http://ukoln.ac.uk/models/models3.html>

37 COPAC. Web pages.
<http://copac.ac.uk/copac>

38 *Electronic Libraries Programme, Long-term preservation of electronic materials: a JISC/British Library workshop*, (British Library R & D Report 6238). London, British Library, 1996.
<http://ukoln.bath.ac.uk/elib/wk_papers/>

39 Commission on Preservation and Access/Research Libraries Group, *Preserving digital information: report of the task force on archiving of digital information*, 1996.
<http://www.rlg.org>

40 Department of National Heritage, Scottish Office, Welsh Office, Department of Education Northern Ireland, *Legal deposit of publications: a consultation paper*, London, DNH, 1997.

41 Joint Funding Councils' Libraries Review, *op. cit.*, 1993, 56.

42 JISC, *Papers on copyright issues in the electronic library*, Bristol, JISC, 1995.

43   IFLA, Position paper on copyright in the electronic environment, 1996.
     <http://ifla.inist.fr/ifla/V/ebpb/copy.htm>

12

Information Technology

IAN LOVECY

Introduction

There are times when the computer would seem to be the modern version of the Philosopher's Stone: plug it into the Internet, and all the information in the world can be yours free of charge. Many have seen the electronic distribution of information as the answer to endless cuts in library budgets and rises in periodical subscriptions. Andrew Odlyzko of AT&T Bell Labs expresses a common view:

> The rapid improvement in communications networks and the impending entry of the entertainment industry, with video and film on demand at consumer affordable prices, suggest that, if a movie to one's home costs $10, then sending much less capacious scientific papers over the Internet should cost pennies.[1]

In this chapter, I want to examine some aspects of the cost of electronic resources to see how far these assumptions may be valid. I will then consider the question of cost-effectiveness, look at the situation of the so-called 'digital library', and highlight some problems which I feel need solutions before the virtual wired-up future becomes a reality.

Costs

However they produce journals, publishers inevitably have costs:

- costs of premises
- costs of staff to deal with correspondence
- to give some thought to layout and design
- to apply some degree of consistency.

Generally publishers quote a figure of 80% of the cost being incurred in the production of the first copy, with 20% being the incremental costs of multiple copy production and distribution.[2] Even if some of those costs reduce in the case of an electronic journal, others will not; and some will be converted into enhanced quality.[3]

In the early days of electronic publishing there was often a premium attached to the cost of an electronic version of a journal. Sometimes this came in the form of an insistence that the subscription to the paper version be maintained; sometimes there was little difference in the cost of a single-user copy, but a network licence (even for 10 simultaneous users) could bring the price to twice that of the hard copy, or even more (as in the case of *PsycLit* on CD-ROM). In other instances, the cost was hidden, or varied from library to library: the Adonis CD-ROM contains a package of journals which, taken as a whole, may not be costly; but it is a package which *must* be taken as a whole, and could be more expensive than the selection of journals to which the library was previously subscribing. (This parallels the concept of a periodical subscription, where one pays for the whole journal even if only 10% of the content is of interest.)

By now, the situation is becoming far more complex. There are deals (usually in the UK negotiated by the Combined Higher Education Software Team (CHEST)) which use the collective muscle of the HE community to obtain an acceptable subscription price – as in the case of Bath Information and Data Services (BIDS). (In such cases there has often been an added complication of a premium charged for those who did not commit themselves in advance.) There has been the recent initiative of the pilot Periodicals Site Licence project, where the bulk of the payment comes from a hefty Funding Councils' top-slice. No-one is yet quite clear what happens when that comes to an end. The present EBSCO offer appears extremely generous, but the comments of Richard West come to mind: 'What happens when the licence expires? What happens if users are by that time "hooked" on using the information? Libraries should beware of low initial costs for licences.'[4]

If the periodicals site licence has effectively transferred costs from individual libraries to the community as a whole, in other cases costs are being transferred to individuals. Adonis makes a charge for articles printed out, and while the library *may* bear that cost, many regard it as similar to the charge a user would make for a photocopy, and pass it on. The Blackwell UnCover/Reveal service, or OCLC First Search, will set up arrangements for individuals, and these and many other services will supply hard copy of full texts against entry of a credit-card number. The example of the student in the Follett Report is notable for the fact that she uses a credit card to order a document,[5] which many would see as an unlikely scenario.

Behind all this stands the unavoidable reality that publishers are in business to make a profit, and that the limits on that profit are driven by commercial considerations and not the convenience of Universities. The competition for the publishers comes from individuals or institutions publishing on the Internet, where the majority of the costs are lost within the organization. However, there are issues of quality involved in non-refereed publication and issues of bibliographical control involved in individual publication, to which I shall return.

Some savings can be anticipated, although they are indirect and often long-term. They relate mainly to storage: to a diminishing need to provide new accommodation if new publication is to be in electronic format, and possibly the ability to relinquish current stack space if back runs can be digitized. One of the more ambitious projects in this area is the JSTOR project, funded by the Andrew W. Mellon Foundation.[6] Bowen argues convincingly that the process of digitization, storage and retrieval, shared among a number of institutions, can be less than the cost of continuing to store a hard copy.[7] Michael Lesk in his Follett Lecture makes a similar point, coupling it with the observation that to obtain cheap storage of hard copy often involves renting accommodation well away from the campus, with a consequent reduction of service.[8]

The other main areas in which savings can be made are those of circulation and re-shelving activities, and possibly the fetching of material from a store. Having digital versions of articles available online to readers, or allowing them to request delivery of an article (whether it be to their desk or simply to the library) takes away many of the traditional functions of a library. Serials check-in may also vanish in the electronic world, although some method of checking that the 'volumes' paid for have been made available may still be needed – and CD-ROMs need to be checked-in conventionally.

However, digital technology has associated costs. Networked information requires a network, and although most people regard the Internet as free it has to be paid for somewhere. In the UK, Higher Education accesses it through the SuperJANET network, paid for by a top-slice of Funding Councils' money; that payment, of course, subsidizes all traffic on the network. Messages transmitted by UK HE, or information returned, may travel over the wires of a number of different networks and telephone systems, but at some point someone has to fund the setting up and maintenance of each of these. Where the network costs are genuinely free to the end user, as for example in the case of local telephone calls in the USA, it is the carrier who has to bear the costs. In the USA this is leading to saturation of the network, because the carrier has no revenue to balance against the costs of increasing bandwidth.

Overall, the costs of the Internet may not be great;[9] the provision of hardware is still a requirement, and hardware at the moment needs replacement on a cycle of between three and five years. The level of hardware required will depend on the nature and quality of the material being used – you do not need a multimedia pentium to read ASCII e-mail, but you cannot view a video on a dumb terminal, or print a high-quality colour illustration on a dot-matrix printer. Libraries that are heavily reliant on electronic resources will need to provide a high number of terminals, either within the library or across the campus as a whole (possibly in student rooms). The latter has implications for the cost of networking, but also of support (an amazing number of students have problems printing from the Web, and there is no reason to suppose that these will magically vanish at 3 am). Assuming that students will supply their own computers is another example of transferring costs to individuals. Against this it may be argued that some of these facilities are supplied for what are not strictly 'library' purposes – for students to write essays, use CAL materials, or communicate with tutors, for example. The apportionment of infrastructure costs between services could be one of the more futile issues to be addressed by universities.

Staff savings may be partially balanced by increased costs of user training and user support, and by administration costs – licence management, billing of users and departments – which are specific to electronic services.

Cost-effectiveness

Computers rarely save money outside large-scale routine activities; they do, however, offer the possibility of an enhanced service at little or no extra cost. In the field of electronic information resources, the two major benefits can be summed up as the greater facility for searching and the improved availability.

Searching

The searching of printed sources is cumbersome, and takes time; time costs money. Universities in general have a very cavalier attitude to how their highly-paid staff spend their time, and have not been concerned if a professor (or even his research assistant) is wasting half a day in searching printed indexes. This attitude is changing, partly because of pressure from the Funding Councils[10] and partly from the realization that the time could be spent writing papers to count in the next Research Assessment Exercise (RAE).

Many systems are allowing users to store personalized search profiles. The UnCover/Reveal system does this with contents page searches, and the Institute of Physics is introducing customization to its full-text services available to UK HE under the pilot site licence agreement. Inclusion of tables of contents of monographs in searchable records is now becoming more usual, and Michael Lesk refers to four projects on this taking place in the United States.[11]

Within the UK e-Lib programme the EDDIS, INFOBIKE and SEREN projects are developing approaches to end-user searching of databases and requesting of documents which can be supplied to the user's desk top. INFOBIKE is concentrating on journal articles supplied by a document supplier; EDDIS is doing the same, but with provision also for dealing with returnable hard-copy items. SEREN has provision for using document suppliers, but is concentrating in the first instance on sharing the resources of Welsh HE, rather as the LAMDA project has done with London and Manchester libraries. All these projects (apart from INFOBIKE) are prepared initially to use hard-copy deliveries to satisfy copyright law.[12]

Two projects have looked at the effect of resource sharing. In the State University of New York, which has 64 campuses, a survey was undertaken to assess the relative costs of local holding of materials as opposed to document delivery throughout the consortium. The results suggested that in many cases local holding was not justified, even when some estimates were made for the costs to users of having to wait for articles.[13]

In the UK, the BIODOC project at Cranfield[14] looked at the effects of replacing journal subscriptions in a specialized area by a reliance upon document delivery. Although the costs of the latter were greater than the previous subscriptions, the interesting finding was the *spread* of literature requested. Most of the journals purchased failed to justify their subscription price by usage, and a large number of other journals were used. There is a suspicion that when journal subscriptions are being considered the tendency is to go for the large journals covering wide fields, which are of limited use to research specialists.

In both these cases there is a clear benefit justifying (in the second case) the additional cost. At Cranfield the ability to search electronically-held databases by stored profiles, and to e-mail the results to users, was crucial. Electronic delivery was successfully tested, but not implemented because of copyright restrictions.

Availability

One advantage of holding items in digital format is the improved availability to readers. Computers do not go home at night; they do not go on holiday; and their record of 'sick leave' is probably better than that of many of their human counterparts. Literature stored on a computer is therefore available for significantly more hours than literature stored on shelves. While this is of value to any user, it is particularly important in the context of part-time and distance-learning students. There are currently more students studying at UK HE institutions on a part-time than on a full-time basis, so this is a real need. Distance learning is growing in the UK, but is becoming a very major factor in the USA.[15]

Also important to distance learning is the availability of digital information simultaneously in a number of locations. The tendency has been to talk of the delivery of documents to the desk of the researcher, or to the student study-bedroom; but delivery to the factory where someone is undertaking a work-based study programme is not a useful adjunct to study but a basic necessity. However, a word of warning: delivery to the user's desk rather than to a central location has always seemed to me to apply to a sub-set of documents. Many users will lack the appropriate equipment for printing out high-quality illustrations.[16]

The other major advantage of resources in electronic formats is that they can be accessed by more than one user simultaneously. This is obviously important when a resource is being shared between a number of institutions, but it really becomes vital when the resource in question is a standard text book in an electronic reserve. Projects such as the ELINOR project at De Montfort University have demonstrated both the feasibility and value of such an approach to the increasingly vexed question of supplying standard texts to classes of 150 students.[17]

Other benefits

Digital storage plays a part in conservation. Paper copies are stored where moth and dust corrupt, and thieves break in and steal. Perusal of computerized facsimiles of rare books or manuscripts minimizes the handling of often-fragile items; it also minimizes the chances of conventional theft, although the potential for stealing the images remains. The avoidance of loss, damage or deliberate theft is also important in the case of digitized collections of slides used for teaching purposes.

A further benefit is the increased knowledge of what users use. There are problems in tracking accurately what is happening. A 'hit' on a web site does not mean that the item has been fully read, even less does it mean that it served a useful purpose. Nevertheless, journal publishers can see which articles are causing the greatest interest and librarians can follow which areas of study are most interesting their clients. The latter may help to focus future collection development, or to highlight areas of weakness in either local provision or in the provision of information about external sources.[18]

The digital library

The phrase 'digital library' has been in use for a number of years, and the concept goes back at least as far as 1945.[19] Yet we have still to see anything which can be termed a 'digital library' outside specialist libraries in industry or commercial firms. Some more general libraries have gone some distance down the route. The best-known example in Europe is probably Tilburg in the Netherlands, but the British Library now has its own Digital Library Programme. In the USA the Library of Congress is aiming to have five million items digitized by the year 2000.[20]

In the UK the e-Lib programme, funded by the Joint Information Systems Committee of the Higher Education Funding Councils, is sponsoring a number of projects aimed at both providing the infrastructure for digital library services of the future and identifying the sort of problems which will need to be faced. It is interesting because it is essentially a practical programme, and as such recognizes the 'mixed economy' in which libraries are likely to be working for a number of years; the printed book will not disappear overnight. Even if the Library of Congress achieves its goal of 5 million digitized items by 2000 AD, it will only be a fraction of that library's collections.

What will it be like managing a digital – or indeed a partially-digital – library? Experimental projects so far have thrown up a number of problems which may themselves be considered transitory. There are new skills required by support staff in libraries, and these are being investigated by some e-Lib projects.[21] Constantly expanding network requirements are another problem, particularly for the more remote or less well-off institutions, and those in the Developing World. As with data storage, data transmission technology is, however, constantly advancing and it is not unreasonable to look to a time when all UK HE institutions will have network connection capable of coping with real-time video and large image files. Connections at an international level are likely to remain a problem, but it is possible to see even this improving.

The question of user resistance is a more vexed one. Michael Lesk sees this as one of the factors which prevented digitization from replacing the spend on new buildings for the British Library and the Bibliothèque Nationale,[22] yet the 3,108 accesses to papers in the e-journal *Information research* in one year[23] suggests that a number of people find this form of access satisfactory. End user reaction to the Tulip project has also been generally positive, although it has raised problems of both hardware and what the project report calls users' 'emotional' ties with paper.[24] Bernard Naylor expresses a very common feeling when he writes:

> In most instances, except where genuinely interactive content is involved, scholars would simply prefer to have a printed copy in the library which they could then access in traditional form and photocopy if they wanted to.[25]

Some of this has to do with the type of material involved. Much of the Digital Library effort has been directed at reference material which is consulted in small sections, or journal literature which is also in manageable sizes. Some projects have dealt with the provision of chapters of books rather than the whole work, but it has to be recognized that there are times where working in sections of this size is not appropriate. I find myself wholeheartedly agreeing with another of Bernard Naylor's points:

> In the electronic world, yesterday's fantasy is tomorrow's reality, but I still find the idea of down loading (and printing out?) 650 pages on the personal rule of Charles I or the Tudor constitution fantastic.[26]

There is an implication here that the 'mixed mode' of operation may continue for longer than anticipated. This will bring problems of management, since it will both delay the potential space-saving of digitization and reduce the perceived advantages for the user – if a humanities researcher has to visit the library anyway to borrow a monograph, a printed journal which can be photocopied could be as convenient as an electronic version. One outcome might be a need to consider delivery of printed materials, if not to the user's desk at least to his or her department.

Electronic resources bring their own managerial problems, and some of these need solutions before the virtual library can become a reality.

Copyright / IPR

Most of the work on copyright which has gone on within the e-Lib programme and elsewhere has been concerned with the technical aspects of being able to control who has access to materials. Many of the requirements militate against the full implementation of the digital library: the e-Lib document delivery projects are having to consider printing out copyright material transmitted electronically. As yet, a signature on a paper copyright declaration is still essential.

There is a need for a major new look at the whole question of the purpose of copyright. Protecting the legitimate financial interests of the publisher is obviously important, although as considered above the level of the publisher's investment in an electronic journal may need to be re-assessed. Proper reward for the author is also a growing theme, although moderated both by a suggestion that the rewards come indirectly through status, promotion and research funding, and by the more frequent claims by academic institutions that as employers the copyright of articles produced during employment belongs to them. Tracing rights owners to request copying permission could become a full-time nightmare for a member of staff. Whether in the case of a journal the proper rewards for all parties can be satisfied by initial purchases, implying that the digitization of back runs – which are hardly a major source of revenue to a publisher – could be undertaken with little in the way of compensation, is a question which needs to be further explored.

The other side to copyright is the ability to establish an absolute version of a text. This can be done in electronic format; but the question is rather, is it desirable? The bulletin board, computer conferencing, the e-mail discussion list are all forms of publication (normally forms for which no royalties would be expected) but they do not lead to the production of an authoritative version of a document.[27] It may be that we have to wait for a complete change in the culture of scholarly communication, one which is beginning but which is not yet recognized in exercises such as the RAE.

Bibliographic control

Without an authoritative text, what becomes of bibliographical control?. A monograph or journal issue deposited in the British Library or the Library of Congress is catalogued, and classified by one or more systems so that the reference can be retrieved. With information published on the World Wide Web, the subject approach is to some extent catered for by services such as YAHOO, which attempt to impose order on the material, or Lycos and InfoSeek, which are search systems. Their success is patchy, both because of the quantity of material and because of the speed with which it is published and withdrawn. One of the e-Lib programme areas is concerned with the tracking of sources in specific subject areas.

The problems encountered include the changes in URLs which still seem to happen with some frequency. Projects such as SOSIG run software to check the validity of the URLs they refer to, but correcting those which prove invalid is a manual, and therefore timetaking, operation. OCLC among others has been working on a project to provide permanent URLs (PURLs) but no definite proposals have yet emerged.

A related difficulty is illustrated in this chapter, that of giving references to the sources. A reference to a printed journal will always be valid; moreover, the reference to a page will always take the reader to the same place if s/he is using the same edition. However, WWW documents are not always paginated, and if they are not the paging will depend on the browser, printer and font being used by the reader; someone reading online will have to translate screens into pages. It becomes very difficult to give readers a precise reference to an item in a document, and we may have to adopt conventions of paragraph numbering to assist this process.

Continuity of access

A vast amount of both scholarship and literature, which was written in manuscript in a single copy, has been lost to us irretrievably. In the age of multiple printed copies there have been casualties even among major and influential works: only eight copies of William Morgan's sixteenth-century Welsh translation of the Bible survive, and only two of these are complete. At least whatever does survive in written or printed form can still be read: eyes have not changed, and the conventions of writing, which may vary from culture to culture, can be applied to scrolls, bound manuscripts, books, letters or anything else.

Electronic formats are vulnerable to all the dangers which beset printed works: fire, flood, vandals, war, sheer carelessness. Precautions in the form of back-ups can be taken, but these will usually be stored within the same city at the very least, and are therefore potentially *more* vulnerable to total destruction than a book distributed over three continents. Electronic sources can also be mirrored across the world, of course, but there is a danger, as there is with back-ups if they are not taken constantly, that the reserve site will be slightly out-of-date compared with the original.

More worrying is the question of whether the material will be usable. Truly online material may be if it is stored in a standard format; but we have already run through a number of versions of HTML and may come to a point at which the backward compatibility no longer reaches far enough into the past. CD-ROMs may seem likely to go on for ever, but the same was probably thought to be true of the 78 rpm record; now it is becoming difficult to find equipment which will play 45 rpm discs, and one can foresee a time when only museums, collectors and libraries will have equipment to play any sort of vinyl disc. I can still read a Caxton book; how many CD-ROMs will be playable in 500 years' time? Libraries run a risk of having to support out-of-date hardware; enter, perhaps, the Rare CD-ROM Librarian! Or perhaps we should take note of Douglas Van Houweling's suggestion that we should preserve the content, not the package.[28]

Will the online versions of things even still be stored? We are constantly being told about the reduction in costs of disks, and economically this will not necessarily provide a problem; but if all this material is to be kept online, the processors to cope with the quantities of disk store will need to be larger, and they will require constant (if infrequent) upgrading. Who is going to undertake such work? Publishers are in business, and if the archive is not making money, and still has costs, they can hardly be expected to continue to support it for the public good. So either the licence revenues for access to back runs will have to be high enough to cover such costs, or another institution will have to take on the responsibility. If the average academic library is to benefit from digital storage *elsewhere*, there is going to be pressure on national libraries and the larger research libraries to be the depositories. The answer may eventually lie in some sort of co-operative agreement, possibly with a subsidy, on the lines of the Anderson Report in respect of printed sources.[29]

The situation is even worse when one considers publication by individuals. Richard Rockwell of the Inter-University Consortium for Political and Social Research has a neat illustration of the problem:

Had there been a World Wide Web on which Beethoven distributed copies of his sheet music, who would have run his file server in 1828? Who would have ensured that even if the file server burned up, there would have been a backup copy of the music somewhere else? Who would have answered questions from musicians who thought something had gone wrong in the transcription? and who would have adapted Beethoven's network service to the new TCP/IP protocol when it displaced the old one?[30]

Quality control

It has to be admitted that a lot of what is published by individuals on the World Wide Web is of questionable value to scholarship.[31] The ease of publishing will always attract the self-publicist; but equally such individual publishing is the only way to provide a degree of competition to prevent publishers from exercising the same near-monopoly which they have now in printed journals. Unless therefore some way can be found to enable online refereeing and the selection of the more valuable of these items, we shall continue to be overwhelmed with an uncontrollable quantity of material. How will libraries react? Faced with similar problems in conventional publishing, we have tended to focus on known authors or reputable publishers. Will the same become true in an electronic context? Will newcomers paradoxically find it *harder* to be read?

Whither (or wither?) libraries?

Faced with the problems and opportunities identified here, perhaps the only certainty is that libraries – and librarians – will change. Clearly there is no evidence that we can expect digitization and electronic publishing to be a panacea for our financial troubles. We may see it as a route to develop more user-friendly – or at least user-satisfying – services. As professionals, we may have an enhanced role as guides in the maze of potential sources. As managers we may need to change the expectations of both our staff and our users.

For all the lip-service paid to 'access vs holdings' few institutions have gone down the route taken by Cranfield and relied totally on external provision, even in such a limited area. The recent publication *The effective academic library*[32] displays a continuing emphasis on size of collections which is almost nineteenth-century – note the use of indicator P3-7, 'Volumes in collection per FTE student'. Periodical runs in our libraries are sacrosanct; anything we obtain for a user should be kept and catalogued 'in case someone needs it again'. The additional costs of cataloguing and storage will vary, but are measurable in pounds per item; we bind runs of periodicals, and the dust grows ever thicker on their tops.

The effect of the increasing availability of information in electronic form will be to remind librarians of their function not of hoarding but of transmitting information. We shall have to cease agonizing over incomplete runs of journals; performance indicators will have to relate to the satisfaction of users.

With this may go a decentralization of the subject librarian, to become an information gatekeeper within a department or even a research group – and perhaps funded from that source. The parallel with Departmental Computing Officers is easy to draw, and as we move into the digital age the blurring of these two professions will inevitably increase, at least in the area of user support. For the foreseeable future the library building with its printed volumes will remain; but its catalogue will be only one of the available resources on the network, and in some disciplines not even the primary one.

References

1   Odlyzko, A. M., 'Tragic loss or good riddance? The impending demise of traditional scholarly journals', *International journal of human–computer studies*, **42**, 71–122, 1995; quoted by Ann Okerson in Butler, M. and Kingma, B., (eds), *The economics of information in the networked environment*, Washington DC, Association of Research Libraries, 1996, 111–12.
2   Garson, Lorrin R., 'Can E-Journals save us? – a publisher's view', in Butler, M. and Kingma, B., (eds), *The economics of information in the networked environment*, Washington DC, Association of Research Libraries, 1996, 116.
3   Noll, Roger, ' The economics of information' in Butler, M. and Kingma, B., (eds), *The economics of information in the networked environment*, Washington DC, Association of Research Libraries, 1996, 41.
4   West, Richard, 'Changing costs of information in the networked world', in *Networked information in an international context: a conference organised by UKOLN in association with the British Library, CNI, CAUSE and JISC.* URL: http//www.ukoln.ac.uk/fresco/net_info/west.html; section on Information pricing.
5   *Report of the Joint Funding Councils' Libraries Review Group*, December 1993, paragraph 271, 'The Virtual Library: an undergraduate's day'.
6   Bowen, William G., 'JSTOR and the economics of scholarly communica-

tion', in Butler, M. and Kingma, B., (eds), *The economics of information in the networked environment*, Washington DC, Association of Research Libraries, 1996, 23–34.

7   *Ibid.*, p 30.

8   Lesk, Michael, 'Why digital libraries?', URL:http://ukoln.bath.ac.uk/follett_lecture_series/why_digital_libraries.html

9   Varian, Hal, 'The economics of the internet and academia' in Butler, M. and Kingma, B., (eds), *The economics of information in the networked environment*, Washington DC, Association of Research Libraries, 1996, 43.

10   *Management information for decision making: costing guidelines for Higher Education institutions*, KPMG Management Consulting, 1996.

11   Lesk, *op. cit.*, section 4.

12   Details of these and other projects in the e-Lib programme can be found through the e-Lib pages of the UKOLN server, URL: http://ukoln.ac.uk/e-Lib

13   Butler, Meredith A., 'The economics of resource sharing, consortia and document delivery'; Bruce R. Kingma, 'The economics of access versus ownership: the costs and benefits of access to scholarly articles via interlibrary loan and journal subscriptions'; both in Butler, M. and Kingma, B., (eds), *The economics of information in the networked environment*, Washington DC, Association of Research Libraries, 1996, 93–7 and 99–107.

14   Evans,Janet, Began, Simon J. and Harrington, John, 'BIODOC: access versus holdings in a university library', *Interlending & document supply*, **24** (4), 1996, 5–11.

15   Ryan, James H., 'Measuring costs and benefits of distance learning', in Butler, M. and Kingma, B., (eds), *The economics of information in the networked environment*, Washington DC, Association of Research Libraries, 1996, 157–64.

16   Noll, *op. cit.* p 41.

17   Arnold, K., Collier, M., Ramsden, A., 'ELINOR: the electronic library project at De Montfort University Milton Keynes', *Aslib proceedings*, **45** (1), 1993, 3–6.

18   E-mail from Tom Wilson to lis-link and lis-e-Lib, 4 October 1996, archived at http://www.mailbase.ac.uk/lists/lis-link ('electronic journal: some usage data'); Hal Varian, 'The economics of the Internet and academia' in Butler, M. and Kingma, B., (eds), *The economics of information in the networked environment*, Washington DC, Association of Research Libraries, 1996, 51.

19 Bush, Vannevar, 'As we may think', *Atlantic monthly*, **176**, July 1945, 101–8.

20 Davis, Hiram L., 'Economic considerations for digital libraries: a Library of Congress perspective' in Butler, M. and Kingma, B., (eds), *The economics of information in the networked environment*, Washington DC, Association of Research Libraries, 1996, 131–6.

21 See for example the SKIP project, http://www.plym.ac.uk/faculties/research/skip.htm, or the NetLinkS project, http://netways.shef.ac.uk/netlinks.htm.

22 Lesk, *op. cit.*, section I.

23 Tom Wilson, e-mail, 4 October 1996.

24 TULIP: final report, 1996. URL http://www.elsevier.nl:80/homepage/about/resproj/trchp5.htm, V 1.2.

25 Bernard Naylor, e-mail to lis-e-Lib, 2 August 1996; archived at http://www.mailbase.ac.uk/lists/lis-e-Lib ('internet archaeology 3').

26 Bernard Naylor e-mail, lis-e-Lib, 6 August 1996; archived as above.

27 Varian, *op. cit.*, 51

28 Van Houweling, Douglas E., 'Knowledge services in the digitised world: possibilities and strategies', in *Electronic access to information: a new service paradigm*, Mountain View CA, Research Libraries Group, 1994, 11.

29 Joint Funding Councils' library review: *Report of the Group on a National/Regional Strategy for Library Provision for Researchers*, [chaired by Michael Anderson], revised 1996.

30 Rockwell, Richard C., 'Funding social science data archiving and services in the networked environment', in Butler, M. and Kingma, B., (eds), *The economics of information in the networked environment*, Washington DC, Association of Research Libraries, 1996, 64.

31 See e.g. e-mail from Ian Winship to lis-e-Lib, 24 January 1997, 'Quality of data on the Web', reporting a survey of chemical data.

32 *The effective academic library: a framework for evaluating the performance of UK academic libraries. Consultative report by the Joint Funding Councils' Ad-Hoc Group on Performance Indicators for Libraries*, 1995.

Bibliography and further reading

Communications of the ACM, **38** (4), 1995. The issue is devoted to Digital Libraries.

Butler, M. and Kingma, B., (eds.), *The economics of information in the networked environment*, proceedings of a conference, Washington DC, Association of Research Libraries, 1996.

Win-Shin S Chiang and Elkington, N. K. (eds.), *Electronic access to information: a new service paradigm. Proceedings from a symposium held July 23 through 24, 1993*, Mountain View CA, Research Libraries Group, 1994.

13

Operating Costs

ELIZABETH HART

Introduction

Academic libraries have faced a period of unprecedented change in the last decade which has included a large growth in the student population; the impact of electronic information with its emphasis upon user-centred information provision; changes in the methods used in teaching and learning and a general climate of budgetary constraints. A large proportion of institutional resources are allocated to academic libraries and, in times of reduction and restraint, libraries have had to examine their operations and services in terms of value for money and efficiency and effectiveness. In recent years this has led to an emphasis on performance measurement, benchmarking, full costing of services and an increasing reliance on issues which are important to the customer.

Before examining operating costs within this context, it is necessary to provide a clear outline of an academic library's purpose and nature of business. We can broadly define that purpose as follows: academic libraries exist in an educational environment which in itself indicates that they generate economic value for their nation. They support teaching, learning and research; sometimes they act as significant repositories of materials for the region or nation and, finally, their staff promote all the above and also help to deliver skills to their users. These skills usually relate to finding and using information and are transferable into the work environment. Academic library staff do not, as for example in special libraries, deliver a finished product in the sense of an 'answer' to a query but, more usually, deliver advice, guidance and support as part of the educational process.

All this implies an academic library's nature of business is high contact customer services[1] delivered in an educational environment. The automatic supposition which might result is that the 'front of house' must take a priority but this neglects the focus on 'back room' operations which are usually there to *add value* to information resources primarily by acquisition or organization. Such an assumption also ignores the large differences between libraries within the same sector which affect their operational focus, the most obvious examples being those with responsibilities for national or regional collections of significance.

Staff

As a high contact customer service[2] the largest operating cost for any academic library will be staff. Despite the developments of electronic information and the concept of a virtual library, the current situation is that academic libraries are staff intensive and likely to remain so for some time to come.

The staffing structures of academic libraries are as numerous as the libraries themselves. The operating costs of such structures are typically dominated by the balance between staff who have qualifications in librarianship and information science (usually paid on higher salary scales) and those who do not (usually paid on lower salary scales). The most recent SCONUL statistics[3] illustrate this balance in the UK. Here the *average* number of professional staff was 26.28 FTE at a cost of £633,681 while the average number of non-professional staff was 39.96 FTE at a cost of £459,505. While this balance can be affected by a whole range of factors, it is a key driver of operating costs and one which can be influenced by the changes in use, emphasis and activity currently ongoing in the sector.

Staff are the key to maintaining service quality, which is the principal element in good customer relationships. Basic operating costs relating to staff are numerous and begin with holidays, sick leave, retirement and overtime. If you operate on a number of sites then, depending on the contractual position, there will also be travelling expenses and time allowances for movement between locations and the inevitable duplication of services and staffing provision. Another major operating cost is staff turnover which is directly related both to overtime, advertising and/or the costs of retirement. Most organizations wish to recruit the best and most suitable staff and many are willing to invest in that process. Elements in that operation include: a minimum of two or three meetings of a recruitment panel; advertising costs; administration of personnel; travelling expenses of candidates; organization of interview process, tours, tests, etc.; appointment and contractual agreements; and a substantial induction and training programme on appointment.

Balanced against a (presumed) lifetime of payment to a valued staff member this investment is relatively small but a repeat of this process many times per year is a major operational overhead. There are ways of minimizing these costs somewhat, particularly for smaller, but operationally vital, posts such as shelving assistants. Some libraries invest heavily once or twice a year and produce pools of available recruits; others use student labour sometimes organized via institutional-based student job clubs. Many libraries have also sub-contracted some staffing overheads. Daily cleaning operations can often be more cheaply sub-contracted when compared with the costs and overheads of employment by the library of cleaning personnel. Other staffing efficiencies have been introduced through technological developments, the most obvious being the downloading of records from electronic sources. This has tended towards at least part of the cataloguing operation being carried out by staff who do not possess a professional qualification in librarianship and information science. This can substantially reduce process costs but must be balanced against payment made for the records.

Staff are regarded by most institutions as their most important resource and staff development and training are key tools in maintenance of the operational effectiveness of that resource. Attempts to put a percentage figure on investment in staff development are difficult and depend very much upon the infrastructure of each institution. For example, some institutions provide a wide range of staff development for all as a central resource. The Fielden Consultancy[4] recommended that a minimum of 5% of LIS staff time should be allocated to training and development and quotes the related LISU survey as indicating that some academic libraries already exceeded that level. For service organizations highly dependent upon customer contact such investment could be seen as a necessity. Whatever the situation, yearly operating cost estimates will require a provision for staff development and for the related time, travel and expenses incurred.

There are other more general issues which affect staff costs. Geographical location of the library is one example which can often dictate the actual remuneration of individual jobs. This can also heavily influence the ease or otherwise with which vacancies are filled. A library with numbers of disparate sites is a further obvious influence as are remote storage locations, which affect the staffing levels of, for example, the deposit libraries such as the University of Oxford. The Bodleian has remained a reference library since its foundation and houses 85% of its holdings in closed access. The supply of this material to 16 physically separate reading rooms from 18 different storage areas is a major logistical operation which currently requires 431,000 fetching operations per year.[5] This is a unique example but clearly illustrates the wide variation within the sector and the importance of the nature of the business and purpose of individual libraries on their operating costs.

Finally there is the issue of managing the staff resource. Staff development and training have already been mentioned. There is also the simple logistics of ensuring that the right people are in the right place at the right time. Costing the efficient staffing of sites and services is often an essential requirement if the concepts of equity, quality and cost effective service are to be ensured.

Architecture and building design

Architecture and building design have a major long-term effect upon library operating costs. Unfortunately beauty and aesthetic merit do not necessarily equate with practical layout, and operating costs depend in large measure upon how well the facilities are designed.[6] Consider what libraries require:

- seating, space, light, shelving, reinforced floors (with ducting for electronic cabling, if possible);
- PC facilities and printers;
- the inevitable bank of photocopiers;
- audiovisual media.

All of these must be accessible, easy to find and placed in a comfortable environment. Simple but basic features such as a proliferation of dividing walls can and do lead to operational difficulties. Similarly, additional floors with more than one entrance demand staff and security, time getting from place to place and the relocation of materials to their correct position. Libraries also change over time and buildings designed around the library operations of 25 years ago are not necessarily able to cope with subsequent developments and different or new types of activity. While it is not always possible to change these elements, it is essential to be aware of them when planning and producing yearly financial estimates of operating costs. One is reminded of the Follett Report's[7] vignette of the virtual librarian, with the library building partially converted into a car park because it was so strong and the floors had successfully resisted the introduction of cable.

Finally, many academic libraries are mixed resources, ranging from modern buildings constructed within the last few years to grade 2 listed buildings and buildings of international significance. The first might have good facilities with excellent access for the physically impaired, well designed for the full range of library activity, hold the bulk of the collection and be far less expensive in operational terms than the second example which might only house a single subject-based collection and have imposed building and alteration restrictions. Ironically, it may well be the listed building which provides the photo-opportunities and excels in terms of public relations.

Environment

Libraries are meant to hold people as well as materials, which can sometimes be a difficult mixture. The type of use now made of libraries has altered over recent years. Many libraries, particularly in the 'new' universities, have moved towards a resource centre approach to services. Others now offer merged services where a mixture of computing, audiovisual, media and educational support staff are linked together in one unit and offer services within a common building. Often users are provided with large open access group study areas where discussion combined with the use of a wide range of printed and electronic sources are encouraged and (naturally) noise is often an issue. How this type of environment is balanced against the equally important need for traditional quiet study areas can cause a conflict in operational focus and also variations between the operating costs of the two different types of area if they exist within one building.

Building design will also influence the need for heat, ventilation and light but equally, the costs will also be affected by opening hours. Currently these are commonly seven days a week during the academic year and often over long hours. Even when the library is closed the need for power must continue for the teams of cleaning personnel who must clean and tidy up the environment on a daily basis. The timing of such operations is also a cost factor. Power is often cheaper late at night than in the early hours of the morning and the shift pattern of the cleaning operation can have a major influence on the power costs particularly over a whole year.

The environment, i.e. the look and feel of a library, is important to library users and library staff, for the latter both in terms of professional credibility and also morale. Rubbish, dirt and dust do not convey a constructive image. Conversely, comfortable and practical furniture and equipment and hardwearing but colour co-ordinated carpets can promote your public relations enormously. All this must be maintained whether via internal departmental recharging or external maintenance contracts (both preferably negotiated with guaranteed attendance and response times, full replacement cover and the like). Unfortunately, none of this will protect against the inevitable losses whether it be books, torn pages from a journal, a plug or a PC. All are likely to need replacing, with the consequential administrative overheads. Investment in security does have proven advantages. A recent cost-benefit analysis on the advantages of theft detection systems in academic libraries[8] concluded that the installation of such systems would be justified both in the short term and over 5 years. Provided the average price of the materials to be replaced was equal to or greater than £13.56 the initial cost of the detection system and its first year's operating costs would be met by the savings in replacement costs. Insurance cover should also be considered here. Most institutions have an overall policy which may mean the loss of a single PC or small piece of equipment is not covered as the policy may limit individual claims to less than, for example, £2500 or £3000. Cumulative losses of small pieces of equipment (typically staplers and hole punches) can lead to a large investment having to be made by the end of the financial year. Sometimes such losses can also lead to library policy regarding the loan or use of pens, staplers, glue and hole punches by users.

There are also the 'strange' occurrences such as the (never apprehended) individual in my library who regularly insisted on dismantling the chairs. Such chairs were discovered, usually in the mornings, neatly piled up with screws and bolts arranged ready for reconstruction. Aside from the irritation factor, time and resources were required to put the chairs back together!

The operating cost for security also changes over time. All academic libraries now contain PCs which, if they are to be secured, must be either bolted down or fitted with security cuffs. Such measures are necessary but require additional original costs, require staff time in maintenance and installation and inhibit movement and easy alteration of layouts and environment. PCs in libraries also necessitate the introduction of appropriate furniture and adjustable seating, which is now a legal requirement.

Developments in new technology such as access control systems seem to offer the combination of security and access to buildings over long hours. They can also be very expensive to install and barriers to appropriate access. For example, if the library offers local community access for reference purposes, holds a local collection of archives, or a bequest which specifies public access must be provided. Ensuring appropriate access in these circumstances will cause administrative overheads which will be a permanent feature over time and have to be balanced against the investment in and advantages of such systems.

Services

The operating costs of services relate firmly back to the nature of business of academic libraries outlined in the introduction to this chapter. In terms of services the nature of business is affected by changes in information provision, access and technological developments. Libraries are beginning to offset expensive staff-intensive operations onto the users, for example with the development of self-issue systems. Here the user is actively participating in the operational process allowing resources and time used in that operation formerly to be allocated elsewhere. This applies to information as well with the development of electronic information services which aim to provide information direct to the user. In the 'new' model, libraries need to consider user needs. Traditionally they have always done so. They provide services, collate, preserve and organize knowledge which in turn allows access. However, libraries have provided these services on their own terms. Users come into libraries and must follow certain rules and regulations, cataloguing and knowledge organization methods to find information. The Internet, for example, offers no such restrictions and is, by complete contrast, an anarchic mix of services and information. Currently, attempts to use artificial intelligence to catalogue the Internet are not working. A program cannot as yet define the quality and level of similar material that might be appropriate for individual use of say a child or a professor. The Internet is also full of information which is redundant, inaccurate and sometimes undesirable. Libraries are beginning to tackle these changes by providing access to quality information, employing user-friendly methods and effectively adding value to electronic resources in much the same way as they do already with printed materials. Such changes of emphasis are vital to operating costs and need to be constantly borne in mind as developments progress. Changes in teaching and learning have also brought the developments in electronic information into sharper focus. The developing role of the librarian as teacher or as a key partner in the academic teaching process is attaining a higher significance. In the confusing world of the Internet more and more users desperately require the necessary skills to find and evaluate sources of information. The role of the librarian in adding value both in terms of information skills and organization becomes more critical, in this scenario, to the success of the educational process overall.

Acquisition policies also dictate the essential balance for most institutions between access and holdings. In a paper from the early 1980s[9] the annual costs associated with investment in book stock were weighed against the extra operating costs that would be incurred through reliance upon Inter Library Loan (ILL). It was concluded that ILL was more economical, though significantly ignored such factors as in-house use and delays associated with ILL borrowing. Increased costs of materials combined with the continued increase in the volume of published materials and electronic developments have led to a greater variety of response to access issues. These include the development of co-operative and consortium agreements and the decision, sometimes on economic grounds, to pay for full text electronic access rather than provide space and storage. Despite these changes there are still basic operating costs for services which cannot be avoided regardless of the scenarios applied. These include:

- telephone charges
- fax
- postage
- stationery
- photocopying costs
- printing
- binding (in-house or external)
- payment for electronic licenses (which directly relates to permitted user access).

Others are dependent upon policy. Inter Library Loan, for example, now usually requires a charge to be made before use though this again relates to the nature of business of the institution. Some institutions allow free use of ILL for postgraduate and research students and academic staff while allowing no use at all for undergraduates. Others restrict the numbers of requests that an individual can make.

The issue of cost recovery and charging for services is one which faces the whole sector in a climate of reduction and restraint. Some academic libraries have developed or are developing service level agreements with their academic departments which provide a clear framework for services provided. These are also linked to a charging policy where 'basic' services are provided at a set cost with extra services incrementally charged. This model can only work if all services and operations have been clearly defined, accurately costed and are delivered to a common standard, the clear implication being that a full cost model including all the marginal operating costs is required and essential.

Changes in teaching and learning and the widening role of

libraries has led to certain types of supplies being 'sold' to users. The development of small scale 'shops' or supply points has led to basic materials such as paper, binding materials, overhead transparencies, floppy disks and laser printing being sold to users, often at highly cost-effective prices. This is a service which supports educational developments but may not necessarily be cost-effective in operational terms. By levying charges and selling materials of whatever kind the operational issues such as increased cash handling, financial management, efficient supply management, unpredictable materials costs and the possible need to guarantee additional staffing must be balanced against the needs of the user and possible 'profit'. Sales of any kind are also subject to the vagaries of Value Added Tax in the UK, where local rules often apply, and what is allowed in one geographical area may not be permitted in another.

Services can also be provided via leasing arrangements, specifically for equipment. This is often a cost-effective option but must be carefully evaluated, be the subject of a business plan and be negotiated with skill. The most common areas where leasing is employed is for large volume equipment with a limited lifespan such as photocopiers or PCs. Such options are also influenced by site and location. Leasing photocopiers, for example, can be more expensive than purchase but not if viewed from the perspective of inclusive maintenance and replacement costs across a number of sites. Leasing also means initial capital or large revenue sums are not required in a single year. Automation of libraries can also benefit by good leasing options but this does not reduce the annual operating and maintenance costs for the automation systems to the originating company. Similarly, as such systems grow and develop there will be resulting additional licenses and yearly maintenance to fund which can be substantial. As automation affects almost every aspect of a library's operation it is significant that many more library management systems are introducing sophisticated financial and management information modules which support sound financial management and performance review.

Special collections and services

Some libraries have responsibilities for national collections, some for local collections of significance, still more are given grants, gifts and bequests of all kinds. Sometimes these are the subject of one-off or non-recurrent funding, sometimes bequests arrive with specific requirements attached to them. All will undoubtedly have operating costs which, unless they are remarkably well and consistently funded, will have an effect upon the overall operation of the library. If they are separately funded there are financial management overheads; if they are not entirely separately funded decisions must be made as to what contribution will come from the library recurrent funding. There are also the 'hidden' elements such as the varying nature of business and purpose of such collections and the perception that they are special and possibly a burden upon the whole and therefore, perhaps, the subject of discontent. All such issues must be balanced against the prestige, marketing and public relations benefits such collections may bring to the library and institution.

Some academic libraries have also ventured into entrepreneurial activity for external users with mixed success. This activity was well reviewed and summarized in a report by Brenda White.[10] Here the difficult balance between the flexibility of operations required to allow innovation to prosper and the control needed to keep the library functioning normally was explored. Often there are external entrepreneurial possibilities but these are usually related to an opportunity which can be pursued as an integral part of the library's role within the institution. In theory, this allows the service to continue without creating tensions between those that pay and those that do not. Here again the consistent quality of the service offered is a key factor. In the future this type of entrepreneurial activity could relate to value added services which are becoming increasingly more important as library roles alter in the face of technological change.

Management

The extent to which operating costs can be controlled by library managers is directly related to the nature of business of the library, and also to the policies of the parent institution. For example, in financial terms the ability to 'vire' resources between budgets may be restricted. Similarly, the devolving of resources to departments and services to cover certain operating costs, previously held centrally, such as postage, telephones or hospitality might be linked to restrictions as to where such services can be obtained. Such restrictions can often create artificial internal monopolies which could mitigate against cost-effective services. Other issues, such as internal definition as to what is meant by equipment (e.g. a stapler, PC or shelf unit) and controls on the timescale in which revenue or capital allocations can be made, can all restrict the effective use of financial resources.

Government policy and influence should not be underestimated. The recent KPMG report, (at present in draft form), produced for the Joint Funding Councils[11] takes a very serious look at costing guidelines for HE institutions in the UK. Essentially KPMG has created what the report refers to as a set of useful tools which can be used by institutional managers to cost Higher Education institutions. It is significant that this report sees the primary benefit of the exercise as giving institutions a better understanding of cost structures and hence a better basis for resource allocation and planning.

Libraries are likely to be ahead of this game as the costing of services and functions (cost per lend, cost per entry) has been under discussion as part of the performance measurement debate for some time. The consultative report *The effective academic library*[12] from the Joint Funding Council's Ad Hoc group on Performance Indicators for Libraries primarily considered issues relating to library effectiveness.

In practical terms, library managers have to be astute judges of financial opportunity and have the information available to make confident and competent decisions. These do not necessarily have to be major to affect operating costs. Minor adjustments or alterations to operating costs across a number of budgets can add up to substantial savings which allow allocations elsewhere. In this context, budgets should be viewed as powerful management tools. However, for this to be truly effective it is not only the most senior managers who require financial management skills but those to whom individual budgets are devolved. This is both a policy and a staff development and training issue. Similarly, there is a need for skills at all levels in contract negotiation (internal contracts and service level agreements between the library sections can often be as valuable in operational terms as external ones), and in the development of strategic alliances between institutions or between departments within institutions or with suppliers of services.

Summary

If it is possible to develop a broad rule for operating costs it must be that they are not either ignored or marginalized because they have a major influence on cost effectiveness. A lesser rule might be that they should not inhibit decision making either, providing operations and services have been fully costed out initially. Operating cost advantages can be secured by radically reconfiguring activities undertaken within libraries, by using budgets as an active management tool, by the development of financial skills in library managers at all levels and the management of strategic alliances of all kinds.

References

1 Armistead, C., Bowman, C. and Newton, J., 'Managers' perceptions of the importance of supply, overhead and operating costs', *International journal of operations and production management*, **15** (3), 16–28, 1995.

2 *Op. cit.*

3 *Annual Library Statistics 1993–1994*, SCONUL Standing Conference of National and University Libraries, 1995

4 *Supporting expansion. A report on Human Resource Management in Academic Libraries, for the Joint Funding Councils' Libraries Review Group*, John Fielden Consultancy, July 1993.

5 With grateful thanks to Richard Bell, Head of Reader Services, Bodleian Library, for this information.

6 Cohen, E., 'The architectural and interior design planning process', *Library trends*, **42** (3), 547–63, 1994.

7 Joint Funding Councils' Libraries Review Group, *Report. A report for the HEFCE, SHEFC, HEFCW and DENI December 1993* (The Follett Report).

8 Foster, C., 'Determining losses in academic libraries and the benefits of theft detection systems', *Journal of librarianship and information science*, **28** (2), 93–104, 1996.

9 Brown, A. J., 'Some library costs and options', *Journal of librarianship*, **12** (4), 211–16, 1980.

10 White, B., *Maintaining the balance. External activities in academic libraries*, (British Library Research paper 100), London, British Library Research and Development Department, 1992.

11 Joint Funding Councils, *Management information for decision making: costing guidelines for Higher Education institutions*, Draft report by KPMG

Management Consulting, 23 October 1996.

12 *The effective academic library: a framework for evaluating the performance of UK academic libraries. A consultative report to the HEFCE, SHEFC, HEFCW and DENI by the Joint Funding Councils' Ad Hoc Group on Performance Indicators for Libraries*, March 1995.

14

Space Planning and Management

Andrew McDonald

Introduction

There continues to be a large number of new academic library projects around the world. This is despite some almost reckless predictions about the end of books and libraries due to the tremendous growth in networked electronic information. Since 1993, there have been no fewer than 96 new academic library projects in the United Kingdom at an estimated cost of £140 million, largely as a result of the influential Follett Report.[1] In the USA, 40 new academic library projects were completed in 1996 alone, at a cost of some $314M.[2]

The management challenge

Space is a precious and expensive resource that should be planned and managed within a strategic framework for the development of the service as a whole, but it has sometimes received less professional attention than the other resources the librarian manages. Space planning must relate to the ethos and culture of the institution and will also be influenced by the newly-emerging strategies for information, learning, research and estates within universities.

The planning of libraries is simply good management, and like all management, involves taking decisions (normally a large number of them) within a finite time scale and within the resources available. It represents a significant managerial challenge, perhaps the biggest one the librarian will face. The librarian has a unique responsibility to ensure a good building capable of delivering high quality services to generations of users. It is the librarian who will have the responsibility for providing library services to users in the building and it is the librarian's name that is invariably linked with the success or failure of the project.

Good space planning is also about creating a great deal of change in order to build an entirely new service that can deliver better quality, greater efficiency and improved responsiveness. The manager must provide the leadership and direction necessary to manage library staff and users through a period of considerable change. On the one hand, this is about managing creativity and ideas, and, on the other, it is about dealing with disruption and uncertainty.

A major project is a massive communication exercise both within the library and the university and also with the whole range of 'building' professionals involved. It requires both a broad vision and great attention to detail. As a rule, the best libraries emerge when there has been good communication between all those involved in the planning process, especially between the librarian and the architect.

A fundamental question is how far ahead should we plan? Any predictions about the size and type of building required for the future will be influenced by our view on how libraries will be used in the future and how services will be provided in the 'information age'. At one recent conference concerned with the impact of information technology on library buildings,[3] it was suggested that the building structure should be planned for fifty years, the utilities for fifteen years, and the fixtures and fittings for seven years. These time scales seem unduly short, but they reflect the pace of change in higher and further education and, more particularly, in telecommunications and the computer industry. Pragmatists might suggest that we should look as far ahead as we can, or perhaps as far as we can afford to.

Space planning and management is not primarily about architecture and taste or about bricks and mortar. The responsible library manager simply wants an attractive library that functions well and lasts a long time. It should enhance the academic work of the institution and be responsive to change. It must be delivered on time and within budget, and be affordable both in capital and recurrent costs. Quite simply, good, well-planned space enables the library to fulfil its mission, and underpins other library resources. On the other hand, poor space often conflicts with what readers and library staff are trying to achieve, and inhibits the library's ability to fulfil its aims and objectives efficiently. More seriously, it can constrain the development of the service.

Library space is one of the attributes by which the quality of academic work in universities is judged. The amount of space and the number of reader places provided have both been recognized as indicators for evaluating the performance of academic libraries in a Consultative Report by the Joint Funding Councils' Ad-hoc Group on Performance Indicators for Libraries.[4] The availability and accessibility of learning resources are now an accepted part of the assessment of teaching quality. For example, assessors for the Higher Education Funding Council (England) may now consider the adequacy (quantity) and suitability (quality) of library study accommodation and of computer workstations and networking facilities for student needs.[5]

Learning resource centres

A number of universities, particularly the new universities, have built learning resource centres or converged services rather than traditional libraries, in which there is generally a much stronger emphasis on providing reader places, information technology and a wide range of learning media, rather than on printed collections. Some also house other learning facilities, such as computer services, media centres, information skills laboratories, learning development services and curriculum support units. Others provide teaching accommodation and seminar rooms. Some planners regard learning resource centres as a new building type with distinctive qualities[6] whilst others suggest they bear much in common with traditional libraries.

Fundamental principles

There are three key fundamental principles affecting the planning and design of academic library space – functionality, ease of use and economy of operation.

Functionality

In simple terms, the purpose of library buildings is to provide the envelope within which the library can fulfil its role. Functionally, the space must facilitate the delivery of high quality services in an economic way in support of university teaching and research. Functional interests should take priority over any purely aesthetic considerations in architecture and planning. This is not to say that aesthetics are not important: they are a crucial element of functionality. Indeed, we want libraries that look good and work well, and a skilful and creative architect can achieve both these requirements. The design should recognise the crucial importance of people, books and information technology in modern library and information services. The building must also enable the library to develop, and provide services that are responsive to the changing library and information needs of the academic community.

Ease of use

A new library must be easy to use. Its layout should be as straightforward as possible, and it should simplify and encourage use. New undergraduates may not have experienced a library of the scale and sophistication of a university library before. The service must be easily comprehensible to the growing number of part-time students and returners from a wide range of backgrounds. Students should be encouraged to learn at their own pace, in their own time, using a variety of learning styles, with particular attention paid to the trend to group study and open and distance learning.

Economy of operation

At the same time, the library must be as efficient and economical to operate as possible. It is a well-rehearsed principle in library planning and design, as in other spheres, that the capital sums involved should be spent so as to ensure that the recurrent running costs, especially staffing costs, are controlled and, where possible, unit costs reduced. Clearly, more staff will normally be required in expanded libraries but the challenge is to meet the additional demand without a proportionate increase in staffing levels. Some architects may disagree, but universities would stress the need for special attention to be given to planning for minimum or low maintenance. Library managers are now often required to meet running and maintenance costs from devolved budgets.

Important qualities

A number of qualities are important in the planning and management of academic library space. Many of these were first defined by Harry Faulkner-Brown, a famous British architect responsible for designing a number of library buildings around the world. He identified ten important qualities that became known as the 'ten commandments' of planning libraries. He suggested a library should be:

- flexible
- compact
- accessible
- extendible
- varied
- organized
- comfortable
- constant in environment
- secure
- economic.

These basic concepts were first published in the sixties and although they have remained relevant to planning good libraries, it is not surprising that some of the words now have rather different meanings and that emphases have changed.

The qualities important for today's and tomorrow's buildings relate to a society and a higher education system with much-changed attitudes and aspirations, and to a rapidly growing networked electronic information culture. Academic library space should be:

- adaptable
- inviting and accessible
- varied
- interactive and well-organized
- conducive
- suitable in environmental conditions
- safe and secure
- efficient
- environmentally appropriate

- suitable for information technology.

The priority given to these qualities will vary according to the mission and culture of the university and the emphasis may be very different in traditional libraries and learning resource centres. There are sometimes tensions and conflicts between and within these qualities. Nevertheless, they form a coherent set of critical issues and challenges for the planning of academic library space. Indeed, it is these qualities that set academic libraries apart from other building types and, as a result, considerable skill is required by all those involved in creating this special space.

I believe that these qualities are equally relevant to any space planning exercise. You may be building a new library or extending an existing one. You may be refurbishing a building or adapting a building for library purposes. You may simply be making better use of existing space. Indeed your project may involve a mixture of these.

Adaptable

It is important to achieve a high degree of adaptability or flexibility in the building so that the use of space can easily be changed merely by rearranging the furniture, shelving and equipment. However, achieving long-term flexibility in a changing and uncertain environment can be expensive, and may be more costly than delivering short-term functionality. Planners are now adopting a more pragmatic approach and are choosing an appropriate balance between cost and adaptability requirements.

It has been generally held that in order to achieve a high degree of flexibility, the floor loading should be sufficient for bookstacks throughout the building. This high level of flexibility can only be achieved at the cost of building to the floor loading suitable for bookstacks throughout ($6.5\text{kN}/\text{m}^2$). However, the growing use of information technology, often at the expense of bookstacks, has challenged this view. Some learning resource centres housing predominantly IT-based resources have been constructed to office, rather than traditional library, floor loading standards. Savings can also be made by reducing the floor loading around the perimeter of the traditional library building where reader places, rather than books, will be accommodated. Any savings should be assessed against the loss of long-term flexibility.

Flexible provision for information technology is also important to enable a PC to be provided virtually anywhere in the library with access to all the networks required, but the necessary infrastructure provision can be quite costly.

Inviting and accessible

The library is the central academic focus of the university with a strong 'social' role. It should, therefore, be as inviting as possible, 'enticing' or even 'inspiring' people to make full use of the services provided. It should feel and be accessible to both the able-bodied and those with disability, and must meet current legal requirements for access by the disabled.

Access from the exterior into the building, and from the entrance to all parts of the library, should be as straightforward as possible, requiring some but not too many additional signs and guiding. The layout should be self-evident, requiring little assistance from library staff.

Students appear to have an insatiable appetite for longer opening hours with a demand for 24-hour access in some institutions. This brings security concerns for readers, collections and the building but, potentially, 24-hour access allows flexible study times and may reduce overcrowding.

It is crucial to make good provision for staff and users with disability and specific learning difficulty, not least because good design for the disabled is generally good design for the able-bodied. For example, the absence of internal doors in public areas facilitates the flow of book trolleys and wheelchairs alike, and automatic entrance doors have found favour with readers carrying books as well as with the disabled. Disability can range from physical to allergic and may be temporary or permanent. Adequate provision goes well beyond consideration of the physically handicapped in wheelchairs who, in many libraries, continue to be unable to pass through the aisles, or reach the books on the higher shelves, or gain unimpeded access to the counter services.

Varied

The library should give readers some freedom of choice of study environment to suit different learning styles and the needs of researchers. It should also provide access to a wide range of learning media and information sources, both print and IT-based.

A variety of reader places is desirable, and these range from single person to multi-person tables, casual reception seating, study rooms and group study facilities. Some readers like an 'active' or noisy social learning environment. Others have a preference for quiet study places with good acoustic and visual privacy, and this can be achieved to different degrees with table dividers, book stands, mesh screens, partial carrels, and even fully enclosed carrels. Single person carrels around the outside of the building have often proved to be popular with readers. Rooms and facilities are increasingly provided for seminars, skills training and teaching purposes.

Interactive and well-organized

It is important to achieve an appropriate level of interaction between the space given over to the collections, services, information technology and readers. The well-organized library not only makes optimum use of the space available but is also easy to use. Libraries should promote human interaction, and therefore main counters and other service points where readers and staff interact, require special attention.

Conducive

As the academic heart of the university, the library should convey a sense of quality and value. The ambience should be conducive to academic work and reflection, and readers, many of whom study for long periods, should feel comfortable. The environment should also facilitate access to information and the delivery of high quality services, and should be responsive to user needs.

Imaginative architecture and cultural artwork enhance the ambience of the learning environment. An investment in a high standard of internal finish and furnishings will also create this sense of quality and will withstand heavy use over an extended period with the minimum of maintenance. Unimaginative 'swotting sheds' with a high density of regimented study places and open staircases through which unwelcome noise can permeate to other parts of the building, should be avoided.

Noise, particularly from computer clusters and the readers themselves, is an increasing problem in libraries. Every attempt should be made to 'design-out' the effects of noise and, wherever possible, to arrange potentially noisy activities away from quiet study areas. The suppression of noise is also achieved by attention to finishes, especially ceiling and floor finishes, and planners have sensibly begun to engage acoustic engineers to advise upon ways of reducing noise in the building. Carpet is generally regarded as the best floor finish in this respect, but there is growing concern about the health problems associated with carpets, especially the underestimated effect on asthma sufferers.

Suitable environmental conditions

Suitable environmental conditions are required, not only for the comfort of readers and the efficient operation of computers, but also for the preservation of library materials. Ideally, temperature, humidity, dust and pollution levels should all be controlled. The most suitable conditions for reading areas in libraries are held to be 20°C and 50 to 55% relative humidity but cooler temperatures, lower humidity and reduced light levels are better for the long-term preservation of books and other materials.

Sophisticated air-conditioning systems may be necessary in some libraries but, in others, mechanical or natural ventilation (or a mixture of these) may be a more affordable and appropriate solution. The choice of ventilation system may be a major factor influencing the shape of the building. It is not uncommon now for temperature to be controlled within a fairly wide comfort range from 19°C in winter to as high as 26°C in summer.

Air-conditioning systems have proved to be expensive to run (it costs four times as much to cool as to heat air by one degree) and often difficult to maintain. The running and maintenance costs of any mechanical ventilation system (throughout its anticipated life-time) should be estimated before any decisions are taken to proceed so that the financial responsibility involved is fully understood. Full air-conditioning may be required in areas housing special collections and certain computers.

Mechanical and natural ventilation (openable windows and adjustable radiators) are increasingly common. Architects have exploited ingenious 'natural' systems, such as thermal chimneys and the building mass venting system, to provide air circulation and environmental control in an economical and environmentally-friendly way.

Any building or energy management system fitted should be designed to the lowest common denominator of building management. Universities often underestimate the real cost of running sophisticated systems and the need for properly-trained maintenance staff.

Ambient lighting, whether natural or artificial, should be sufficient both for bookstacks and reader places, and must take account of the growing use of computer terminals by both readers and library staff. Fluorescent downlighting (the most economical form of artificial lighting) must be well-diffused to prevent glare. Uplighting can create an attractive 'feel' in the library, and the resulting reflected light causes less glare on screens. Lights can be automatically controlled in well-lit areas and in stacks by photocells. Task lighting may be the only alternative for illumination at night in huge glazed reading rooms without artificial lights overhead.

New window and glass technology mean exterior vistas and natural daylight are now possible without many of the familiar hazards to people and paper. Double glazing (even triple glazing), tinting, solar film, blinds and architectural shading remain necessary to alleviate the worst effects of noise, solar gain and glare.

Safe and secure

Every precaution should be taken to ensure personal safety and security, and the design must be in accordance with current health and safety legislation. Particular attention may need to be paid to non-standard working hours.

Security and vandal resistance should be considered at an early stage of the planning process. There are security risks associated with the building, the people using it, the collections, equipment and also data. Special attention may be required to secure computers and their chips. Unfortunately, good security measures can often be in conflict with convenience, aesthetics and even safety.

Efficient and environmentally appropriate

There is an increasing concern about operating costs, energy efficiency and environmental issues. Buildings should be designed so as to minimize running and maintenance costs. Space efficiency and life-cycle costs have also come under close scrutiny. The need to demonstrate good value-for-money in relation to the large capital sums made available for major projects, is almost a world-wide requirement.

There is an enhanced awareness of the importance of conservation and many universities now have environmental policies, and architects themselves are often taking the necessary initiatives.

The electronic library

One of the major challenges to the planners of buildings is creating space with appropriate provision for information technology. This will enable the library and its users to benefit fully from rapid advances in library automation, the growth in electronic information networks, and developments in technology-enhanced teaching and learning and research. The number of computers and peripheral devices used in libraries has grown significantly and readers are also bringing in their own portable machines. The ultimate challenge for the library is to be able to have a fully networked computer at virtually any point in the building from which users and library staff can access all the information and services they require. Effective planning requires the combined wisdom and experience of architects, librarians, computer specialists and networking experts.

Cabling infrastructure

Many new library buildings have been fully wired-up. The cost of trunking, flood wiring and connections, together with the cost of the equipment and the growing need for effective security, are all significant.

Provision must be made for getting cabling into the building to a data communications cabinet or hub room, and then for distribution to the various floors through risers, and finally across each floor to clusters and individual machines. A structured cabling system will ensure future flexibility and minimize the need for rewiring.

Trunking is required for the distribution of power, data and telephone cables, ideally around the perimeter of the building, across the ceiling, under the floor, to the pillars, and to individual rooms. Large accessible cable trays are needed to accommodate the many changes of cables that may be necessary during the life of the building.

Networking standards are changing with the convergence of video, data and telecommunications cable technology. Cabling specification must not only accommodate existing network standards but must also be suitable for emerging technologies which are likely to raise data transmission rates from the current 10 megabits per second to 100 megabits per second and beyond. The trend is to upgrade speed and performance through connecting equipment rather than by frequent re-cabling.

Some argue that only minimal provision is needed for data cables because of the possibility of wireless networking in the future using broadcast or microwave technology. At the moment, so long as the resources are available, it seems sensible to make good provision for trunking and flood-wiring in new libraries. Blown fibre cabling may be an alternative, and some institutions lease dark fibre, preferring to make decisions about the speed of operation at a later stage by upgrading the connecting equipment.

Docking stations are required for readers to connect portable computers to the library or campus network, and attention is needed to the quality of the frequently-used connections provided.

Wired-up study places

Planners often choose to wire-up a certain proportion of the reader places, not least for reasons of cost. Indeed, some institutions have developed a ratio for the number of PCs per student in the institution as whole, following the 1:5 ratio recommended in the Nelson Report.[7]

Computer tables arranged around the perimeter can easily be serviced from the wall. It has been customary for tables to be positioned at right angles to the wall but in some cases a continuous perimeter bench has been fitted where readers face outwards and the computer screens inwards. Because of problems of solar glare and gain, reader tables housing computers may also be placed in the centre of the building.

In many libraries computers are simply placed on ordinary tables and this gives a flexible arrangement. Special computer tables are available from furniture suppliers, and architects and interior planners often design computer tables specially for new library buildings. The variety is limitless, but common features include VDU shelves and adjustable keyboard supports. Screens and dividers can be used to protect people from any harmful emissions from other computers. A useful feature of some special tables is the physical enclosure of the central processing unit for security reasons, sometimes beneath the table to give more space at the work surface. Computer screens have even been set beneath a glazed panel in the surface to free space at the work surface, and this offers an alternative physical relationship between eye and screen. The design of workstations for both readers and library staff should take account of the appropriate health and safety regulations, such as those published by the EC[8] and by the Health & Safety Executive[9] for work with visual display equipment. The large number of wires in networked libraries makes wire-management in the furniture a necessity both for safety and aesthetic reasons. Where it can be afforded, IT workplaces should be provided with fully adjustable chairs.

Clusters of PCs are now commonplace in libraries and have been given a variety of interesting names (Barn Cluster, Tarn Cluster, Apple Orchard, IT shed, IT pit and Information Commons). They often double up as teaching clusters too. In designing the layout, there is an inevitable tension between achieving the maximum number of machines and creating an attractive space conducive to learning. Recently, Y-shaped or star shaped tables have been used, where one or two computers are placed on each wing with shared drives or printers located in the centre portion. It is suggested this gives a greater density of workstations and a welcome relief from more rectangular and formal arrangements. Large clusters can produce a surprising amount of noise and heat and attention is needed to fire protection and security.

Self-services

Self-services are increasingly being offered in academic libraries as a way of meeting the growing demand from users where staffing resources are limited and also as a way of avoiding the risk of repetitive strain injuries. Self-issue and return systems have the potential radically to change our approach to designing entrance areas and counters, since readers can undertake these transactions anywhere in the library. Smaller counters may then be required to deal only with those transactions where staff intervention is really necessary. Indeed, some automated services could even become available on a hole-in-the-wall basis. Card-entry and smart cards have begun to be used for entrance control and cashless financial transactions.

Space standards and norms

There are space standards or norms for academic libraries in many countries, but none specifically for learning resource centres, converged services or other academic support services. They usually indicate the amount of space required by readers or bookstock. Others give an appropriate number of reader places in relation to the size of the user population. The most credible standards are those agreed at national level by government or professional bodies, but individual institutions have sometimes adopted their own norms in relation to local circumstances and aspirations.

Norms or guidelines for the size of a university library in the United Kingdom were last approved some twenty years ago by the then University Grants Committee when it accepted the recommendations of the Atkinson Committee Report (1976) on *Capital provision for university libraries*.[10] According to what have become known as the Atkinson Norms, the appropriate net size of a university's central library should be assessed by the following formula:

> 1.25 m²/FTE student numbers
> *plus* 0.2m²/FTE student numbers in 10 years' time
> *plus* assessed provision for special collections
> *plus* adjustment for special circumstances.

The gross size of the library can be derived by adding the balance area (for toilets and staircases etc.) to this net figure. Depending on the shape of the building, this balance area is commonly about 25%.

The figure of 1.25m² was based on 0.40m² for seating and 0.62m² for bookstacks with an additional 20% allowed for administration (library staff). It was also suggested that there should be one reader place for every six students (FTE) on average, and the space required for each reader place was 2.39m^2. It was recognized that different provision was appropriate for different academic disciplines, for example one place for every two law students was recommended. Interestingly, a different guideline of one place for every 3.75 students is used in the Republic of Ireland, reflecting the relatively heavy use of academic libraries.

These Atkinson Norms have been widely adopted not only in the UK but also around the world, and have been used by many universities in planning their libraries and bidding for the necessary resources. The quantitative assessments and funding recommendations in the Follett Report were based upon them. On the other hand, some universities regard them as an irrelevance because the level of funding necessary even to approach these minimum standards has never been made available.

It is widely accepted that the UGC norms are now outdated and no longer reflect the real pressure for library space.[11] The shift from teaching to learning and the increased emphasis on independent learning across the sector have intensified the pressure on learning resources. Despite predictions to the contrary, the widespread use of information technology has made proportionately greater demands on space, and has also increased the cost of library buildings.

A number of other factors have increased the pressure on learning space in universities:

- the move from ownership to access
- semesterization and modularization
- use by the increasing number of non-traditional students
- the growth in collections
- the greater range of services provided
- the variety of reader places
- provision for people with disability
- space for library staff
- the decentralization of service provision.

Ideally, norms should reflect good practice and should recognize the heterogeneity of the sector. They should not be prescriptive, but leave institutions to decide upon local provision and priorities within a broadly accepted nationally determined framework.

The library as a 'place'

The future of the library as a physical 'place' is a matter of considerable professional speculation and debate. Despite some hasty predictions about the imminence and inevitability of the virtual library, universities have continued to build 'scholarly' environments in which learning and research can be pursued, often, as it happens, with growing printed collections. These buildings provide a physical focus where people can come together, preferably without disturbing each other too much, to undertake a number of important activities central to the educational process. People come to study, learn, reflect and exchange ideas. They consult the collections, retrieve information and use serviced equipment and computers. They seek professional assistance and support and make use of the whole range of managed services provided. Increasingly, they learn information skills and use other learning development and support services. The library building remains the 'place' where these essential services can be provided efficiently and economically. It is interesting that many of the electronic libraries in the world are still buildings, and most often very pleasant ones.

However, there can be little doubt that information technology will have an effect on the need for library space in the long term. As networking, electronic publishing and digitization progress, the exciting potential to deliver information and services directly to end users will almost certainly reduce the need for ever-expanding traditional library buildings. For the moment, as the pressure on learning space intensifies, we can observe that library buildings continue to be built, and that they must provide access to both print-based and electronic information services in support of the scholarly aspirations of the universities they serve.

Standards of design continue to improve throughout the sector, and we are seeing a growing diversity of wonderful new library buildings in which exciting architectural expression, satisfying internal spaces and good functionality have been successfully combined. Some new universities have recently built outstanding new libraries and learning resource centres in order to improve the quality of their learning support services in an increasingly competitive higher education sector. These 'premier' buildings are often the most distinguished on campus and some have been designed by internationally renowned architects.

The library manager requires a clear 'vision' and has a crucial role to play in the planning and management of academic library space. New libraries must encourage and support learning and research in the changing world of higher education and global information. They must also enable our universities to be key players in lifelong learning and 'virtual' higher education, and to play a full part in the learning cities and networked culture of the Information Society. As higher education, technologies and management continue to change, the building shells we create today will remain as a lasting tribute, whether in stone, brick, or now more likely in glass, either to our commendable foresight or our regrettable lack of vision.

References

1   Joint Funding Councils' Libraries Review Group: Report, December 1993, *A Report for the Higher Education Funding Council for England, Scottish Higher Education Funding Council, Higher Education Funding Council for Wales and Department of Education for Northern Ireland*, Bristol, HEFCE, 1993 (The Follett Report).

2   Fox, B-L. and Cassin, E., ' Beating the high cost of libraries', *Library journal*, December 1996, 43–55.

3   Institute of Advanced Architectural Studies, *Building libraries for the information age: based on the proceedings of a symposium on the future of higher education libraries held at the King's Manor, York, April 1994*, edited by S. Taylor. York, Institute of Advanced Studies, 1995.

4   Joint Funding Councils' Ad-hoc Group on Performance Indicators for Libraries, *The effective academic library: a framework for evaluating the performance of UK academic libraries*, Bristol, HEFCE Publications, 1995 (Consultative report to the HEFCE, SHEFC, HEFCW and DENI).

5   *SCONUL Briefing Paper: Aide-mémoire for assessors when evaluating library and computing services*, by J. Sykes. London , SCONUL, 1996.

6   Higher Education Design Quality Forum and SCONUL, *The development of learning resource centres for the future. Proceedings of a conference held at the Royal Institute of British Architects, 1995*, London, SCONUL, 1996.

7   Computer Board for Universities and Research Councils, *Report of a Working Party on computer facilities for teaching in universities*, London, Computer Board, 1983 (The Nelson Report).

8 European Community Directive No. 90/270/EEC, 'Minimum safety and health requirements for work with display screen equipment', *Official journal of European Community (L Series)*, **156**, 1990, 14.

9 Health & Safety Executive, *Display screen equipment work – guidance on regulations*, London, HMSO, 1992.

10 University Grants Committee, *Capital provision for university libraries: a report of a Working Party under the chairmanship of Professor R. Atkinson*, London, HMSO, 1976.

11 *SCONUL Briefing Paper. Space requirements for academic and national libraries and learning resource centres*, by A McDonald, London, SCONUL, 1996.

15

Special Bids

DAVID BAKER

Introduction

Increasingly, librarians have to make special bids for resources, whether to carry out one-off, out-of-the-ordinary projects or to develop new services and even, in some circumstances, to maintain existing activities. The trend in many academic institutions is towards the creation of special funds, whether made up of 'new money' or created from a 'top-slice' of existing (normally recurrent) allocations. This is a prime example of the changing culture in academic institutions – from an environment where librarians could expect a given level of resourcing almost 'as of right' to one where everything has to be justified.

The bidding process is in any case now a central aspect of most academic environments – certainly in Britain and many other western European countries. Even if the academic library manager is not directly involved, it is important to know and understand what academic colleagues are 'up against' as they work to attract funds into the organization. The library may also be asked to be a partner with an academic unit, or be relied upon to provide direct or indirect support to other bids within the institution.

If the library resource manager is careful and thorough and uses an appropriate blend of foresight, attention to detail and political nous, then good ideas are more likely to become successful bids and effective projects for the library in its own right. Successful 'special bids' may well allow library resource managers an opportunity to introduce, experiment with and develop new services, systems and even resource management techniques when it might be difficult to do so (in the short- to medium-term at least) in the more traditional areas of library operations.

It also gives librarians a chance to 'prove their worth' within the institution, whether as managers who can 'lever' money from inside/outside the organization or as effective and trusted members of that organization. A successfully completed project, with tangible results and benefits – not least to the academic community and the reputation of the institution – will do much to enhance the reputation of the senior librarians and of the library as a whole, making it that much easier to win or retain resources in the future.

The discipline of bidding for funds and completing 'special projects' is a good one to practice. It makes library resource managers ask fundamental questions about what they wish to do, to what standard, at what cost and to what effect. Much of the approach described in this chapter is also applicable to 'mainstream' resource management, especially at a time when much library and information work is project-driven.

Prerequisites of good bidding

Effective and successful bidding requires much time, effort, thought and planning. Successful proposals must set out clearly the aims and objectives and the ways in which they will be met. The larger the activity or special project, the more detailed the bid will need to be. Information which the bid may need to contain will include the overall costs, the personnel, the timetables for completion of given parts of the project and a host of other factors which inform both the process of gaining the approval of the funding body and the management of the project. Within reason, the more detail provided, the more chance of success the bid is likely to have.

Framing a bid

There are several key issues which will have to be considered before, during and after the 'project' has been completed. In any bidding process, large or small, it is of vital importance to 'read the rule book'. In larger, external calls for bids, failure or inability to comply with the requirements set out by the funders is likely to result in either immediate rejection or failure before the end of the evaluation process.

The factors to be considered before framing a bid may include 'eligibility criteria', the duration of projects or the available budgets for successful submissions. These may rule out a given bid or a particular unit/institution, however worthy the idea behind the proposed bid. The politically adept library resource manager will know – or make sure that s/he finds out – what is expected. If possible, the views, prejudices and predilections of the evaluation committee will also be identified.

An often quoted piece of advice is to decide what one wishes to do and then to describe the main aims using the terminology and in the context of the aspirations of those who are likely to provide the resource. Care must of course be taken to ensure that there is not too great a mismatch between what the library wishes to do and what it says it will achieve as part of the bid. Successful bids are only really successful when they achieve – and are perceived to have achieved by those who provide the resource – what they set out to do, as stated in the submission.

However, it is not simply a matter of saying the right words to the right people. 'Packaging' the bid is of paramount importance. Unit heads who consistently send in wordy, twenty-page documents when the institution's policy/planning and resources committee is looking for two sides of A4 paper with bullet points *and no more* should expect (and deserve) their bids to be turned down. Given the pressure on most management committees, such a manager should not be surprised to find that these overlong bids are not actually read, let alone considered. The person's or the unit's reputation in this regard will eventually precede their submissions.

The successful resource manager will find out in as much detail as possible the ways in which the library may participate in either an internal or an external project bid. It is often the case that planning and resource committees in academic institutions do not immediately think of the library as a candidate for special funds or as a go-getting bidder for contract or innovation or similar funds outside the institution.

Avoiding pitfalls

Library resource managers need to be aware of the pitfalls as well as the attractions of following a 'high profile' policy in the area of special bids or projects. Reference has been made earlier in this book to the importance of the political dimension in resource management; it is no less important in the development of 'special projects' and bids than elsewhere.

In making bids or developing project work as a regular aspect of library resource management, it is assumed that the political climate in which the bidders are working is conducive to such activity. In some instances, it is the only way to obtain additional resources from within, as well as outside, the institution. Success in a sphere in which the parent organization wishes to see units such as the library succeed is all to the good. But what if the political environment is not conducive to this sort of activity?

Academic libraries form part of the support service infrastructure which allows an institution to carry out the activity – study, teaching, research – which it has been set up to undertake. The library is an indirect rather than a direct cost to the organization. It is one remove from the actual process of attracting funds, although it often has a vital role to play in helping others to 'lever' money and often benefits from others' efforts in this field.

There is therefore a danger in direct external bidding for funds if this detracts from the library's prime purpose, or, just as worryingly to the library resource manager, is seen by the powers-that-be as detracting from that mission, however inaccurate the latter perception. In this situation, political judgement has to be applied. The same is true, though perhaps to a lesser extent, of internal bidding. In an environment where support services have to bid against each other for funds, there is the need on the part of the library resource manager to maintain a balance between friendly contact and arch-rivalry with other support service units.

This is perhaps especially true of relationships with computing centres, at least in institutions where they, and the libraries, remain separate cost centres. It is also an issue in terms of relationships with academic colleagues and departments, who may be suspicious of a library which appears to be too proactive and envious of significant success in attracting special funds – especially if this has come from a top-slice of academic departments' own income.

Anticipating outcomes

It is also important to think ahead, both in terms of success and failure. If the bid is successful, it will have to be implemented. It is important to ensure that the library resource manager is not 'caught by surprise' in this context; there is nothing worse than being given the money for a project or an innovation when the bidders are ill-prepared (or even unwilling) to undertake the project. This relates back to the earlier point about making a proposal based on an aim or aims which one actually wishes to fulfil.

Similarly, it is important to anticipate the effects of a failed bid. What message will this give within the library or the institution? How can the aspiration be met regardless of the non-appearance of additional resources? It is assumed that the proposed project was a desired enhancement or activity (if it was not, why was the bid being submitted?).

Many worthwhile projects fail – especially when resources are limited and there are more bids than money available. Provided that the proposal is a technically and financially sound one, there is no reason why the library resource manager should not try other funding bodies, if the objectives meet with theirs in respect of the project.

The politically aware manager will also look out for opportunities within the organization to re-submit a bid, or to re-use parts of it in a later, revised submission, when the chances of success – whether because of improved funding, a culture change or some other factor – seem to be greater than on the first, unsuccessful occasion.

As with the 'packaging' of bids, however, it is important to avoid the wrong kind of reputation. A small number of carefully-targeted bids, each of which is successful in terms of the winning of resources and the delivery of results will do far more for reputations than too many undisciplined and regularly unsuccessful ones.

Then there is the question of the success or failure of the special project or initiative itself. Here again, it is important for the library resource manager to anticipate every eventuality. The more carefully thought out the bid, the clearer and more realistic its timescale and objectives; the more carefully monitored and the more efficiently managed the experiment or project, the less likelihood there will be of failure. The politically-sensitive library manager will nevertheless ensure that even partial failure will not leave the library with an unduly tarnished image if at all possible.

Resource implications

All resource management takes time. The library manager has to take decisions on how best to deploy resources in order, amongst other things, to attract resources, or to improve their long-term management. Bidding processes also take time and time is a precious resource and costs money. Time spent on a special project is time not spent on other work. The library resource manager has to identify where the greater benefit actually lies.

Proposals will have to be evaluated by those who are to fund the chosen bids. In major (mainly external) projects and initiatives, successful proposers could well be involved in contractual negotiations. The detailed preparation of technical and related documentation requires time and expertise (which may have to be paid for). The post-bidding negotiation and agreement process could take anything from a few weeks to several months, depending on the complexity of the project and the involvement and approach of those funding it.

There is therefore no escaping the fact that the key personnel in the bidding process will have to spend time working on the proposal from beginning to end – anticipation of all eventualities being one of the key ways of avoiding pitfalls, as noted above. Gone are the days (if ever they really existed) when project proposals were just 'roughed out on the back of an envelope'. The time involved in preparing a full and detailed bid cannot be overestimated. In this context, it should be noted that even the pithy, two-sides of A4 bid to an internal resource allocation committee takes time: indeed, the shorter the paper, the more important it is to structure the argument, target the points and aim for the maximum effect.

Major projects may well involve other partners, whether inside or outside the library/institution, for example the computing centre, another library or a commercial organization. Time will have to be spent consulting and working with them. This may involve meetings and visits. Even internal bidding processes may necessitate arguing one's case as well as negotiating details with the evaluators/funders of the bid.

There will also be indirect costs such as telephone, fax and travel expenditure. The assumption is that in an internal bidding process, these 'overheads' would be subsumed within normal operating or administrative expenditure, but they cannot be ignored when a library engages in any major internal or external bidding process. 'Up-front' costs can rise to several thousand pounds in such situations. Once again, the library resource manager has to decide on the risks to be taken and the value of the investment to be made in any bidding process.

The unit's contribution

Just as knowing what resources are available in any given context is an important aspect of effective resource management, a key part of the bidding process is the identification of the bidding unit's actual resource contribution to the project/innovation/special bid if successful.

More importantly, before a proposal is even submitted, the bidding manager needs to be confident that s/he is able to raise the necessary matching resource. Many funding agencies will only contribute 50% or less of the costs of a project, possibly with an upper-level cash limit, regardless of size of project or funding agency contribution. This may also be true of internal bidding processes.

Even where the contribution is the greater part or even all of the perceived resource required, there is no escaping the fact that the bidding unit will have made some contribution to the project, even if it is only time, use of existing infrastructure or opportunity cost.

Some funding agencies – including internal resource committees – may impose conditions on the award of resources. These might range from the ownership of copyright on the end-product to the self-financing nature of the innovation once the 'pump-priming' funds have run out. Some funding committees might ask the bidding unit to rank the project/innovation/new activity in relation to existing areas of work and then make the unit pay for the bid, at least in part, by the cessation of activity in some of those areas, where the activity is ranked lower than the proposed project, etc.

Making a bid

In making bids for resources, then, it is important to pay particular attention to the basic principles, the detailed submission requirements and procedures and the criteria for evaluation of submitted projects bids, all as enumerated by the funding body or organization. It is also as well to anticipate any contractual arrangements which may have to be made if the bid is successful. A 'contract' may be a simple understanding that a report has to be written when the project/experiment, etc. is complete; or, at the other extreme, it could be a legally binding document which needs careful consideration before the bidders agree to sign it.

In more formal and larger-scale bids, it is at this stage that the detailed breakdowns of work to be undertaken – and at what cost – need to be as accurate as possible. It is also necessary -where the project involves one or more other partners – to gain complete commitment from those involved. In this context, it is assumed that partners share the same objectives as the initiating library but complement the strengths of the initiator of the project. It goes without saying that any partnership must be a realistic one.

Defining the topic

This chapter is not the place to provide detailed advice on defining the topic of a bid for resources, but it is worth summarizing the kinds of question whose answers will influence the resource aspects of any bidding process. Reference has already been made to the need to bid for resources on the basis of a desired aim or objectives. Defining the subject of the bid is arguably the key aspect of the whole process – not simply because of the need to frame what one wishes to do in terms of the funding body's requirements and objectives – but also because a full and definitive description of the project/initiative/service, etc. will help to determine the required resource – nature and level – and to identify any major problems at an early stage in the process.

The headings under which information will have to be supplied will vary from funding organization to organization. The fundamental question is 'What do you want to do?' The answer should include concise and comprehensive descriptions of the overall aims and the specific objectives. It should give the rationale for the project and demonstrate the need that has to be met by the project and the benefit that will ensue from it if it is successful. It should demonstrate that the bidders have 'done their homework' in terms of: previous work in the field; understanding of the area; interest and experience in the activity; aims and objectives of the funding body.

The aim is to persuade the evaluation panel or committee that your bid is the one in which resources should be invested. In this context, it is useful if likely short-term results can be listed alongside longer-term benefits when the submission is made.

Methodology

Of crucial importance to the funding body and the bidders themselves is the description of *how* the work will actually be carried out. It is on the basis of this element in the bid (assuming that the overall aims and objectives of the proposal are favoured by the evaluation committee) that the resource implications and the ability of the bidders to manage the project are likely to be assessed.

Phasing

The 'backbone' of any bid or project is likely to be the main phases of its development. Depending on the requirements of the funding body to whom the submission is being made, the submission will also include a detailed statement of methodology. It is essential for both bidders and funders to know how a project will be phased and what will be delivered in each phase. The number, nature and length of phases will depend upon the project.

Milestones

'Milestones' is an increasingly common term in project management and project-based bids for resources. A milestone may span several phases, or a single phase may include more than one milestone. A milestone is basically a point in time during the project plan when something can be marked off as having happened. This could be the writing of a report, the production of a service or the creation of a database. It is a target date by which to achieve a given 'deliverable' and a point on a critical path or timetable by which progress can effectively be measured. Setting the milestones within an overall work plan will enable both bidders and evaluators to assess the best flow of work within a project and the realism with which the project is being tackled.

Work packages

In the more complicated and more formal project-type bids, submissions may well have to included detailed work packages. A work package is a separately identifiable, discrete block of work to which resources and costs are to be allocated. A package will typically have a title, objective(s), a list of specific tasks to be performed, and a timescale.

Whether or not work packages are formally required as part of the submission, working out the 'parameters' of a project (time, schedule, duration) using the work package framework is a valuable way of managing resources in the specific context of special projects. Putting the work packages into the most logical and effective/efficient relationship by using a flowchart will also aid good quality management when the time comes to implement a project proposal and will also impress the prospective funders.

Time assessment

Exactly how the work packages will be assembled into a flow chart will vary from project to project. However the mapping is done, it is of paramount importance that time assessment is carried out thoroughly and effectively. In this context, it is important to bear in mind that there are different ways of assessing the time required, depending upon the goal, the context and the particular resource to be managed.

Project management

The larger the project, the more important it will be to have a dedicated project manager and perhaps also a project management team. Small-scale, internal projects can be led by staff partially seconded from their existing work, with or without a 'buy-out' from other duties and responsibilities, as appropriate. For a major project, however, there will have to be a commitment to a proper project management approach. This will necessitate the deployment of resources either within the project budget or, depending upon the rules of the funding agency, outside it. The resource manager will need to take this latter point into consideration before embarking upon a bid. In addition, it must be remembered that no project is ever truly 'standalone' and that existing employees are likely to be involved in any project, including the senior management, who may be responsible overall for the project's direction and success.

Resource allocation

Reference has already been made to the resource implications of the project formulation and bidding process and to the development of phases, milestones and work packages, organized into a meaningful, coherent and effective order through some form of flow chart. This structure will allow resources to be allocated and used in the most effective and efficient way possible – though in any major project, there will always be confounding variables. Standards may change, or equipment prove to be faulty; staff may resign in mid-project, or a new tax be imposed that increases costs. Unforeseen technical difficulties may emerge in any 'leading edge' work where the products being used or developed are not 'tried and tested' ones. In this context, as with any resource management operation, the creation of a contingency fund is strongly recommended.

The resource allocation process will be made easier if those constructing the bid or project have 'ready reckoner' tables on which to base their calculations. These could relate to the standard costs for employing different grades of staff, including 'on-costs', or the time taken to carry out a given operation (e.g. convert a card-catalogue record into machine readable form). These 'price lists' can also be useful when bidding for additional resources for existing services, or to support new groups of students or subjects, for example.

Summary

This chapter has concentrated on the general resource management issues relating to special bids for funds, whether for special projects or new activities, and whether to internal (parent-body) sources or to external funding organizations. Not all the aspects of special bidding covered here will apply in all cases, though many of the principles enumerated are appropriate to good resource management in any circumstance. In addition, while the chapter has assumed that, in general, libraries will be bidding for funds to carry out a project, it may be that they are in fact putting together a proposal to provide a service, at a price, to a given user group. The same principles of thorough preparation, detailed analysis of the elements of the project or activity to be carried out, comprehensive and accurate costing of all aspects of the proposal, the judicious employment of complementary expertise and the willingness and ability to take careful but imaginative resource management decisions apply whichever is the case.

16

Models for the Future: Implementing a Resource Management Strategy

David Baker

Introduction

Academic librarians of the 21st century will have to use every means at their disposal to attract, manage and exploit to best advantage the available resources. This book has looked at the specific challenges posed by information technology, space, research collections, special bids, operating costs and some of the key approaches to resource management in the future. This chapter aims to look in general at the future development of resource management in academic libraries, in the context of the role and nature of academic libraries, past and present approaches to resource management and the future environment in which library resource managers are likely to be working. In this context:

> Change is not an option, if the information manager does not do it, it will be done to him. The most difficult thing is that any cultural change takes time. The manager is not working in a vacuum, outside pressures will disrupt plans and he will often have to go faster than he wanted. But if he is clear about what he is doing, where he wants to be and has the trust and cooperation of staff he will be better able to adapt to change and to manage more on less.[1]

Redefining role and context

As Enright pointed out some years ago, it is not so much a question of redefining our role as reminding ourselves of it:

> 'What is our business?' The task now (as it probably in reality was before) for the academic library is to achieve 'stock management' balance, to be in con-

trol of its operations (avoiding demoralizing backlogs and costly commitments which threaten to outstrip available funds), to treat space as a resource, and above all to maintain 'working' collections and network access arrangements which are relevant and responsive to the institution's teaching and research needs. In attempting to demonstrate their utility in maximizing document exposure for the user, it will be essential for libraries to 'differentiate carefully in their statements of institutional goals between archival responsibilities with one set of values and library information system responsibilities with a different set of values'.[2]

However, the context in which academic library resource managers fulfil that role has changed considerably, as this book has shown. Much of the literature relating to academic librarianship in the 1970s and 1980s, and also of the literature relating to higher education in general, had at its base an assumption that:

- the 'lean times' would gradually pass and, at some point in the not too distant future the existing model for higher education and academic libraries would be more adequately resourced
- the basic pattern of delivery of higher education and of associated library provision would remain the same.

More recent literature has suggested otherwise.[3] Major change can 'creep up' on organizations without them fully realizing it.[4] This is as true of higher education as it is of other public (and private) institutions.

In the context of resource management in academic libraries, it could be argued that a number of fundamental, irreversible and, to use Handy's terminology, 'discontinuous' changes have taken, or are taking place. These perceived changes lead me to make the following statements – all crucial to the future development of resource management. The following premises are put forward as the basis for the context in which future resource management in academic libraries is likely to be carried out:

- Never again will institutions of education be able to rely on a guaranteed level of support for their activities. Income will be allocated primarily on the basis of the resources required to produce a given product (graduates, research results) and continued on the basis of perceived and measured performance in producing quality and quantity at low cost.

- Libraries in education will never again be accepted automatically as a necessary part of academic activity, whether teaching or research. Where they are accepted, it will be because they are deemed to be an integral part of the teaching/research activity and add value or worth to that activity.
- The challenge for the future is not a technical one, but a managerial and a professional one – how to adapt to significantly changed circumstances and how to adopt new or revised approaches to the best advantages of users, ourselves (as academic librarians) and our institutions.

Competition

Writing in 1990, Maurice Line commented that:

> Simple market criteria will not work because for academic libraries there is at present no real competition...and because academic users do not generally pay directly for library and information services.[5]

While this may still be largely true, the internal competition for resources is increasing and, when competition for resources increases, so does the prospect of success or failure. The prize for winning is likely to be a level and possibly an increased resource base, at least in the short- to medium-term. The reward for the library in its contribution to the financial success of the parent institution is a restatement of the service's value and importance to the continued wellbeing of the campus as a whole. But the prizes and rewards will be hard-won, by a combination of politics, skill and good management; hence the importance of resource management in academic libraries in the 1990s and beyond.

Thinking long-term

However successful the academic library manager might be in terms of 'levering' money and allocating it to best advantage, there is no telling when attitudes may turn sour and budgets fail. Having a resource management strategy in place, together with the appropriate tools for implementing and adapting that strategy over a period of time, and to suit changing conditions, will act as an 'insurance policy' against the worst effects of any sudden and/or drastic changes within the parent institution or the library itself.

Despite the annual nature of budgetary allocation, there can be few academic institutions which have not adopted some form of longer-term strategic planning. The organizational planning process can and should stimulate the development of a long-term approach to resource management. If the strategic planning process is taken seriously and the library is allowed to play an important role, then there is both the opportunity and the justification for a library resource management strategy to be developed. In any case, 'most systems acquire inefficiencies over time, and a thorough analysis every few years is likely to yield worthwhile savings'.[6] A coherent approach to resource management, whether formally approved within the institution or locally devised by the library resource manager, seems appropriate.

Aims of a resource management strategy

The first aim must be to attract the necessary (financial) resources to fulfil the aims and objectives set down by the parent institution and, in consequence, those determined by the librarians themselves in respect of the library and its role. The second should be to allocate and manage those resources efficiently and effectively. The third must be the monitoring of the effects of the resource allocation and management process with a view to making changes to improve efficiency or effectiveness and/or to increase the likelihood of fulfilling the library's and the parent institution's aims and objectives.

A holistic approach

There are clear signs that academic institutions are now taking a much more holistic approach to central support services than ever before. The UK Higher Education Funding Councils' initiative to encourage both national and institution-specific information strategies has stimulated such an approach.[7] The JISC guidelines define the objective of an IS as being:

To have a clear, accepted and efficient means by which information of all kinds is created, handled and used to support and deliver the aims of the institution.

There is more to it than mere compliance with the HEFC and JISC guidelines. Information is the life-blood of any organization. Without a coherent approach to information provision, management, flow and exploitation, we are not going to be well prepared for the future, whether academically, administratively or strategically. Information is itself a resource and much of the philosophy of a good information strategy could be applied to resource management in general.

Key characteristics of a resource management strategy

In Chapter 1, it was argued that, despite the diversity, academic libraries had much in common with each other. It is argued here that a resource management strategy (like any other strategy within the academic sector) can be applied across a wide range of institutions. The following key and common characteristics of a successful strategy are suggested:

There must be commitment 'from the top' and widespread support within the institution.

This should be self evident. A library-specific resource management strategy which is not actively supported by the institution's senior management is unlikely to be successful, at least not on the scale necessary to justify the inevitable input of time. In this context, the nearer the library's resource management strategy can approximate to the philosophy and approach of the parent institution the more likely it is to be supported by that institution and accepted by those who have to live with the results (typically the academic departments).

At the University of East Anglia, for example, the Library chose to introduce a formula to divide up the acquisitions budget between subject areas (see pp.119–135). This was after years of 'historic' funding and in order to respond to considerable academic change within the institution – new subjects, growth in some existing areas and contraction in others – together with differential price increases between subjects and types of material. The University was looking to central budget managers who could control expenditure and re-allocate it strategically. The Library's initiative was applauded centrally. Departments were harder to convince initially, though transitional funding and a high degree of consultation with and involvement of, academic staff resulted in a general approval of what was seen as a 'firm but fair' allocation process.

The University itself subsequently adopted a formulaic approach to resource allocation across the academic and central support units. This took as its basic principle the distribution of resources to academic units in direct relation to the units' contribution to the University's overall income. As with the Library formula, there was a good deal of frank debate, but an eventual 'ownership' of the result. The Library then revised its own formula to ensure that it mirrored the basic philosophy of the University's resource management model, whilst maintaining a subject distribution of the funds, once the school-level allocations had been determined.

The strategy must grow out of the organization's overarching strategic plan.

The success of a resource management strategy, and the performance of those charged with implementing it, will in large part be measured by the extent to which the strategy aids the fulfilment of the institution's broader objectives. If, for example, a university has decided to improve its research ratings, then the library must aim to contribute to that drive for improvement, reallocating resources accordingly. The recent research assessment exercises (RAEs for short) in the UK have concentrated effort in many universities on the targeted use of resources to improve performance in subsequent exercises. The university library will have to seek, and be given, a clear indication of the ways in which research activity is to be developed and supported. Even with selective support of given areas, the resources available to the priority areas is unlikely to be sufficient to fulfil all the demands that researchers might reasonably (or unreasonably) place on the library service, the strategy will also need to encompass modes of delivery (on-site versus remote; hard copy versus electronic, etc.) as well as level of support (postgraduate taught course; postgraduate research; research group; individual academic research requirements, etc.).

The critical issues identified by the parent institution will drive the strategy at any one time and the order of priority for any particular activities associated with it.

A 'critical issue' might be the drive to research excellence in given subject areas, as noted above, or a new subject area, an emphasis on excellence in teaching, of particular types of delivery of teaching or of learning support or some other area, whether locally or nationally led. In some institutions (as noted in earlier chapters of this book) the effective use of existing space consequent upon the institution's inability to acquire additional quantities of this resource might be a particularly important 'critical issue'. This will inevitably affect the library's resource management strategy and, as discussed elsewhere, space will naturally be seen as a resource. The astute library resource manager will ensure that use of library space is – and is seen to be – an effective and integral part of overall management of the unit.

The strategy will recognize the diversity within the institution and the importance of 'ownership' of its aims and objectives.

It is clear that ever more difficult decisions will have to be made. It has not always been easy to allocate funds. A resource management strategy must make life easier in this respect, even if the decisions continue to seem harsh to those who are at the receiving end. Whether or not a formula is adopted, there must be a clear and widely-owned approach to the disbursement of resources at the librarian's disposal. Reference has been made earlier in this book to the fact that universities and higher education colleges are internally very diverse institutions.

The longer-term development of the strategy will be informed by major national initiatives.

There can be very few academic institutions which do not need to take account of national level activity, whether in relationship to teaching quality assessment, research selectivity, initiatives leading to regional cooperation and many more areas where national guidelines or directives have been issued in respect of the way in which an individual university or college might or must allocate and manage its resources. In this context, the most important national 'initiative' is likely to be the way in which funds are allocated centrally to individual institutions. A higher education system which, for example, explicitly separates out the funding of teaching or of research or consistently top-slices for 'central' initiatives such as networking provision is likely to be mirrored, at least to some extent, at individual institutional level and, hence, at library resource management level. Even if the end results do not overtly affect the library budget distribution, an awareness of the ways in which the income has reached the library is important, as is early warning of any major changes in the shape and nature of the broad income streams.

The strategy should be a flexible, rolling plan.

Futures in education are uncertain. Technological change is equally unpredictable. In a 1992 report, the UK's Department of Trade and Industry noted that the main reason for success or failure in achieving high quality business systems depended on the state of readiness of the organization: that is, on a combination of circumstances that encourage or even determine success at four key levels – in the organization overall, in the development team overall, in the specific project teams allocated to particular areas of work and amongst individuals themselves.[8] As far as is humanly possible, the strategy should be adaptable to rapidly changing circumstances. Again, to use the example of the University of East Anglia's formula approach to resource distribution: both at library and institutional level, there is general acceptance that a formula model is the best way of allocating resources and as a base for measuring the effectiveness of targeted allocation. However, the formula has changed over time to take account of changes in central funding (e.g. the gradual withdrawal of separate capital funding) and allowed for the creation of separate 'pots' of money which could be used for new initiatives – new subjects, major infrastructural change, and so on.

Developing a resource management strategy

A library can only develop a resource management strategy within the context of the parent institution's strategy. The library has to be accountable for the resources made available, not simply in terms of their deployment but also in relation to their origin. The service provided has to be one which is perceived as being relevant to the needs of the parent institution as well as being one which is efficient and cost-effective. The academic library resource manager must be aware of the perceived dispensability of support services in times of financial restraint.

A resource management model has to begin with the library's fundamental role. It could be argued that the role of the academic library is to be what the parent institution wants the library to be, and especially to appear to be so. It must be a positive factor in the continued survival and growth of the organization rather than an expensive and unpopular millstone round the administration's financial and strategic plans and ambitions; to be 'cheap' (as defined by the institution), cost effective, responsive and proactive.

Key questions need to be asked as part of the process of managing resources in the academic library. They include the following:

* Is the library supporting study and teaching or research?
* Is it providing just-in-time information or long-term research collections?
* Does it exist for the scientist or the humanist, the scholar or the teacher? – Is it an archive or an information centre?
* Does it have a hard copy or a technology base?

Only when these questions have been asked and answered can the assessment of effective performance be properly undertaken.[9] Good resource management presupposes a long-term (3-5 years) strategic plan, a well-run accounting system and effective financial reporting mechanisms. It also presupposes estimating and budgeting systems which feed into the longer-term plan and which are capable of being well and easily managed and changed at relatively short notice if strategy dictates it. Good resource management implies a high degree of freedom within the budget to transfer resources to where, in the opinion of the library manager, they are most needed and where they will bring the greatest return on their allocation. That freedom will, of course, be in the context of clear lines of responsibility and accountability for decision-making, monitoring and control in relation to available resources.

Increasingly, effective resource management also requires detailed and (as far as is possible) precise information on the cost of all library activity, enabling the resource manager to plan ahead in terms of future expenditure requirements in new and existing areas and to identify relative levels of efficiency within the library.

Finally – though not part of the remit of this book – it requires people to make it work. Being a good resource manager is not just about being good at managing resources. To be a good one must also have leadership skills and an ability to motivate others. Staff involved in resource management must also have training and develop expertise in its various aspects:

- forecasting
- budgeting
- accounting
- risk assessment
- analysis of information
- decision-making.

Senior resource managers must also have leadership skills and an ability to motivate others, not least at times and in areas where perhaps those who collect the data which makes effective resource management possible are less than convinced of the need to do so.[10]

Costings information

Models must be developed which are flexible and sensitive to change and which allow the resource managers to take long term and short/medium term decisions. The first step is to define the basic activities associated with library services and then to identify all the costs which can be attributed to each separately defined activity. This is a simple enough objective, but in practice can prove to be difficult to achieve.[11] Yavarkovsky[12] describes a step-by-step approach to costing out library operations. Webster[13] asks a number of questions of financial management systems in academic libraries – questions which are as pertinent now as when originally posed:

- do they help people become aware of the financial issues?
- do they provide incentives for saving money and innovating?
- do they truly allocate resources fairly and equitably?

- do they permit assessment of the effects of various changes on the university?
- do they help ensure effective management of resources?
- do they tie resource allocations to goals and objectives?
- do they merely provide new formats for bureaucratic and political in-fighting?

Costing information is not currently kept nor analysed on any large or consistent scale, other than in some individual libraries where the librarian has shown local initiative. This is despite the fact that cost-effectiveness studies have been carried out for many years in library and information services.[14] Developing costing mechanisms which can be applied across the system as a whole must now be an essential prerequisite for the effective long-term planning and management of a library system. Costings will:

- inform local, regional and national management of library systems and operations
- provide key funding and decision-making agencies with data which can be used as part of any allocation process and as part of negotiations regarding the development of new services, systems and subjects/research projects
- be an aid to forward projections of national, regional and individual library budgets
- be an aid to cost-cutting/prioritization
- be a mechanism for 'tendering' for the library support of new developments/additional growth/changes of direction in teaching and research
- act as a means of setting charge levels to ensure either cost-recovery or income generation on the activity being costed
- be an aid to cost-benefit analyses of library support in relation to student performance and research effectiveness.

'You don't have to be an accountant to use cost analysis as an effective management tool' wrote Michael Vinson. There is much already written on the subject and the library and information studies literature gives many examples of good and useful practice.[15] While the exercise will be labour-intensive in the short term, it is important to carry out this

work on the library system by working from a *zero base* wherever possible and politically realistic to do so. As Richmond summarizes:

> Cost data can bring an understanding of unit costs and cost behaviour in relation to overall library operations and organization, long-range planning, and setting priorities. Cost finding provides data for making models and projecting costs. But, there are pitfalls in using cost information. The cost finding process ... requires time and thought – from data collection to interpretation. It is not a quick fix and not without caveats.[16]

Even when working in primarily a political arena, the availability of seemingly 'hard' data on resources and costings can prove to be a powerful weapon in budget meetings.[17] It should be remembered, of course, that the collection of the necessary 'management information' is itself a resource management process and there is a cost to the activity which has to be justified in terms of the purpose of the exercise, its contribution to the service being provided and the results achieved.[18] However,

> costing needs to be regarded as an area of strategic management. Its aim has to be to assist in better decision-making and it cannot do this unless it reflects business [sic] realities ... perhaps the really fundamental question is what would happen if the costing system were abolished. If it is not part of the decision-making machinery of your business then it really has no role at all.[19]

Units of currency

The basic unit of currency in these exercises will vary from institution to institution and from purpose to purpose. However, it is argued that the basic unit should be the cost per student (undergraduate/postgraduate – taught/research) and/or per member of staff, as appropriate. Provision should also be made for the costing of activity relating to external usage of a library's services and collections and to 'atypical' students (e.g. part-time, self-funding, overseas, validated/federated, etc.). Costed activity should be based on each discrete operation within each major area of activity (accessions, cataloguing, circulation, information work), with each subset of costs being capable of adding up to a matrix of costs. This matrix should be capable of manipulation to provide costings for particular packages of activities and services.

Ready reckoners

Costing out activities takes time. The more a library resource manager can draw on 'ready reckoner' figures to facilitate the calculation of all the costs associated with a particular activity, service, option or new activity, the better. This might relate to the cost of constructing, maintaining, heating and lighting space, or of the total salary costs of staff on particular grades, including superannuation and other employer overheads. It might be the cost of undertaking a particular activity (as for example issuing a book to a user). Some of these ready reckoner costs, especially where activity based, can themselves become performance indicators.[20]

Fundamental questions and answers

The effect of any costings exercise should be to provide answers to fundamental questions such as the following:

- How much does it cost to add a volume/similar unit to stock?
- How much does each service transaction (issue, return, enquiry, etc.) cost?
- What is the relative spend (using the basic unit of currency) between different subject areas?
- What effect on spend would expansion/cessation of activity in given areas of library activity/service have?
- Where are parts of the system/individual libraries expensive/ cheap relative to the overall average costs?
- Where can the system/individual libraries most easily accommodate growth/change in academic direction?
- What is the correlation between spend in given areas and the quality/nature of teaching and research output?

Cost reduction

Too often in the past, libraries have reacted to budget cuts by one-off cuts to achieve a percentage reduction and then, once the 'savings' have been achieved, continued as before. There are strong arguments for saying that in the present and likely future climates, library resource managers must be more concerned with *continuous* cost reduction.[21] Richardson[22] lists the characteristics of a good cost management strategy:

1 Fits with overall corporate and business strategies
2 Establishes clear long- and short-run goals for cost reduction.
3 Balances human, capital and technological inputs into cost reduction.
4 Identifies and aims at reducing the important costs, even if they are hard to measure.
5 Recognizes that there are high costs associated with capital when used as a cost-cutting source.
6 Generates a sense of excitement and challenge in participants.
7 Continually reduces in real terms.
8 Rewards the people who 'make it happen'.
9 Recognizes that information is a key resource and communication is essential.
10 Provides a distinct competitive advantage.

Summary: what, then, is good resource management?

Just as there can be no single definition of resource management, so is it difficult to give a definitive answer to the question 'what is good resource management?' The following list is offered as an aid, both for those librarians wishing to develop a resource management strategy relevant to their parent institution and their library/information service, and as a summary of the key elements of this book.

Good resource management is about:

- Deploying all available resources to best effect in the interest of the parent institution and the library's users
- Spending money to 'lever' money, whether directly or indirectly
- Knowing what your costs are
- Achieving the best balance between collection and usage of management information
- Developing accounting and allocation systems which are simple, transparent and relevant
- Remembering that good resource management in an academic institution is as much about politics as it is about finances
- Remembering that resource management is about people as much as about money.

References

1 MacLachlan, L., 'How to manage more on less: the management challenge of the new world', in *New roles, new skills, new people*, Hatfield, University of Hertfordshire Press, 1995, 70.

2 Enright, B., 'Concepts of stock', in Line, M., *Academic library management*, London, Library Association Publishing, 1990, 45.

3 Thompson, J., *Redirection in academic librarianship*, London, Library Association Publishing, 1991. Martyn, J., *et al.* (eds.), *Information UK 2000*, London, Bowker-Saur, 1991.

4 Handy, C., *The age of unreason*, London, Hutchinson Business, 1989.

5 Line, M., 'The concept of "library goodness": user and library perception of quality and value', in Line, M., *op. cit.*, 191.

6 Ford, G., 'Acquisitions: books', in Line, M., *op. cit.*, 69.

7 Joint Information Systems Committee [of the Higher Education Funding Councils] *Guidelines for developing an Information Strategy*, Bristol, The Committee, 1995. See also: Joint Information Systems Committee, *Five-year strategy, 1996–2001*. Bristol, JISC, 1996; Joint Information Systems Committee, *Electronic libraries programme*, 3rd edn, Bristol, HEFCE, 1996.

8 Department of Trade and Industry, *Key issues affecting quality in information systems*, London, HMSO, 1992, 2.

9 Winkworth, I.R., 'Into the house of mirrors: performance measurement in academic libraries', *Journal of British academic librarianship*, 8 (1).

10 See, for example, the Follett Report, paras 117ff.

11 See, for example, Innes, J. and Mitchell, F., *Activity based costing*, London, Chartered Institute of Management Accountants, 1991.

12 Yavarkovsky, J., 'Planning and finance: a strategic level model of the university library', *Journal of library administration*, 3 (3/4), 1982, 37–54.

13 Webster, D., 'Issues in the financial management of research libraries', *Journal of library administration*, 3 (3/4), 1982, 14.

14 See, for example, Burgess, T.K., 'A cost effectiveness model for comparing various circulation systems', *Journal of library automation*, 6, 1973, 75–86.

15 Vinson, M., 'Cost finding: a step-by-step guide', *Bottom line*, 2 (3), 1988, 15-19. See also Mitchell, B.J., *et al. Cost analysis of library functions: a total system approach*, Greenwich, Conn., JAI Press, 1978 ;Kantor, P.B., 'Levels of output related to cost of operation of scientific and technical

libraries', *Library research*, **3** (1–2), 1981, 1–28; 141–154; Wood, M.S. (ed.), *Cost analysis, cost recovery, marketing and fee-based services: a guide for the health sciences librarian*, New York, Haworth, 1985; Schauer, B., *The economics of managing library service*, Chicago, American Library Association, 1986; Brockman, J., *The costs of academic libraries: an econometric interpretation*, Perth, Curtin University Library, 1988; Kingma, B.R., *The economics of information: a guide to economic and cost-benefit analysis for information professionals*, Englewood, Colorado, Libraries Unlimited, 1996.

16 Richmond, E., 'Cost finding: method and management', *Bottom line* **1** (4), 1987, 17. See also Getz, M. and Phelps, D, 'Labor costs in the technical operation of three research libraries', *Journal of academic librarianship*, **10**, 1984, 209–19.

17 See, for example, Pierce, A. R., and Andrew, L., 'Using Delphi for more efficient goal setting', *Journal of library administration*, **5** (1), 1984, 35–44.

18 Carter, M. P., 'Costing management information: a more formal approach', *Journal of information science*, **9**, 1984, 117–22.

19 Sheridan, T., 'Don't count your costs – manage them', *Management accounting*, 71–4, February, 1989.

20 Ford, G., 'Lending services', in Line, M., *op. cit.*, 131. See also, for example, Hardy, E.D., *Statistics for managing library acquisitions*, Chicago, American Library Association, 1989.

21 See, for example, Pitkin, G., *Cost-effective technical services: how to track, manage and justify internal operations*, New York, Neal-Schuman, 1989.

22 Richardson, P., *Cost containment: the ultimate advantage*, New York, Free Press, 1988, 40.

Index